# Energy Efficiency

*Dedicated to Sophie
who brought light, warmth and
renewed energy to our lives.*

*7th September 2011 to 10th January 2013*

# Energy Efficiency

The Definitive Guide to the
Cheapest, Cleanest, Fastest
Source of Energy

STEVEN FAWKES

Routledge
Taylor & Francis Group

LONDON AND NEW YORK

First published in paperback 2024

First published 2013 by Gower Publishing

Published 2016 by Routledge
4 Park Square, Milton Park, Abingdon, Oxon OX14 4RN

and by Routledge
605 Third Avenue, New York, NY 10158

*Routledge is an imprint of the Taylor & Francis Group, an informa business*

**British Library Cataloguing in Publication Data**
A catalogue record for this book is available from the British Library.

**The Library of Congress has catalogued the printed edition as follows:**
Fawkes, Steven, 1959-
  Energy efficiency : the defini   e guide to the cheapest, cleanest,
fastest source of energy / by Steven Fawkes.
     pages cm
  Includes bibliographical references and index.
  ISBN 978-1-4094-5359-8 (hardback) -- ISBN 978-1-4094-5360-4 (ebook)
 -- ISBN 978-1-4724-0802-0 (epub) 1. Energy policy. 2. Energy
consumption. 3. Energy conservation. 4. Energy policy--United States. I.
Title.
  HD9502.A2F383 2013
  333.79--dc23
                                                                    2013010235

ISBN: 978-1-4094-5359-8 (hbk)
ISBN: 978-1-03-283740-6 (pbk)
ISBN: 978-1-315-57954-2 (ebk)

DOI: 10.4324/9781315579542

# Contents

# List of Figures

# List of Tables

# List of Abbreviations

Note: Not all of these terms are used in the text, but they are commonly encountered in discussions of energy efficiency.

| | |
|---|---|
| A | Ampere – unit of current |
| A&E | Architecture and Engineering (as in A&E firms) |
| AC | Alternating Current |
| ACEEE | American Council for an Energy Efficient Economy |
| AEE | Association of Energy Engineers |
| aM&T | Automated Monitoring and Targeting |
| AMR | Automated Meter Reading |
| ARRA | American Recovery and Reinvestment Act 2009 |
| ASE | Alliance to Save Energy |
| BAMF | Biological Alternative Methane Fuels |
| bbl | Barrels – unit of volume |
| BMS | Building Energy Management System |
| BOE | Barrels Oil Equivalent |
| BOO | Build, Own and Operate |
| BPIE | Buildings Performance Institute Europe |
| BTS | Base Transceiver Station |
| BTU | British Thermal Unit |
| CEM | Contract Energy Management |
| CERT | Carbon Emissions Reduction Target – mandatory energy efficiency supplier obligation for UK utilities – (operational 2008–2012) |
| CESP | Community Energy Saving Programme – mandatory energy efficiency supplier obligation for UK utilities – (operational 2009–2012) |
| CFL | Compact Fluorescent Lamp |
| CGE | Computable General Equilibrium – a type of economic model |
| CHP | Combined Heat and Power |
| CO | Carbon monoxide |
| $CO_2$ | Carbon dioxide |

| | |
|---|---|
| COP | Coefficient of Performance – usually applied to heat pumps |
| CSR | Corporate Social Responsibility |
| D3 | Shorthand for Demand Management (DM), Demand Response (DR) and Distributed Generation (DG) |
| DC | Direct Current |
| DCF | Discounted Cash Flow |
| DEC | Display Energy Certificate |
| DECC | Department of Energy and Climate Change (UK government department) |
| DG | Distributed Generation |
| DH | District Heating |
| DHW | Domestic Hot Water |
| DM | Demand Management – permanent reduction of load through energy efficiency |
| DNO | Distribution Network Operator (UK term for regional electricity distribution companies) |
| DOE | Department of Energy (US government department) |
| DR | Demand Response – short-term reduction in load or time shifting of load |
| DSM | Demand Side Management |
| EBRD | European Bank of Reconstruction and Development |
| ECCJ | The Energy Conservation Center, Japan |
| ECEEE | European Council for an Energy Efficient Economy |
| ECM | Energy Conservation Measure |
| ECM | Electronically Commutated Motor |
| ECO | Energy Company Obligation (UK scheme to mandate spending on energy efficiency by energy suppliers) |
| EDF | Électricité de France |
| EDF | Environmental Defense Fund – US-based NGO |
| EDR | Electricity Demand Reduction (used by DECC in the UK) |
| EE | Energy efficiency |
| EEC | Energy Efficiency Commitment – mandatory energy efficiency obligation for UK utilities (operational 2002–2005) |
| EEDI | Energy Efficient Design Index (design standard introduced by International Maritime Organization) |
| EEDO | Energy Efficiency Deployment Office, office within UK Department of Energy and Climate Change |
| E-FiT | Energy efficiency Feed-in Tariff |
| EIA | US Energy Information Administration |
| EIB | European Investment Bank |

| | |
|---|---|
| EJ | Exajoules – unit of energy |
| ELENA | European Local Energy Assistance – an initiative of the European Investment Bank and the European Commission to provide technical assistance to towns and regions to help develop large energy efficiency and renewable energy projects |
| EMA | Energy Managers Association (UK) |
| EMR | Electricity Market Reform – major changes to the UK electricity market being implemented in 2013/2014 |
| EPC | Energy Performance Contract |
| EPC | Energy Performance Certificate |
| EPS | Energy Efficiency Portfolio Standard – mandatory requirement on utilities (USA) |
| ESA | Efficiency Services Agreement (similar to MESA) |
| ESCO | Energy Service Company |
| ESKOM | South African utility |
| ESPC | Energy Savings Performance Contract |
| ESTA | Energy Services and Technology Association – UK trade association for energy efficiency industry |
| EVO | Efficiency Valuation Organization – international not-for-profit organization administering IPMVP |
| FCM | Forward Capacity Market |
| FHFA | Federal Housing Finance Agency |
| FiT | Feed-in Tariff |
| FM | Facilities Management |
| GAO | General Accountability Office – the audit, evaluation and investigative agency of the US Congress (formerly General Accounting Office) |
| GHG | Greenhouse Gases |
| GIB | Green Investment Bank (UK) |
| GSA | General Services Administration – US government agency supporting the functioning of federal agencies |
| GSHP | Ground Source Heat Pump |
| GSMA | Organization representing mobile telecommunications operators |
| GW | Gigawatts – unit of power |
| GWh | Gigawatt hour – unit of energy |
| GWP | Global Warming Potential |
| HTS | High Temperature Superconductivity |
| HVAC | Heating, Ventilation and Air Conditioning |
| ICAO | International Civil Aviation Organization |
| ICP | Investor Confidence Project |

| | |
|---|---|
| IDM | Integrated Demand Management – demand side programmes run by ESKOM |
| IEA | International Energy Agency |
| IFC | International Finance Corporation |
| IFI | International Financial Institution |
| IGA | Investment Grade Audit |
| IHD | In Home Display |
| IIGCC | International Investors Group on Climate Change |
| IISD | International Institute for Sustainable Development |
| IMO | International Maritime Organization |
| IOU | Investor-owned utility (USA) |
| IP | Intellectual Property |
| IPMVP | International Performance Measurement and Verification Protocol |
| IRR | Internal Rate of Return |
| ISO | Independent System Operator (USA) |
| ISO 50001 | International Standard 50001 Energy Management |
| ISO-NE | Independent System Operator – New England |
| JESSICA | Joint European Support for Sustainable Investment in City Areas – initiative of the European Commission, the European Investment Bank and the Council of Europe Development Bank |
| KEMCO | Korean Energy Management Company |
| KPI | Key Performance Indicator |
| kW | Kilowatt – unit of power |
| kWh | Kilowatt hour – unit of energy |
| LBNL | Lawrence Berkeley National Laboratory – US Department of Energy national laboratory |
| LED | Light Emitting Diode |
| LEED | Leadership in Energy and Environmental Design |
| LNG | Liquefied Natural Gas |
| M&T | Monitoring and Targeting |
| M&V | Measurement and Verification |
| MACC | Marginal Abatement Cost Curve |
| mCHP | Micro-Combined Heat and Power |
| MEE | Mobile Energy Efficiency – benchmarking programme run by the GSMA |
| MESA | Managed Energy Services Agreement |
| MIT | Massachusetts Institute of Technology |
| Mtoe | Million tonnes of oil equivalent |
| MUSH | Municipal, University, School and Hospital sector (in USA) |
| MW | Megawatt – unit of power |
| MWh | Megawatt hour – unit of energy |

| | |
|---|---|
| NDEE | Non-Domestic Energy Efficiency – term used by UK Green Investment Bank to describe non-residential energy efficiency |
| $NO_x$ | Oxides of nitrogen |
| NPI | Normalized Performance Indicator |
| NPV | Net Present Value |
| OBR | On Bill Repayment |
| ODP | Ozone Depletion Potential |
| OECD | Organisation for Economic Co-operation and Development |
| OEM | Original Equipment Manufacturer |
| OPEC | Organization of the Petroleum Exporting Countries |
| ORC | Organic Rankine Cycle |
| ORNL | Oak Ridge National Laboratory – US Department of Energy National Laboratory |
| PACE | Property Assessed Clean Energy |
| PE | Private Equity |
| PEMFC | Proton Exchange Membrane Fuel Cell |
| PGE | Pacific Gas & Electric – Californian utility |
| ppm | Parts Per Million |
| PV | Photovoltaic |
| PWR | Pressurized Water Reactor |
| QBTU | Quadrillion British Thermal Units |
| R&D | Research and Development |
| R, D & D | Research, Development and Demonstration |
| RE:FIT | London-based programme to encourage use of Energy Performance Contracts |
| RF | Radio Frequency |
| RHI | Renewable Heat Incentive – UK support mechanism for renewable heat |
| RMI | Rocky Mountain Institute |
| ROC | Renewable Obligation Credit – UK renewable electricity support mechanism |
| RTG | Radioisotope Thermal Generator |
| RTO | Regional Transmission Operator (USA) |
| SAAS | Software as a service |
| SEC | Specific Energy Consumption |
| SEEMP | Ship Energy Efficiency Management Plan (management system for ships introduced by International Maritime Organization) |
| SME | Small or Medium Enterprise |
| SMUD | Sacramento Municipality Utility District |
| SOFC | Solid Oxide Fuel Cell |
| $SO_x$ | Oxides of sulphur |

| | |
|---|---|
| SRI | Socially Responsible Investing |
| TJ | Terajoules – unit of energy |
| toe | Tonnes of oil equivalent – unit of energy |
| TSO | Transmission System Operator (USA) |
| TVA | Tennessee Valley Authority |
| TWh | Terawatt hour – unit of energy |
| UAA | Utility Alliance Agreement – multi-utility contract form used by RWE and Diageo in UK and Ireland |
| UNDP | United Nations Development Programme |
| UNEP | United Nations Environment Programme |
| UNFCC | United Nations Framework on Climate Change |
| USAID | United States Agency for International Development |
| USGBC | United States Green Building Council |
| V | Volt – unit of electric potential, difference in electric potential or electromagnetic force |
| VC | Venture Capital |
| VOC | Volatile Organic Compound |
| VRLA | Valve Regulated Lead Acid batteries |
| VSD | Variable Speed Drive |
| W | Watt – unit of power |
| WEC | World Energy Council |
| WHO | World Health Organization |
| WHP | Waste Heat to Power |

# Acknowledgements

As ever, the process of writing a book is in many ways a solitary one, but the end result is based on the inputs of many people over many years which somehow get processed into new ideas, new connections and a linear sequence of words that attempt to describe a complex, interconnected world. It is impossible to catalogue and acknowledge all these inputs, but major ones this time round include: Dr Keith Jacques who introduced me to soft systems a long time ago; the late Mr Peter Morimura for giving me opportunities and an excuse to learn about Japan over a 20-year period; MCC for introducing me to the financial world; Graham Meeks of the CHPA for collaborating on D3 and policy matters; numerous energy efficiency practitioners around the world, including Dipak Shah and the Energy Excel team, John Romano of Telstra and Peter Garforth of Garforth International, to name only a few; numerous innovators of amazing new technologies, including the late Dr Jens Müller, Scott White of Autonomic Materials, the teams at Nanoco and Ilika, and many others; and the numerous experts I have met and interacted with who are working to move the energy efficiency financing market forward, notably Amory Lovins, Greg Kats and Matt Golden in the USA, Sean Kidney and Ingrid Holmes in Europe and Flora Kan in China. On the work front I would also like to acknowledge the friendship and efforts of Bayju Thakar and the entire Day One Energy Solutions team for advancing the UK market and also introducing me to Indian concerns. Thanks are also due to Paul Blanchard for introducing me properly to the world of Twitter and blogs, Sarah Nutter for editing, and the Gower team. The final thank you, as ever, goes to my dear wife Kathy, whose commitment to family, profession and education always inspires and encourages me. As always, any errors are my responsibility.

Steven Fawkes

# About the Author

Dr Steven Fawkes is an internationally recognized, award-winning energy efficiency, new energy and clean technology expert with more than 25 years' experience of implementing energy management programmes and advising governments on energy efficiency policy. He has worked in the UK, Europe, Asia and America, developed large-scale energy programmes in both the private and public sector, built a number of energy services businesses from start-up and advised governments in Europe and Asia. Much of his current work is concerned with the issues of aggregating energy efficiency projects and financing them.

Currently Steven is an adviser to a number of energy and clean technology companies and also a Director of Energypro Limited and a Non-Executive Director of Bglobal plc, an AIM-listed smart meter and energy services company. Prior to these posts he was Corporate Finance Partner at Matrix Corporate Capital, leading the team specializing in energy and clean technology. While at Matrix, Steven also led the research team rated by Extel as number one in the New Energy and Clean Tech sector.

Steven has worked in Japan, advising a leading Japanese consulting engineering company on energy efficiency projects, including for the British Embassy in Tokyo. He has also worked for the EU Phare programme, the United Nations Development Programme, the United States Agency for International Development (USAID) and the World Bank implementing national energy efficiency programmes in Romania, going on to co-found one of the first industrial energy service companies in Romania. In 2000 he joined Enron and was part of the team that implemented innovative energy supply and efficiency contracts for Sainsburys and Diageo, and in 2002 Steven led that team in their transition to RWE Solutions, going on to build a successful business that became part of RWE npower in 2006.

Steven has an interdisciplinary BSc focused on energy resources from the University of Bimingham, a Diploma in Technological Economics and a PhD concerning the potential for energy efficiency in UK industry from the University of Stirling, and a Postgraduate Diploma in Sustainable Business from Cambridge University. Steven is an experienced public speaker and has undertaken engagements in the UK, Europe, the USA, Asia and Africa. He has published more than 150 articles and papers, and a previous book on energy efficiency: *Outsourcing of Energy Management*. Steven advised the UK government on energy efficiency policy and to establish the Energy Efficiency Deployment Office (EEDO) within the Department of Energy and Climate Change (DECC). He was an Adviser to EEDO during its formation phase. In November 2012 he was awarded the Energy Institute's Individual Achievement Award.

As well as his interests in energy, Steven has been a Non-Executive Director of Autonomic Materials Inc., a company spun out of the University of Illinois, which is commercializing self-healing materials. Steven is also an aviation and space travel enthusiast. He has flown in the Russian zero-g cosmonaut training aircraft and a MiG-25 to 25,000 metres. He has also authored papers and articles on space tourism. Steven is married and lives in London.

Steven's blog can be found at: www.onlyelevenpercent.com

# Foreword

I have long been committed to ensuring that energy efficiency is given the proper role and precedence in our national energy policy that it rightly deserves.

In a global race for limited resources, it will be those countries which are the greenest and crucially those which are the most energy efficient which will succeed in the long-term and whose economies will prosper. Energy efficiency therefore has a key role to play in all our lives. For it will be those businesses which are best protected from energy price shocks which will have a clear competitive edge and in the domestic sector, it is those consumers who are least vulnerable to changing energy prices whose household bills will be the lowest.

Greater energy efficiency therefore belongs at the very heart of our low carbon economy. Finding ways to do more, or even the same, with less makes real economic sense. It improves the energy security of our country, reduces our carbon emissions, stimulates growth and creates jobs.

So, this Coalition Government is determined to break with past indifference to energy efficiency. We have a clear mission to seize the energy efficiency opportunity, which is why we published our Energy Efficiency Strategy in November 2012, identifying the untapped energy efficiency potential in the UK economy and setting out the barriers to this potential and how we can address them.

I firmly believe the public and private sector must work hand in hand to deliver this opportunity, to unlock investment and stimulate innovation. By working collectively we can lead the world in becoming more energy efficient. We are at the early stage of an exciting journey in terms of greater energy efficiency but Steve Fawkes has been a powerful and expert advocate of efficiency for many years. I very much welcome the contribution Steve's new work can play in helping us navigate an exciting path forward.

The Rt Hon Gregory Barker
Minister of State for the Department of Energy and Climate Change

# 1

# What Do We Mean By Energy Efficiency?

*What gets us into trouble is not what we don't know. It's what we know for sure that just ain't so.*

*Will Rogers, American humourist*

*Everything has changed but our way of thinking.*

*Albert Einstein, Theoretical physicist*

## Growing Interest in Energy Efficiency – Again

Interest in energy efficiency has grown significantly over the last five years, particularly so in the last three years. This growth has been driven by increasing energy prices and environmental concerns as well as increasing recognition of the value opportunity that energy efficiency presents in all parts of the economy. For those of us who have been active in energy efficiency for decades, since 1980 in my case, this increase in interest and activity represents the second up-wave during our careers. The last time there was as much interest in energy efficiency was between the mid-1970s and the mid-1980s in response to the oil crises of 1973 and 1979 which saw oil prices rise to $34/barrel, about $100/barrel in today's money.

This book is broad in scope rather than deep in any one aspect. It seeks to give a current overview of the issues and tries to offer insight into how we may effectively tackle the significant challenges ahead. Many other excellent texts exist which go much deeper on the various topics within energy efficiency, and some are referenced throughout. This book focuses on the various broad aspects of energy efficiency and covers:

- what do we really mean by energy efficiency?

- what is the potential (in different dimensions)?

- why is it important?

- what management processes lead to optimization of energy efficiency?

- what technologies are useful for improving energy efficiency?

- what policies can be used to promote energy efficiency?

- how can energy efficiency be financed?

- how can energy suppliers engage with energy efficiency?

Other topics could have been covered, and any of these could have been covered in depth, but that will have to await future books.

## Where Are We Today?

I believe that we are at a critical inflection point for energy efficiency. Over the last two to three decades we have identified the potential and learnt and codified what works in energy management through standards such as ISO 50001 and IPMVP (International Performance and Measurement Protocol) – see Chapter 6 for more details. At the same time, incredible advances in technology, particularly around data, communication and materials, are giving us new approaches and new tools to allow us to design better equipment, systems and buildings that improve energy efficiency. In addition, new business and financial models are evolving and transforming energy efficiency into an attractive and practical investment opportunity, one which will continue to get attention from managers, entrepreneurs and investors even if there are reductions in energy prices.

As is often the case, however, government policy lags market reality on the ground, and in many countries governments are trying to catch up and accelerate the processes of improving energy efficiency. The challenge for policy makers and practitioners alike is how to massively scale up the deployment of energy efficiency. I believe that we know enough to do that; the question over the next decade or so is how successful will we be?

## What Is Energy Efficiency?

We need to start a book on energy efficiency by defining energy efficiency and then putting it into its proper place in the context of the global energy scene. Definitions are needed as there is still confusion about the term 'energy efficiency', as well as associated terms such as 'energy productivity', 'energy intensity' and 'energy conservation'. Putting energy efficiency into its wider context powerfully illustrates both the potential for improvement and the vital importance of the topic.

So what do we mean by energy efficiency, and some of the associated ideas and terms such as energy conservation, energy intensity, energy productivity and energy management? The term energy efficiency is widely used but is sometimes misused. It conjures up different images, associations and models for different people. The term also carries with it a lot of baggage, bringing with it outdated ideas that inhibit understanding, hinder acceptance and block effective action. It really is important that everyone who has any interest in energy efficiency starts from the same basic set of concepts, and this is particularly true today as the growth of interest in the subject has inevitably and necessarily brought in many new entrants without a solid technical grounding in energy matters or long experience of energy efficiency.

### ENERGY EFFICIENCY IS THE WRONG TERM

There is a view, and it is one I am sympathetic to because it is technically correct, that the use of the term energy efficiency is misleading in the sense that we normally use it. First of all, as Walt Patterson, one of the great energy gurus, pointed out (Patterson 2005), using the term 'energy', which came into widespread use in the 1970s, is in itself misleading because it fails to distinguish between two very different things: fuel and electricity. As Walt says, you cannot power your computer or smart phone using gasoline, only electricity of the right voltage and current will work, and you cannot run your gasoline engine car on diesel fuel. Each specific type of technology requires fuel or electricity with very specific characteristics. Walt also points out that the term energy conservation is technically incorrect because, as all energy engineers know, energy is always conserved under the First Law of Thermodynamics. The term energy efficiency is also problematical because, for example, you cannot measure all the inputs of ambient energy from the sun or the atmosphere, occupants or equipment, or the useful energy output of a building. Ideally we would change the language of energy and energy efficiency, but the terminology is in widespread use and any attempt to avoid it or change it will lead to even more confusion.

Cullen and Allwood (2010) make a very useful distinction when considering energy efficiency. They distinguish between 'conversion devices' (power stations, engines and light bulbs, for example), which convert energy from one form into another, and 'passive systems' (such as buildings), where useful energy is finally 'lost' by degrading to low-grade heat in exchange for it providing us with useful services. You can measure the energy efficiency of a conversion device, i.e. the useful energy out as a proportion of the total energy in, but you can't measure the useful energy out/total energy in of a passive system such as a building. You can only measure energy productivity, i.e. energy in/some useful output.

## INEFFICIENCY EVERYWHERE

Whatever level we look at, the degree of energy efficiency, or perhaps more accurately inefficiency, is quite stunning. The energy efficiency of many everyday conversion devices is surprisingly low. A filament light bulb converts electricity into light with an efficiency of about 2 per cent; the rest of the energy put into the device is emitted mostly as heat, which is not usually useful. Fluorescent lamps have efficiencies of about 10 per cent, and power transformers for devices like computers and mobile phones are typically only 50 per cent efficient. At a global level, Cullen and Allwood (2010) reported that for a total input of 475 exajoules of primary energy (oil, coal, gas, biomass, nuclear and renewable), we get 55 exajoules of useful energy services (motion, heat, light, cooling and sound): an overall efficiency of 11 per cent. Although some of this is, of course, unavoidable because of the laws of thermodynamics and the limitations of practical machines, with all our 'advanced' technology it is still a surprisingly low number.

## 'ENERGY EFFICIENCY' EQUALS ENERGY EFFICIENCY AND ENERGY PRODUCTIVITY

So the all-enveloping term 'energy efficiency' really incorporates two concepts. First, energy efficiency, useful energy out/energy in – usually reported as a percentage, for conversion devices. Secondly, energy productivity, usually reported as energy in/useful output, for passive devices. We are familiar with some everyday measurements of energy productivity, such as miles per gallon or litres per 100 kilometres for car fuel efficiency, and others including energy input to a building per square metre to produce a certain temperature for a certain period of time; energy use per passenger mile for aircraft; or energy per 1,000 tins of beans produced in a factory.

## ENERGY EFFICIENCY AS A PROCESS

When we talk about energy efficiency in a macro sense we often mean a series of processes rather than a status at a single point in time. The energy efficiency of all technologies tends to improve over time because there is a basic human desire to spend less, invent new technologies and improve existing technologies. The process of making many small changes to improve things could be called 'tinkering', although applying that term to modern, focused development engineering seems disrespectful. As well as these constant incremental technological changes, there are the major paradigm-busting changes, such as a complete change of processes, that work to improve energy productivity over time. Improvements in energy efficiency are generally mirrored by improvements in the productivity of other resource use.

The process of improving energy efficiency or reducing energy input for a given output is a process of technical and/or behavioural change that is driven by technological, financial, management, social and political drivers and constraints. 'Energy', in the form of oil, gas, coal, or uranium, is made up of a set of unique physical resources. Therefore, the process of improving energy efficiency is actually the process of improving the productivity of energy resource use – in the same way as the process of improving productivity of any other resource, physical or human. So when we commonly talk about 'energy efficiency' we really mean 'the process of improving the productivity of energy use'. In later chapters, this book addresses the management of the process, the technologies that can be used, the social factors and policies that can accelerate or impede the rate of improving energy efficiency.

## ENERGY INTENSITY

Energy intensity refers to the overall energy efficiency of an economy measured as energy usage per unit of Gross Domestic Product (GDP), typically in tonnes of oil equivalent (toe) per $1,000 of GDP. The inverse of energy intensity, which is not so widely seen, is 'economic energy efficiency' – how many units of GDP are produced for each unit of energy. Energy intensity is influenced by the stage of economic development of an economy, the structure of the economy, climatic conditions, as well as overall energy efficiency. As countries start to industrialize, energy intensity tends to increase as the economies move from primarily agricultural activities to industrial activities. Once this change has occurred, energy intensity then decreases. This reduction is driven by structural shifts in the economy, e.g. a move away from heavy industry to lighter industry or services, as well as overall energy efficiency, a pattern that has been seen many times in many countries (Rühl et al. 2012).

## ENERGY MANAGEMENT

Energy management includes the management processes and tools used to manage both the supply side and the demand side of energy systems. Primarily, energy managers are the people who focus on the energy management processes, although energy management can, and must, involve far more people than just dedicated energy managers. Some energy managers are more involved in the issues of energy supply such as securing supplies at the best price and assessing risk levels, while some are more involved in energy demand, i.e. reducing energy input for a given output. Since the 1980s, the term 'energy manager' has been most associated with the demand side, i.e. managing the process of improving energy efficiency, but an integration of supply and demand functions is sensible to obtain optimal results. We will explore the demand side of the energy management process in Chapter 6.

## ENERGY CONSERVATION

The other term often heard in discussions of energy efficiency is energy conservation. Energy conservation is often used interchangeably with energy efficiency although they are not the same, and fortunately this does appear to be happening less frequently. The term energy conservation became popular in the wake of the oil crises of the 1970s. Policy makers at the time talked about the three pillars of energy policy: coal, nuclear and conservation, all three together summarized as 'conuco'. Energy conservation means reducing energy use by reducing output. To use our examples from above, it means reducing the space temperature in the building, i.e. reducing comfort, producing fewer or inferior tins of beans, or driving fewer miles. There are many examples where energy conservation, saving by doing less, can and does make sense. However, it is one of our basic beliefs that people and organizations don't like to make do with less output or comfort and we cannot, and should not, base our energy decisions on conservation.

Development inevitably means increasing economic output, and some proponents of sustainability believe that the future will involve making do with less and giving up output or comfort. I do not think this is either likely or indeed desirable. We live in a world where 1.3 billion people exist without any electricity (IEA 2012) and, despite good progress on global poverty reduction, about the same number live at 'the bottom of the pyramid' (Prahalad 2005) on an income of less than $1.25 a day. An energy strategy based on doing less cannot practically or ethically be applied to the poor people in the developing world, or even the poorer parts of the developed world, an increasing number of whom are in fuel poverty.

We need to generate more wealth and more jobs everywhere in the world, particularly in the developing world where low incomes help drive social and international problems. But we also need to do this in developed countries which have been severely affected by the global financial crisis. What we need to do is grow output and make every unit of output much, much more energy efficient. The evidence at both the micro and the macro levels is that:

- we can do this to an extent beyond what is commonly held to be possible;

- it is financially attractive to do this;

- we know how to do it, we have the technologies and the management tools;

- doing it will reduce costs, reduce carbon emissions, increase the profitability of firms and create real jobs.

## ENERGY EFFICIENCY AND RENEWABLE ENERGY

Perhaps surprisingly there is still confusion between energy efficiency and renewable energy. Energy efficiency is about reducing the end use of energy for a given output. Renewable energy is just another way of generating heat or electricity. Renewable energy does not reduce end-use efficiency, although it is clearly a way of substituting or reducing the consumption of fossil fuels. There is a difference between reducing the end use of electricity or fuel and substituting a renewable source for it. Renewable energy systems can help to achieve a higher overall efficiency in the electricity system if they can reduce peak loads and thereby avoid additional, usually inefficient, power stations being ramped up, e.g. by using solar in sunny climates to reduce peak air conditioning loads. But they should not generally be thought of as part of 'energy efficiency'.

## D3 – DEMAND MANAGEMENT, DEMAND RESPONSE AND DISTRIBUTED GENERATION

Another important area to be clear about is the difference between energy efficiency, demand response and distributed generation. A useful term to encapsulate all aspects of energy demand-side issues is D3, which was first used in the UK a few years ago by a group (including the author) concerned with promoting the demand-side agenda within the context of the proposed UK Electricity Market Reform (EMR). D3 stands for Demand Management (DM), Demand Response (DR) and Distributed Generation (DG). DM is pure energy efficiency, the permanent reduction of demand. DR is the short-term reduction or shifting of load on the electricity supply system, usually in response to market signals at times of peak demand. DG is the local generation of electricity using systems connected directly to the end user (embedded) or the distribution network rather than the transmission network.

DG can use any form of generation technology, including Combined Heat and Power (CHP) of any kind, biomass, solar, wind, geothermal, as well as conventional fossil fuel-driven technologies. DR can reduce on-site energy use if it consists of switching off load to avoid high charges at times of peak demand on the electricity system, or it can involve simply shifting load to another time. It could, in an electricity market regime where there is negative pricing, involve increasing demand to take advantage of negative or low prices, possibly using some form of storage technology. Application of DR, even if there is no energy reduction at the site in question due to the load being shifted in time, may result in energy efficiency in the electricity system as a whole if it prevents the need to operate a standby power station, for example. DG does not reduce on-site energy use but in the particular case of CHP can reduce energy use, i.e. improve efficiency at the whole-system level by substituting CHP with an overall efficiency of up to 75 per cent for electricity and heat, for power and heat generated separately with an overall efficiency of 51 per cent efficiency (EPA 2012).

## THE JEVONS PARADOX – A QUICK NOTE

Of course, as soon as we have defined energy efficiency as improvements in energy productivity, someone counters with the argument that reducing energy use per unit of output only leads to more energy use as people and firms spend some (or all) of the money saved by greater efficiency on more consumption, resulting in more energy use. This is the Jevons Paradox. This issue is so important that it gets a short chapter to itself. The only comment to make here is that we don't say the same things about the use of other resources, e.g. metals. You do not hear the argument that we shouldn't improve productivity of metal use as it will only result in more metals use. It may be equally true in metals as it is in energy, but the argument isn't made nearly so often. Improving productivity of resource use, whether it be metals or energy or land, is one of the basic drivers of increasing wealth. The other main driver is creating resources out of 'thin air' by creative thinking; for example, turning something that has no value or is currently thought of as waste into a productive resource.

## References and Bibliography

Allwood, J. 2010. *Energy and Material Efficiency*. Presentation at Zero Energy Kyoto, 19 August 2010. [Online]. Available at: http://www.energy.kyoto-u.ac.jp/gcoe/en/symposium/2010/pdf/03Allwood.pdf [accessed 26 January 2013].

Cullen, J.M. and Allwood, J.M. 2010. 'Theoretical Efficiency Limits for Energy Conversion Devices', *Energy* 35(201): 2059–69.

EPA. 2012. United States Environmental Protection Agency. *Combined Heat and Power Partnership – Efficiency Benefits*. [Online]. Available at: http://www.epa.gov/chp/basic/efficiency.html [accessed 26 January 2013].

IEA. 2012. *World Energy Outlook 2012*. [Online]. Available at: http://www.worldenergyoutlook.org/publications/weo-2012/ [accessed 26 January 2013].

Patterson, W. 2005. *Getting Energy Right*. Presentation made to London Boroughs Energy Group Christmas Meeting, Southwark Cathedral, 9 December 2005. [Online]. Available at: http://www.waltpatterson.org/gettingenergyright.pdf [accessed 26 January 2013].

Patterson, W. 2008. *Managing Energy Wrong. Working Paper One*. Chatham House. [Online]. Available at: http://www.waltpatterson.org/mewfinal.pdf [accessed 26 January 2013].

Patterson, W. 2009. *Managing Energy Data. Working Paper Two*. Chatham House. [Online]. Available at: http://www.waltpatterson.org/medfinal.pdf [accessed 26 January 2013].

Patterson, W. 2010. *Managing Energy Technology. Working Paper Three*. Chatham House. [Online]. Available at: http://www.waltpatterson.org/metfinal.pdf [accessed 26 January 2013].

Prahalad, C.K. 2005. *The Fortune at the Bottom of the Pyramid*. Upper Saddle River NJ, Pearson Prentice Hall.

Rühl, C., Appleby, P., Fennema, A. and Schaffer, M. 2012. *Economic Development and the Demand for Energy: A Historical Perspective on the Next 20 Years.* [Online]. Available at: http://www.bp.com/liveassets/bp_internet/globalbp/ STAGING/global_assets/downloads/R/reports_and_publications_economic_ development_demand_for_energy.pdf [accessed 26 January 2013].

# 2

# The Global Energy System – Stresses and Strains

*… America will be forced to rely on the Persian Gulf, which is a part of the world, I assure you, that you do not want to allow yourselves to rely upon.*

*Sheikh Yamani, Saudi Arabian Oil Minister, 1988*

*Where oil fields are really found … is in the minds of men …*
*Wallace Everette Pratt, 1885–1981, pioneer petroleum geologist*

In this chapter we look at the current global energy situation and review the stresses and strains on the energy system, all of which can be reduced by improving energy efficiency.

## A Historical Perspective

The use of energy in industrial quantities, i.e. commercially available fuel of various types plus electricity, is central to modern life, economic growth and the maintenance of society. The history of human development can be framed in terms of energy use. Prior to the start of the industrial revolution in the 1760s the only energy sources open to humans were muscle power, biomass in various forms – mainly wood, charcoal and animal dung – and a small amount of renewables in the form of wind and water power, driving machines mechanically. By the mid-1800s, the Industrial Revolution, through the use of the steam engine, greatly increased the use of fossil-fuel sources, mostly coal, and built economic wealth on a scale never before imagined. Of course it also introduced huge social dislocations and problems, including the type of rapid urbanization which we now see in developing countries such as India and China. The Industrial Revolution also created environmental pollution and led to the destruction of ecosystems on a massive scale, issues that are at least being partly addressed in the developed world through better regulation, but again are still growing in developing countries.

The use of electricity, which can be called the Second Industrial Revolution, built on Faraday's early experiments of the 1830s, really got into gear in the 1870s with the introduction of electric lighting and motors. Growing rapidly, electricity brought with it new and amazing technologies such as lighting that provided better illumination, refrigeration which improved health and nutrition, the telephone, and computers, which together have evolved into the worldwide network of internet and communications systems we use – and abuse – today. Anyone who wants to really appreciate how far our energy, specifically electricity, technology has come in less than 200 years should visit the Faraday Museum at the Royal Institution in London and view the first ever electrical generator of 1831/32, and then compare it to a large modern power station generator.

One measure of the effect of large-scale energy use is to compare the work done today using commercial energy to the work that in previous generations would have been done by servants. Richard Wolfson (2012), a Professor of Environmental Studies at Middlebury College in the USA, estimates that the industrialization of energy means that the average American now has the equivalent of 100 servants. In England, even at the height of domestic service in late Victorian and Edwardian times, as popularized by TV series such as *Upstairs Downstairs* and *Downton Abbey*, a large home may only have had up to 40 servants, perhaps four per resident, so the average American citizen now has access to some 25 times more energy services than the typical Edwardian aristocrat.

Fundamentally, demand for energy is driven by two things: the demand for goods and services that require energy to provide, and the energy efficiency with which those services are provided. Demand for goods or services is driven by two things: the size of the population and the level of wealth of the population.

When we look forward 20 to 40 years we see a growing population and rapidly growing affluence. These two factors will drive up energy demand. The United Nations, in their 'medium variant', forecast that the global population is expected to reach 9.3 billion by 2050 (United Nations 2010), 2.3 billion higher than in 2011. If the entire nine billion people used energy in the way that the average European (EU-27) does today (not even the average American), global energy use would reach about 75 per cent higher than today's level. A more realistic scenario for the total energy use is given by the International Energy Agency's 'Current Policies' scenario, which suggests that total global primary energy demand will increase to 18,676 Mtoe by 2035, a 47 per cent increase from the 2010 level (IEA 2012). Increasing energy supply by 47 per cent by 2035 is certainly not impossible, but doing so will greatly exaggerate stresses and strains on the global energy supply system that are clearly visible even today.

Despite a temporary setback caused by the global financial crisis, global affluence is also expected to grow sharply and in the next two decades the global middle class could grow from 2 billion people today to 5 billion. Between now and 2021 it is expected that there will be 2 billion people with a middle-class standard of living in Asia alone (Kharas 2010). China is likely to have more than 670 million middle class compared with only 150 million today. This is important because when people enter the middle class they start to buy more energy-consuming devices such as refrigerators, TVs and cars, and energy demand per capita kinks sharply upwards.

The prevailing view within economics has been that there is a correlation between energy use and affluence (GDP). The difference in energy intensity between affluent countries, e.g. the high usage in the USA and the lower usage in Scandinavia, and the differences within local jurisdictions in the USA, suggest that aggressive energy efficiency programmes can reduce, and even flatten, the growth in demand for electricity. Based on these findings, final energy use in the future will be more a matter of policy and technology choice, and that by adopting more efficient technologies and more aggressive energy efficiency policies we can decouple growth in energy use and growth in GDP. We really can choose our energy future.

## Energy Supply Trends

Despite the growth of renewable energy sources in the last decade, in 2010 fossil fuels still accounted for more than 80 per cent of all primary energy, with nuclear power making up less than 6 per cent and renewables 13 per cent (with large-scale hydro making up 2.3 per cent, traditional and modern biomass 10 per cent and other renewables less than 1 per cent) (IEA 2012). Transport is almost entirely dependent on fossil fuels and despite the introduction of electric and hybrid vehicles there is still little choice other than to use fossil fuels for road, marine and air travel. As John Kay said in the *Financial Times* in 2005 (Kay 2005), 'The most technologically progressive century in history ended with fuel technologies not fundamentally different from those when it began.'

## GROWTH OF RENEWABLES – FUELLED BY SUBSIDIES

Over the last 20 years, there has been a dramatic growth in the use of renewable energy technologies, in particular wind power and solar power. Investment in renewables has grown from close to zero in 1990 to some $257 billion in 2011 (UNEP 2012), and the proportion of global electricity generated by renewables has grown to six per cent of total electricity demand. Although the general principles of these technologies were known for a long time, their large-scale industrialization has been driven by subsidies, put in place as a policy response to concern about man-made global warming. Without those subsidies the renewable industry would have remained tiny, though there is a strong argument that subsidies have actually impeded real innovations that could bring the costs down as resources are focused on deploying uneconomic technologies.

Despite the advantages of renewable power, notably zero fuel costs and zero emissions, the problems of intermittency and high costs remain challenging and large parts of the industry do exhibit the symptoms of subsidy dependence. Declining cost in some areas, notably photovoltaics, holds out the prospect of 'grid parity' in some markets, but whether or not the existing renewable technologies such as offshore wind can ever provide reliable, low cost power remains in doubt. With the general economic problems, pressures on government deficits and consumer resistance to higher energy bills, we may be seeing the beginning of the end for renewable energy subsidies.

## UNCONVENTIONAL GAS

In the last five years, especially in the USA, we have seen a massive boom in the production of 'unconventional' gas and oil, most notably shale gas, which has reduced natural gas prices to new lows and will see the USA as a net exporter of liquefied natural gas (LNG) by 2016 and a net exporter of natural gas by 2021 (EIA 2012). Other countries, notably China, are stepping up exploration for shale gas, while in many countries its use – and the technology of hydraulic fracturing, 'fracking' – remain deeply controversial.

The exploitation of shale gas is inevitable in many parts of the world, including those that have currently banned fracking or are putting barriers in the way, due to its accessibility and the low cost of recovering it. On balance, I believe this will be a good thing and is part of what Robert A. Hefner calls the 'Grand Energy Transition' (Hefner 2009), a historical move from solid fuels to liquid fuels to gaseous fuels. Many of the environmental issues seem to be overblown by the anti-fracking community. On the other hand it has to be said that the industry in the US has been inconsistently, and generally lightly regulated although this is now beginning to change as various states introduce new regulatory frameworks. There is a real need to develop and implement better environmental standards globally, something that the major oil companies such as Statoil and Shell, working with standards organizations such as Det Norske Veritas (DNV), are working on. There is also ongoing innovation in the technology to reduce the use of hostile fracking fluids and the volume of water used. However, even in a future national or global economy with access to large quantities of relatively cheap natural gas (assuming we get to that state), energy efficiency should form a central part of energy policy to minimize the negative effects of energy use, maximize the lifetime of resources and optimize productivity.

## ELECTRIC CARS – AGAIN?

In the last five to ten years we have also seen the return of the electric car. I say 'return' for good reason. In 1900, 40 per cent of cars were steam, 38 per cent electric and 22 per cent gasoline, and in 1899 and 1900 electric cars outsold gasoline and steam cars (Bellis 2006). In 1900, Ferdinand Porsche developed the first functional hybrid car and, interestingly, New York had battery swapping stations in 1910 (*Electric Vehicle News* 2012); these are being proposed today by some companies promoting electric cars such as Better Place (which in May 2013 went into liquidation having had $850 million invested), illustrating that old ideas often resurface with the promise of better technology.

There has been much optimism in recent years about how quickly electric cars can take market share, as well as sensible debate about the true system benefits of electric cars in a world where most electricity is generated from fossil fuels. The optimism over the growth of electric motors often fails to take into account how fast conventional internal combustion engine technologies can be improved, and have improved in the last few years alone, when there is competitive and legislative pressure. All-electric vehicles will probably become the norm one day, but I suspect the market transformation will be measured in many decades rather than the years to a few decades talked about by some analysts.

## Energy System Stresses and Strains

When looking at the global energy scene we see a number of stresses, strains and interrelated problems. Russell L. Ackoff, the great management scientist, once said, 'Every problem interacts with other problems and is therefore part of a set of interrelated problems, a system of problems ... I choose to call such a system a mess.' (Ackoff 1974). On that definition, the global energy scene is a mess. Here we outline some of the more pressing aspects of the mess, those that are likely to become bigger stresses and strains as we try to provide energy services to a growing and more affluent global population in the coming decades.

### THE THREAT OF RESOURCE DEPLETION

There can only be a finite amount of any material resource on planet Earth, including fuels such as coal, oil and natural gas. This basic fact has led to recurring concerns, starting with the publication of *An Essay on the Principle of Population* by Thomas Malthus in 1798, about resources running out in the face of a growing human population. Encouraged by the oil crises, which were politically rather than resource driven, the idea of fossil fuels running out resurfaced in the 1970s in books such as *The Limits to Growth* by Dennis Meadows et al. (1972), which was commissioned by the Club of Rome, an international think tank. *The Limits to Growth* was followed by the work of the Brundtland Commission, formally known as the World Commission on Environment and Development, which was formed in 1984 and in 1987 published its report, *Our Common Future* (United Nations 1987), which largely launched today's concerns with sustainability.

The peak oil concept was introduced by M. King Hubbert (1956) and gained widespread popularity in the mid-2000s. Peak oil refers to the point in time when the maximum extraction of oil occurs, after which production declines terminally. Estimates of when global peak oil will be reached vary, with some analysts saying it has already occurred and some analysts claiming it will never occur. Peak oil remains a controversial subject, but there is little or no doubt that important information on oil reserves is deliberately obscured by some oil-producing countries and so it is difficult to be precise about the real reserves situation.

It may well be that conventional oil production has already peaked, and the significant growth in the production of shale oil and other unconventional oil sources has masked it. As far as conventional oil is concerned it does seem clear that the easy, cheap oil has largely been found and that future discoveries are likely to be difficult and expensive, deep offshore for example, but it does have to be said that many areas of the world still remain relatively unexplored.

The growth of shale gas and unconventional oil in recent years does, however, serve as a warning that we should not be too pessimistic on energy supplies as human ingenuity has a way of creating usable resources. The shale gas existed all along but until companies like Mitchell Energy, with government support, developed the technologies of hydraulic fracking and horizontal drilling, the resource could not be utilized. Resources of any kind are only there when we look for them and have the technology to utilize them; they are not just the simple physical oil fields or gas fields but rather a combination of the physical geology, the available technology to find and map them, the prevailing economics and the human desire, motivation and ability to see them.

Even if the peak oil theory turns out to be incorrect there are very real issues with ageing infrastructure and an ageing work force in the oil industry, as highlighted by books such as *Twilight in the Desert* by Matthew Simmons (2005) and work by the World Petroleum Council (Rimer 2008).

## RAPIDLY GROWING DEMAND IN OIL-PRODUCING COUNTRIES

Another big issue in the oil market, which has not yet been as widely recognized as peak oil, is the rapidly growing domestic demand inside oil-producing countries. According to a report by Chatham House (Lahn and Stevens 2011), internal oil demand in Saudi Arabia, which already accounts for 25 per cent of production, is growing at 7 per cent per annum, a rate that will double consumption within a decade. In a business-as-usual scenario, Saudi Arabia would become a net importer of oil by 2038. This scenario, which according to Chatham House would lead to dependence on debt and economic collapse, explains Saudi Arabia identifying energy efficiency as a key national priority (*Saudi Gazette* 2012), as well as its aim of rapidly expanding solar energy – a $109 billion investment plan announced in 2012 (Bloomberg 2012a) – and nuclear power. Electricity production in Saudi Arabia already struggles to keep up with demand in summer which can increase by 50 per cent, driven mainly by air conditioning to combat the extreme temperatures of 40°C to 50°C. Other oil- and gas-producing countries such as Oman and Indonesia face similar issues and are increasingly raising the priority of energy efficiency. The economic equation of energy efficiency for oil-producing countries is clear – is it worth more to use a barrel of oil meeting domestic energy demand or is it better to invest in greater efficiency and export that barrel of oil?

## RAPID GROWTH IN ELECTRICITY DEMAND

The growth of electricity demand, particularly in rapidly growing economies, puts great strain on energy infrastructure. In the summer of 2011 Shanghai had to introduce power rationing – mandatory power cuts – due to an inability to supply peak loads resulting from air conditioning use during high summer temperatures. With increasing wealth, consumers buy electrical goods such as refrigerators and air conditioning, and electricity demand grows at rapid rates. In developed countries we are seeing increasing electrification as we buy more electrical items; this trend is likely to increase, especially if there is a switch to electrically driven heat pumps for heating and/or electric cars.

## ENERGY SECURITY

Energy security is often cited as a driver for energy policy, and specifically energy efficiency policy, but it is a term that is not often unpacked. What do we really mean by energy security? Energy security is a measure of the vulnerability of maintaining the flow of fuel and electricity into, and within, a country or region. Energy security is, of course, a major concern for politicians, whose jobs would become very insecure very rapidly if the flows of energy we have become dependent on were to be interrupted. It should also be a concern for business leaders and community leaders, as well as ordinary citizens, because even the perceived threat to energy supplies can lead to social disruption and ultimately social breakdown.

In March 2012, the perceived threat of a disruption to UK fuel supplies due to threatened strike action by tanker drivers caused widespread panic. Francis Maude, a senior government Minister, suggested people should keep a jerry can of petrol in their garage, which exacerbated the situation and led to long lines for fuel and petrol stations running out of supplies. In this case the politician kept his job and a strike was averted but it does illustrate the sensitive nature of keeping energy supplies flowing.

Energy security is most often highlighted at the macro level and, in particular, in relation to oil supplies. Twenty per cent of the world's oil output – and 35 per cent of tankered oil – is shipped through the Straits of Hormuz. Any disruption of oil traffic through the Straits of Hormuz, either by a country or a terrorist group, would disrupt oil supplies to many countries and have a major impact on the oil price in the short term. Although in the US and Europe oil demand is relatively flat or declining, these countries, along with the rest of the world, remain entirely dependent on oil for transportation of all kinds, road, rail, air and maritime.

## THE THREAT OF SUPPLY DISRUPTION FOR POLITICAL REASONS

The threat of supply disruption by energy-supplying nations is always going to be a risk for energy-importing nations. In 2011, in response to an EU embargo on Iranian oil imposed as part of the international effort to limit their nuclear programme, Iran threatened to disrupt oil supplies through the Straits of Hormuz. The threat helped drive oil prices higher. This was not the first time the threat had been made and the significant US and international navy presence in the area makes the risk of a clash, deliberate or accidental, quite high. The events of the Arab Spring could still threaten the security of oil and gas production in several countries.

Russia provides about one quarter of the gas consumed in the European Union, and about 80 per cent of this flows through Ukraine. Due to a dispute over gas sales, Russia cut gas supplies to the Ukraine completely in January 2006. After four cold days the dispute was settled. Supplies were also reduced in 2008 and 2009, directly affecting gas supplies in some EU countries.

Importing energy remains a high-risk strategy for any country. In colonial days major powers such as the UK were able to secure oil fields by occupation and military power – but this is not a moral or even practical option in the modern world.

## THE THREAT OF SUPPLY DISRUPTION BY TERRORISTS

Despite success against terrorist movements such as Al Qaeda in some parts of the world, all countries remain vulnerable to terrorist attacks on energy supplies. Choke points such as the Straits of Hormuz or major gas and electricity transmission and distribution centres make enticing targets. Destroying, disrupting or damaging them would lead to high levels of disruption, economic damage – and global publicity. The tragic events in Algeria in January 2013 when terrorists targeted the Amenas gas production facility and killed more than 35 hostages highlighted this vulnerability once again.

Saudi Arabia holds 25 per cent of the world's proven oil reserves, produces 12.5 per cent of the world's oil production, exports 16 per cent of the world's total oil exports, and has the largest surplus oil production – approximately 1.1 to 1.8 million barrels a day, so the security of Saudi oil facilities should be a particular concern to everyone. In 2004, an attack on oil facilities in Yanbu was thwarted by the authorities with no damage, and in February 2006 terrorists attacked the Saudi Aramco Abqaiq facility. This plant includes one of the largest oil fields in the world, with reserves greater than those of Mexico or Canada, and a processing facility with a capacity of seven million barrels a day – about 70 per cent of Saudi oil production – which stabilizes oil for shipment by controlling dissolved gas, natural gas liquids and hydrogen sulphide contents. The attack led to oil prices rising by $2/barrel to around $62/barrel. In 2007 the Saudi authorities arrested 700 alleged terrorists suspected of plotting to attack oil installations. As well as oil fields, processing facilities and export terminals, Saudi Arabia has about 11,000 miles of pipelines which are vulnerable to attack.

The total budget for security of oil facilities in Saudi Arabia was estimated at $1.5 billion in 2005 (Al-Rodhan 2006). This does not include the cost to the US and other countries of securing the Straits of Hormuz, which for the US has been estimated by Stern (2010) at $6.8 trillion between 1976 and 2007, an average of $227 billion per annum. This is roughly $83/barrel of Saudi exports, of which only about 20 per cent go to the US, raising serious questions over the real value of this expenditure to the US and what may happen in future when the US becomes less dependent on imported energy due to the unconventional oil and gas boom.

With continued terrorist activity, particularly in nearby Yemen, and political and religious turmoil throughout the Middle East, the threat of oil disruption in Saudi Arabia remains a major concern. But it is by no means the only area for concern. In Nigeria, rebel groups have repeatedly attacked oil installations and kidnapped oil workers. These attacks led to oil production being reduced by 40 per cent in 2009 and, despite an amnesty, production in 2012 was still one million barrels a day (26 per cent) below capacity (Bloomberg 2012b).

Nowadays it is not only the threat of damage from explosives and other physical weapons that security professionals have to worry about – cyber warfare is a very real danger. The Stuxnet virus was targeted at the controllers of the uranium enrichment centrifuges in Iran's nuclear programme and sent the centrifuges into an unstable condition that destroyed them. In October 2012 it was reported that in August cyber terrorists attacked the computers of Saudi Aramco with a virus that wiped the memories of 30,000 computers (Perlroth 2012). The IT network, which in this case was not linked to the production control systems, was disabled for some time and fortunately the attack did not directly impact on operations. Two weeks after this attack a similar attack was made on RasGas, the Qatari natural gas company.

It is important that we unpack and quantify energy security as much as possible. The Institute of 21st Century Energy (2012a) in the USA has developed a comprehensive Energy Security Index® that takes into account four factors: geopolitical, economic, reliability and environmental. These four factors in turn are assessed using nine quantifiable categories:

- Global Fuels Metrics, which cover security of fossil fuel reserves;

- Fuel Import Metrics, covering security and import expenditures;

- Energy Expenditure Metrics, covering different aspects of expenditure;

- Price and Volatility Metrics, covering price volatilities, refinery utilization and petroleum stock levels;

- Energy Use Intensity Metrics, covering various aspects of energy intensity and efficiency;

- Electric Power Metrics, covering factors such as capacity margin

- Transportation Sector Metrics;

- Environmental Metrics;

- Research and Development Metrics.

The Energy Security Index®, which has been applied to the USA and other countries, is not without its problems, but it does provide a quantitative and consistent way of measuring energy security which could be used as input to formulating policy objectives and measuring progress.

The Energy Security Index® for the USA increased to a record high in 2011, despite some factors improving due to the development of shale gas and unconventional oil coming on-stream. As shale gas and domestic unconventional oil production increase it is expected that the US energy security index will reduce, i.e. risks will reduce, over the next decade.

For the Organisation for Economic Co-operation and Development (OECD) as a whole, the Energy Security Index® has increased over the last few years following a low in the mid-1990s. A similar pattern is shown by the United Kingdom, where the Index reached 878 in 2011 compared to a low of below 600 in the mid-1990s (Institute for 21st Century Energy 2012b), a time when North Sea gas and oil reserves were in high production. UK continental shelf gas production peaked in 2000.

Of course, the Energy Security Index® does not measure the impact of a supply disruption. Starting with the Organization of Petroleum Exporting Countries (OPEC) oil embargo of 1973 we have seen the economic and social impact of supply disruptions and price increases a number of times. There is no doubt that being an energy importer makes a country dependent on the energy-exporting countries, and this carries high political and social risks. However small this risk, the magnitude of the effects of not being able to import energy, for whatever reason, are very large, and should – and do – feature in political thinking and energy policy.

Energy security is an issue that has both short-term and long-term time horizons. In the short term even a small, short-lived disruption on any day can cause major economic and social disruption. In the longer term, given the projected increase in global population to about 9 billion by 2050 and the likely entry of 2.5 to 3 billion into the middle class by 2030, energy demand is set to increase dramatically – particularly in rapidly developing economies such as China, India, Brazil and SE Asia. In the future, these countries will compete to buy energy resources and ensure the supply of energy to their own economies.

The issue of energy security is usually talked about in terms of national energy security but it is – and should be – increasingly viewed as a regional or local issue. Improving energy efficiency can improve energy security by reducing the need to import energy sources.

## AGEING INFRASTRUCTURE AND UNDER-INVESTMENT

At the level of individual countries, energy security is also threatened by ageing electricity generating and distribution infrastructure. A 2008 survey of 500 electricity industry professionals in the USA referenced by the NorthWestern Energy Stakeholders Group (2009) reported that more than half of electricity distribution assets are at or beyond their intended life. The Black & Veatch (2012) *Strategic Directions in the US Electric Utility Industry* survey reports that ageing infrastructure remains a major concern for US utility managers. The US Department of Energy reports that the average large-power transformer in the USA is now more than 40 years old (US Department of Energy 2012a). Ageing infrastructure is a consequence of the spike in investment in the electrical distribution system 40 to 50 years ago coupled with excess capacity leading to under-investment since then – plus the fact that cutting investment is an attractive and easy way to save money with consequences that are usually deferred beyond the decision makers' job tenure.

Electrical networks in many parts of the world, particularly in rapidly growing and densely populated cities, are increasingly under pressure due to increasing demand on the system. Upgrading the capacity of network elements such as substations to meet growing demand in cities such as London and New York is often difficult due to physical space constraints. When much of our existing electrical infrastructure was first installed it was designed with what seemed like ample spare capacity at the time, but electrical demands have greatly increased since they were installed.

Implementing energy efficiency measures has been shown to reduce, delay or even lead to permanent deferment of capital expenditure on network reinforcement. A recent report from the New England Independent System Operator (ISO-NE) (Peterson et al. 2012) stated that both private and state-wide energy efficiency programmes had cut the need for $260 million of planned transmission upgrades for two or three years. Neme and Sedano (2012) cite several examples where energy efficiency and demand response programmes have led to deferral of transmission and distribution upgrades, including an example from Consolidated Edison in New York where some $85 million of planned upgrades may never be needed.

In order to enable these spending reductions, the regulatory regimes must allow distribution companies to invest in energy efficiency and demand response projects to avoid investment in network upgrades. As we will discuss in Chapter 11, a major and usually unresolved issue here is the interaction of the electricity market regime and the economic potential. Unless the electricity market is designed to enable and reward investment in demand-side measures by the network operators, this economic and financial potential, along with its attendant environmental and other societal benefits, will remain unexploited. In the UK, for instance, the distribution network operators (DNOs) are rewarded according to how much capital they spend on infrastructure (on a fixed return) and therefore they have no incentive to invest in demand-side measures that reduce the need to invest in infrastructure upgrades.

## ENERGY SYSTEM RESILIENCE

The effect of Hurricane Sandy in late October 2012 on the electricity system of several Caribbean islands, the north-east United States and particularly New York, once again graphically illustrated the issue of resilience of energy systems – their ability to withstand and recover from shocks caused by major natural or man-made incidents. In the USA, more than 4.8 million customers in 15 states and the District of Columbia had an extended period after the hurricane without electricity. Local officials in many parts of the world are now looking at the issue of energy system resilience and how it may be improved by energy efficiency, decentralization and the addition of 'smart' technologies.

## THE ECONOMIC COSTS OF IMPORTING ENERGY – NATIONALLY OR REGIONALLY

Many countries – and regions within countries – import energy, notably oil, coal and natural gas as well as electricity. As well as increasing security risk, this creates a balance of payments problem as energy imports have to be paid for and the money leaves the country or region. In 2010 the European Union spent €435 billion on importing fuel from outside its borders, equivalent to €2.70 per person of the 503 million population every day (Casey 2011). By 2011, rising fuel prices meant this number had increased to €580 billion, meaning that 3.3 per cent of its GDP left the EU to pay for energy – notably, this was more than the total Greek national debt which has caused so much concern over the last few years. This amount was nearly two thirds higher than in 2009 as a result of increased oil prices. Across the world, oil-importing countries paid out $1.8 trillion in 2011, a number that may have exceeded $2 trillion in 2012 (Boselli 2012).

As well as the national-level picture and the national impact of such large wealth transfers, some regional leaders are now starting to consider the regional economic impact of energy imports into their regions. The US state of Massachusetts, for example, spent $22 billion in 2008 (Massachusetts Executive Office of Energy and Environmental Affairs 2010) on energy imports, with an average of about $20 billion of energy imports between 2007 and 2009 (Breslow 2010). Some $252 million was spent on coal imports alone in 2008, $206 million of which left the USA for Columbia. This kind of information is a powerful motivator for political and business leaders to take action.

## THE THREAT OF CLIMATE CHANGE

The threat of climate change is linked to emissions of carbon dioxide resulting from fossil fuel combustion. As is well known, carbon dioxide levels in the atmosphere have increased from about 200 parts per million (ppm) in pre-industrial times to about 400 ppm today. It is hard to debate that the climate is changing, although for some people even this is still debatable, and of course the Earth's climate has changed many times over geological time periods. Whether or not climate change is really driven predominantly by anthropogenic carbon dioxide emissions remains controversial, but the theory remains a strong driver of policies that affect the energy sector in many jurisdictions, particularly the European Union. There are increasing signs that the EU may pull back from these policies, irrespective of the reality of climate change or what the climate actually does, in response to factors including the advent of shale gas, evidence that the global temperature increase may have slowed or stopped, and of course general austerity.

Globally, reduced energy usage results in lower emissions of carbon dioxide as well as other pollutants. The amount of carbon emissions and other pollution avoided by improved efficiency depends on the energy mix in question, i.e. what sources of fuel are being used and which energy conversion technology is being used. Energy efficiency, however, is a vital tool in reducing emissions.

## INDOOR AND OUTDOOR AIR POLLUTION

Air pollution, particularly in the form of smogs and particulates both indoors and outdoors, causes massive health problems. The World Health Organization (WHO 2004) estimates that indoor air pollution, which is primarily created by heating and cooking using coal and biomass in open fires or leaky stoves, causes approximately two million premature deaths a year, primarily in developing countries, half of them due to pneumonia in children under five years of age. Outdoor air pollution in urban areas is estimated to cause 1.3 million deaths worldwide per year (WHO 2011). The majority of these are in rapidly industrializing middle-income countries, but more advanced countries are not without their problems. A 2012 study by the Massachusetts Institute of Technology (Yim and Barrett 2012) reported that emissions from cars, trucks, aircraft and power plants cause 13,000 premature deaths in the United Kingdom each year and although there may be some questions about the methodology, there is no doubt that air pollution affects health directly through inhalation of particulate matter (PM), very fine particles that are present in exhausts from liquid and solid fossil fuel combustion. London, in particular, has high levels of PM that regularly exceed the standards set in EU air quality regulations.

The effects of pollution from the combustion of fossil fuels, particularly the emissions of oxides of sulphur and nitrogen and carbon particulates, is obvious in rapidly developing economies like China. In January 2013, air pollution in Beijing reached new highs and attracted international publicity. The health effects of this level of pollution are immense and shocking. The Chinese Ministry of Environmental Protection published a report (2010) which showed that one third of the 113 cities surveyed failed to meet China's own national air standards. The World Bank (2007) estimated that 750,000 people in China die prematurely each year from respiratory problems (Spencer 2007). Despite efforts to reduce the problem, air pollution in Beijing reached new highs in early 2013 with particulate matter reaching 20 times the WHO's safe level, and the government had to take emergency action. This is not just a Chinese problem but is common in other rapidly developing economies. It is a terrible human cost that we can, and should, fix. The UK pioneered action in this area through the Clean Air Act of 1956 (and subsequent legislation), a response to the infamous London 'Great Smog' of 1952 which killed several thousand people.

Although the trail of death and illness caused by airborne pollution clearly has to be addressed, mainly by the enforcement of better regulations and cleaner fuels, improving energy efficiency can play a significant role by reducing the amount of fuel burnt, hence reducing emissions. Introducing more efficient stoves could go a long way towards eliminating the problems of indoor air pollution.

## FUEL POVERTY AND ITS HEALTH EFFECTS

Low levels of energy efficiency also create health issues for those in fuel poverty. The term fuel poverty, introduced and championed in the UK and elsewhere by Dr Brenda Boardman in the early 1980s, refers to households where energy costs exceed 10 per cent of household income. Typically the homes of those in fuel poverty have low levels of insulation and low-efficiency heating systems and appliances. This means that the cost of delivering a unit of comfort, such as 24 hours at a normal living-room temperature in December, is far higher for the fuel-poor than it is for the majority who live in better-insulated homes with more efficient systems and appliances and higher incomes. The health effects of fuel poverty include premature deaths from hypothermia (more old people die in winter than summer in cold climates such as the UK and parts of the USA), additional hospital stays due to cold-induced illnesses, and the effects of mould. Action to improve the efficiency of homes of people in fuel poverty can deliver significant health benefits as well as societal benefits in terms of reduced health costs. The Marmot Review Team (2011) and Friends of the Earth reported that the UK's Chief Medical Officer stated that spending one pound on energy efficiency saved 42 pence on health care costs in the National Health Service.

## THE HUMAN COSTS OF THE ENERGY INDUSTRY

The numbers of lives lost due to conventional energy production are large. The highest-profile example of this is deaths of coal miners in China, which, despite dramatic reductions over the last few years, still reached 1,973 in 2011 (UPI 2012), more than five a day. In the USA there were 21 deaths in 2011, a rate – normalizing for production – of approximately one-thirtieth of that in China. Of course, all energy production has its health and safety risks, even rooftop solar and wind power, and it is extremely unlikely that we could ever remove all health and safety risks from any human activity.

## ENVIRONMENTAL IMPACTS OF EXTRACTING ENERGY RESOURCES

The environmental impacts resulting from fossil and nuclear fuel extraction are many and varied. They include deposition of waste materials; water contamination; leaching of contaminants from drilling muds; emissions; oil spills; leaks and blowouts; venting of volatile organic compounds (VOCs); releases of radioactivity both from reactor accidents (such as Fukushima in 2011, Chernobyl in 1986, Three Mile Island in 1979, and Windscale in 1957) and uranium mining; extraction of water resources and destruction of wildlife habitats. High-profile and large-scale cases such as Fukushima and the BP Gulf of Mexico oil spill get most of the attention, but there is a constant and widespread environmental impact from fossil and nuclear fuel extraction.

## SAFETY (AND PERCEIVED SAFETY) OF NUCLEAR POWER

There are currently 435 operable nuclear reactors in the world (World Nuclear Association 2013) with a total capacity of 374 GW, producing about 13 per cent of global electricity production in 2010. The commercial/civilian generation of electricity by nuclear production started in the UK, USA and USSR in the 1950s, and throughout the 1950s and 1960s nuclear power was generally regarded with hope and optimism. The famous quote about 'electrical energy too cheap to meter' was coined by Lewis Strauss, the Chairman of the United States Atomic Energy Commission in 1954; he was apparently referring to the prospect of fusion power rather than fission power, but it captures the spirit of optimism of those early years of nuclear power. Since the 1970s, however, nuclear power has been, and continues to be, controversial on the grounds of safety.

On one side of the nuclear debate is the view that we need to expand the use of nuclear power to help reduce dependence on fossil fuels, reduce carbon dioxide emissions and provide reliable base load power. The alternative view is that nuclear power is too dangerous to use. In the light of the Fukushima disaster, Germany decided to phase out nuclear power by 2022. But in 2012 a number of noted environmentalists in the UK such as James Lovelock appeared to come out in favour of expanding nuclear power. Even in France, where nuclear power produces 70 per cent of total electricity output, there is considerable resistance and concern around nuclear power. Opinion polls show that 40 per cent of the French population are 'hesitant' about nuclear power and 17 per cent are against it (Bloomberg 2011). Under Francois Hollande's Socialist party there may be a partial nuclear phase out.

Walt Patterson (1986), in his excellent history of the UK nuclear power programme, outlines the almost incredible story of mismanagement, overspending and delays throughout the life of the programme from its beginning soon after the war through to the 1980s. I suspect a similar story could be written about every country's civil nuclear programme, including the much heralded – and over-sold – French nuclear programme, in which the latest reactor at Flamanville, the budget for which was originally €3.3 billion, has cost €8.5 billion to date and is now expected to commence operations in 2016, rather than the original target of 2012. These costs and dates should be compared with a 2010 estimate of €6 billion and a 2012 completion date. It is hard to believe that the UK equivalent using the same design from EDF won't be similarly affected by delays and budget overruns.

Since the advent of the nuclear age, the nuclear programme has consumed a high proportion of total government spending on energy. In the UK, nuclear decommissioning still accounts for about half of the entire budget of the Department of Energy and Climate Change (DECC 2012) (circa £2 billion), while in the USA the proportion of the Department of Energy's budget spent on nuclear matters is around 40 per cent (US Department of Energy 2012b).

Safe operation of nuclear power requires the highest standards of security, management and operation at all times, 24/7, and it is extremely difficult – if not impossible – to ensure these standards are maintained for decades in a modern commercial or quasi-commercial organization, or even in a military or paramilitary organization. Furthermore, any reactor-system design needs to be inherently failsafe, and many existing designs are not. Nuclear power, like space exploration technology, is still dominated by its military origins. But the use of a uranium-cycle pressurized water reactor, which evolved from military submarine propulsion systems, is inappropriate for civil nuclear power systems. The thorium cycle could be a better basic technology on the grounds of safety, non-proliferation and ultimate resource base but has never received the level of support it probably deserves because of the dominance of the militarily useful uranium cycle. Global research and development on this technology should be stepped up significantly.

## Energy Efficiency Can Mitigate the Problems

All of these problems within the global energy system can be researched and discussed at much greater length. Expanding energy supply, whatever the underlying technologies, to meet expanding demand from nine billion people and the rapidly expanding global middle class is going to be a major challenge for us all. Aggressively pursuing the improvement of energy efficiency in all sectors and all countries can help to significantly reduce these problems and represents a profitable opportunity which will create jobs and more sustainable growth.

## References and Bibliography

Ackoff, R. 1974. *Redesigning the Future.* Hoboken NJ, John Wiley & Sons.
Al-Rodhan, K.R. 2006. *The Impact of the Abqaiq Attack on Saudi Energy Security.* [Online]. Available at: http://csis.org/files/media/csis/pubs/060227_abqai qattack.pdf [accessed 26 January 2013].

Alyousef, Y. and Abu-ebid, M. 2012. 'Energy Efficiency Initiatives for Saudi Arabia on Supply and Demand Sides', in Morvaj, Z. (ed.) *Energy Efficiency – A Bridge to Low Carbon Economy*. [Online]. Available at: http://www. intechopen.com/books/energy-efficiency-a-bridge-to-low-carbon-economy/ energy-efficiency-initiatives-for-saudi-arabia-on-supply-and-demand-sides [accessed 26 January 2013].

Bellis, M. 2006. *History of Electric Vehicles. The Early Years, Electric Cars from 1830 to 1930.* [Online]. Available at: http://inventors.about.com/od/estartinventions/a/ History-Of-Electric-Vehicles.htm [accessed 26 January 2013].

Black & Veatch. 2012. *2012 Strategic Directions in the U.S. Electric Utility Industry*. [Online]. Available at: http://bv.com/docs/management-consulting-brochures/2012-electric-utility-report-web.pdf [accessed 26 January 2013].

Bloomberg. 2011. 'Atomic Power Heats Up French Election as Sarkozy Rival Backs Reactor Halts'. [Online]. Available at: http://www.bloomberg.com/ news/2011-12-01/atomic-spat-rocks-french-election-as-sarkozy-rival-backs-halts.html [accessed 26 January 2013].

Bloomberg. 2012a. 'Saudi Arabia Plans $109 Billion Boost for Solar Power'. 26 November 2012. [Online]. Available at: http://www.bloomberg.com/ news/2012-11-22/saudi-arabia-plans-109-billion-boost-for-solar-power.html [accessed 26 January 2013].

Bloomberg. 2012b. 'Nigerian Delta Unrest Cuts Oil Output by 1 Million Barrels'. 5 March 2012. [Online]. Available at: http://www.bloomberg.com/ news/2012-03-04/nigeria-s-nnpc-says-unrest-cuts-oil-output-by-1-million-barrels.html [accessed 26 January 2013].

Boselli, M. 2012. 'World Oil Import Bill Heading for Record 1.25 Trillion Pounds'. [Online]. Available at: http://uk.reuters.com/article/2012/03/27/uk-iea-oil-bills-idUKBRE82Q10C20120327 [accessed 26 January 2013].

Breslow, M. 2010. 'Massachusetts $ Savings and Job Gains from Energy Efficiency in Buildings & Transportation'. [Online]. Available at: http://www. epa.gov/statelocalclimate/documents/pdf/breslow_presentation_8-4-2011. pdf [accessed 26 January 2013].

Casey, Z. 2011. 'EU Energy Import Bill Amounted to €355 billion in 2010'. [Online]. Available at: http://www.ewea.org/blog/2011/10/eu-energy-import-bill-amounted-to-e355-billion-in-2010/ [accessed 26 January 2013].

DECC. 2012. *Business Plan 2012–2015*. [Online]. Available at: http://www. number10.gov.uk/wp-content/uploads/2012/05/DECC-2012-Business-Plan. pdf [accessed 26 January 2013].

EIA. 2012. 'US Expected to Become Net Exporter of Natural Gas by End of Decade'. U.S. Energy Information Administration, 5 December 2012. [Online]. Available at: http://www.eia.gov/radio/transcript/aeo-lng-12052012.pdf [accessed 27 December 2012].

*Electric Vehicle News.* 2012. 'The History of Electric Vehicles'. [Online]. Available at: http://www.electricvehiclesnews.com/History/historyearly.htm [accessed 26 January 2013].

Frost & Sullivan. 2012. 'Saudi Arabia puts Energy Efficiency on Radar'. [Online]. Available at: http://www.frost.com/prod/servlet/press-release. pag?docid=266188072 [accessed 26 January 2013].

Hefner, R.A. 2009. *The Grand Energy Transition: The Rise of Energy Gases, Sustainable Life and Growth, and the Next Great Economic Expansion.* Hoboken NJ, John Wiley & Sons.

Hubbert, M.K. 1956. *Nuclear Energy and Fossil Fuels.* Presented to the Spring Meeting of the Southern District Division of Production, American Petroleum Institute, San Antonio, Texas, March 7–9, 1956. [Online]. Available at: http://www.hubbertpeak.com/hubbert/1956/1956.pdf [accessed 26 January 2013].

IEA. 2012. *World Energy Outlook 2012.* [Online]. Available at: http://www. worldenergyoutlook.org/publications/weo-2012/ [accessed 26 January 2013].

Institute for 21st Century Energy. 2012a. *Index of U.S. Energy Security Risk.* [Online]. Available at: http://www.energyxxi.org/us-index-of-energy-security-risk [accessed 26 January 2013].

Institute for 21st Century Energy. 2012b. *International Index of Energy Security Risk.* [Online]. Available at: http://www.energyxxi.org/2012-international-index-energy-security-risk-pdf [accessed 26 January 2013].

Kay, J. (2005). 'Bush's Lack of Guilt on Global Warming', *Financial Times,* 26 July 2005. [Online]. Available at: http://www.johnkay.com/2005/07/26/bushs-lack-of-guilt-on-global-warming [accessed 26 April 2013].

Kharas, H. 2010. *The Emerging Middle Class in Developing Countries.* OECD Development Centre Working Paper Number 285. [Online]. Available at: http://www.oecd.org/dev/44457738.pdf [accessed 26 January 2013].

Lahn, G. and Stevens, P. 2011. *Burning Oil to Keep Cool: The Hidden Energy Crisis in Saudi Arabia.* Chatham House. [Online]. Available at: http:// www.chathamhouse.org/sites/default/files/public/Research/Energy,%20 Environment%20and%20Development/1211pr_lahn_stevens.pdf [accessed 26 January 2013].

Malthus, T. 1798. *An Essay on the Principle of Population.* London, J. Johnson. [Also online]. Available at: http://www.esp.org/books/malthus/population/malthus.pdf [accessed 26 January 2013].

Marmot Review Team. 2011. *The Health Impacts of Cold Homes and Fuel Poverty.* [Online]. Available at: http://www.instituteofhealthequity.org/projects/the-health-impacts-of-cold-homes-and-fuel-poverty [accessed 26 January 2013].

Massachusetts Executive Office of Energy and Environmental Affairs. 2010. *Massachusetts Clean Energy and Climate Plan for 2020*. [Online]. Available at: http://www.mass.gov/eea/docs/eea/energy/2020-clean-energy-plan.pdf [accessed 26 January 2013].

Meadows, D.H., Meadows, D.L., Randers, J. and Behrens, W.W. 1972. *The Limits to Growth*. New York, New American Library.

Ministry of Environmental Protection of the People's Republic of China. 2010. *Report on the State of the Environment in China*. [Online]. Available at: http://english.mep.gov.cn/standards_reports/soe/soe2010/201301/P0201301 10394493041019.pdf [accessed 26 January 2013].

Neme, C. and Sedano, R. 2012. *US Experience with Efficiency As a Transmission and Distribution System Resource*. [Online]. Available at: http://www.raponline. org/document/download/id/4765 [accessed 26 January 2013].

NorthWestern Energy Stakeholders Group. 2009. *Our Deteriorating American Infrastructure and the Role of Electric Distribution Systems*. [Online]. Available at: http://www.northwesternenergy.com/Documents/ISG/Sept-09/ StakeholderSlides9-24-09.pdf [accessed 26 January 2013].

Patterson, W. 1986. *Nuclear Power*. 2nd edition, with Postscript. Harmondsworth, Penguin. [Also online]. Available at: http://www.waltpatterson.org/ nppenguin.pdf [accessed 26 January 2013].

Perlroth, N. 2012. 'In Cyberattack on Saudi Firm, U.S. Sees Iran Firing Back'. *The New York Times*, 23 October 2012. [Online]. Available at: http://www. nytimes.com/2012/10/24/business/global/cyberattack-on-saudi-oil-firm-disquiets-us.html?pagewanted=all&_r=0 [accessed 26 January 2013].

Peterson, P., Hurley, D., Jackson, S. and Schultz, M. 2012. *The Road to Better System Planning: ISO-New England's Revised Energy Efficiency Forecast*. [Online]. Available at: http://www.synapse-energy.com/Downloads/ SynapseReport.2012-04.CT-OCC.ISO-New-England%27s-Revised-EE-Forecast.12-015.pdf [accessed 26 January 2013].

Rimer, P. 2008. *A World in Transition: Delivering Energy for Sustainable Growth*. Presentation delivered at the 19th World Petroleum Congress, 2008. [Online]. Available at: http://www.world-petroleum.org/docs/docs/speeches/wpc%20 Presentation%20the%20Aging%20Workforce%202.swf [accessed 26 January 2013].

Saudi Gazette. 2012. 'Five National Energy Conservation Targets Set'. *Saudi Gazette*, 10 February 2012. [Online]. Available at: http://www.saudigazette. com.sa/index.cfm?method=home.regcon&contentid=20120210117276 [accessed 26 January 2013].

Simmons, M.R. 2005. *Twilight in the Desert*. Hoboken NJ, John Wiley & Sons.

Spencer, R. 2007. 'Pollution Kills 750,000 a Year in China Every Year', *Daily Telegraph*, 4 July 2007. [Online]. Available at: http://www.telegraph.co.uk/earth/earthnews/3299339/Pollution-kills-750000-in-China-every-year.html [accessed 26 April 2013].

Stern, R.J. 2010. 'United States Cost of Military Force Protection in the Persian Gulf, 1976–2007. *Energy Policy*, 2010. [Online]. Available at: http://timemilitary.files.wordpress.com/2011/04/us-miiltary-cost-of-persian-gulf-force-projection.pdf [accessed 27 December 2012].

UNEP. 2012. *Global Trends in Renewable Energy Investment 2012*. UNEP, Frankfurt School and Bloomberg New Energy. [Online]. Available at: http://fs-unep-centre.org/sites/default/files/publications/globaltrendsreport2012final.pdf [accessed 27 December 2012].

United Nations. 1987. *Report of the World Commission on Environment and Development: Our Common Future*. [Online]. Available at: http://www.un-documents.net/our-common-future.pdf [accessed 26 January 2013].

United Nations. 2010. *World Population Prospects: The 2010 Revision*. [Online]. Available at: http://esa.un.org/unpd/wpp/Documentation/pdf/WPP2010_Volume-I_Comprehensive-Tables.pdf [accessed 26 January 2013].

UPI. 2012. 'China's Coal Miners Still at Risk'. [Online]. Available at: http://www.upi.com/Business_News/Energy-Resources/2012/05/08/Chinas-coal-miners-still-at-risk/UPI-44711336506039/ [accessed 26 January 2013].

US Department of Energy. 2012a. *Large Power Transformers and the U.S. Electric Grid*. [Online]. Available at: http://energy.gov/sites/prod/files/Large%20Power%20Transformer%20Study%20-%20June%202012_0.pdf [accessed 26 January 2013].

US Department of Energy. 2012b. *FY 2013 Congressional Budget Request*. [Online]. Available at: http://www.cfo.doe.gov/budget/13budget/Content/Highlights.pdf [accessed 26 January 2013].

WHO. 2004. 'Global Burden of Disease Due to Indoor Air Pollution'. [Online]. Available at: http://www.who.int/indoorair/health_impacts/burden_global/en/ [accessed 26 January 2013].

WHO. 2011. 'Tackling the Global Clean Air Challenge'. [Online]. Available at: http://www.who.int/mediacentre/news/releases/2011/air_pollution_20110926/en/index.html [accessed 26 January 2013].

Wolfson, R. 2012. *The Future of Energy*. [Online]. Available at: http://www.insightcruises.com/pdf/sa11_slides/Wolfson/Future_of_energy.pdf [accessed 26 January 2013].

World Bank. 2007. *Cost of Pollution in China: Economic Estimates if Physical Damage*. [Online]. Available at: http://siteresources.worldbank.org/INTEAPREGTOPENVIRONMENT/Resources/China_Cost_of_Pollution.pdf [accessed 26 January 2013].

World Nuclear Association. 2013. 'World Nuclear Power Reactors and Uranium Requirements'. [Online]. Available at: http://www.world-nuclear.org/info/reactors.html [accessed 26 January 2013].

Yim, S.H.L. and Barrett, S.R.H. 2012. 'Public Health Impacts of Combustion Emissions in the United Kingdom'. *Environmental Science & Technology*, 46(8): 4291–6.

# 3

# Potentials and Barriers

*Regardless of what the skeptics may think, there are indeed 20-dollar bills lying on the ground all around us. We only need the will – and the ways – to pick them up.*

Stephen Chu, US Secretary of Energy

## Introduction

In this chapter, by reviewing a number of studies that have been conducted over the decades, we look at the potential for energy efficiency at the highest levels, globally, nationally and by sector. We also examine the ultimate limits to energy efficiency – the ultimate technical potential based on the known laws of physics. We then examine the other benefits that result from improved energy efficiency and their potential impact on the energy issues we reviewed in Chapter 2. Finally, we review the evidence on the barriers to achieving the potentials.

## What is the Potential for Energy Efficiency and What Do We Mean by Potential?

One of the first questions facing decision makers looking at energy issues, either at the level of the organization or national policy, is what is the potential for energy efficiency? Because energy efficiency brings many benefits, we also have to ask: what kind of potential are we considering? Possible answers include reduction in energy costs (financial savings); energy consumption; reduced risk; reduced environmental emissions; health benefits; job creation. We will consider the various types of potential in turn.

This chapter focuses on the potential at the level of national and global economies rather than that for individual organizations or householders.

Although the potentials referred to here are aggregates across the defined sector or economy, the actual potential benefits in any particular organization, process, vehicle or building will be very specific to the particular situation and site. Their magnitude will be affected by the design, quality of build, condition, operating pattern, maintenance regime of the process, vehicle or building, as well as by the previous effort put into energy efficiency and the design techniques used to develop energy efficiency projects. The scale of the potential benefits will also be affected by the availability and costs of energy-saving technologies, which in practice are driven by a number of site- and situation-specific factors, as well as by soft factors such as attitudes and leadership. Finally, of course, the economic potential will be driven by prevailing energy prices. The actual savings achieved in certain case studies within each sector, a very small selection of which are featured in Chapter 6, and many, many more of which can be found in books, online and in presentations by many authors, serve to illustrate the likely potential and the specific benefits in similar situations, but each case will be different.

When discussing the potential for reducing energy consumption through improved energy efficiency it is important to distinguish between technical potential and economic potential. Economic potential is defined as the potential for energy efficiency improvement that is economic. In my view the only sensible way to measure what is 'economic' in the micro-case of an individual firm or organization is to use the investor's own criteria rather than some arbitrary or academic criteria and sum the resulting likely investments. But, of course, in macro studies it is necessary to take some fixed criteria such as a payback period or an Internal Rate of Return (IRR), as it is not possible in any large sample to measure everyone's definition of economic.

In reality, all potentials are dynamic and affected by shifting technological, economic and management factors. Like other resources, energy efficiency potentials are, in a very real sense, only there when you look for them, in the same way that an oil field, or a shale gas field, is only visible and realizable when you search for it. The size of any potential is driven by energy prices and the cost of energy efficiency technologies. If energy prices increase, the potential increases; if energy prices fall, the potential falls. If the price of an energy efficiency technology falls, the potential increases, and if it increases the potential falls. Therefore, any quantification of potential is only an estimate of a quantity at a fixed point in time under certain prices and a particular stage of technology development. Some studies recognize this dynamic and make their assumptions explicit, while in others they are implicit which makes comparisons of potential studies difficult. The drivers of the size of the energy efficiency potential are summarized in Figure 3.1.

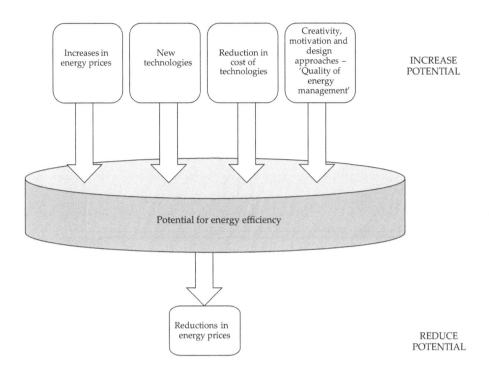

**Figure 3.1    Drivers of energy efficiency potential**

The types of potential for energy efficiency can be extended beyond the simple technical and economic potential and a schema of potentials is presented in Figure 3.2. There is often discussion of an 'energy efficiency gap', which is usually defined as the gap between what is actually achieved in energy efficiency and what is economic. In the schema presented here there are several types of energy efficiency potential and gaps between them.

The ultimate potential for energy efficiency in any particular process is the difference between what is being achieved now and what is theoretically possible as defined by the laws of physics. This potential is essentially fixed unless, and until, we discover new laws of physics.

The technical potential is the difference between what is being achieved now and what can be achieved utilizing existing, available, real technologies. It should be noted that different technologies may carry different performance risks because they are at different stages of technological maturity, and decision makers need to be conscious of their risk preference. The size of the technical potential is driven by technological developments.

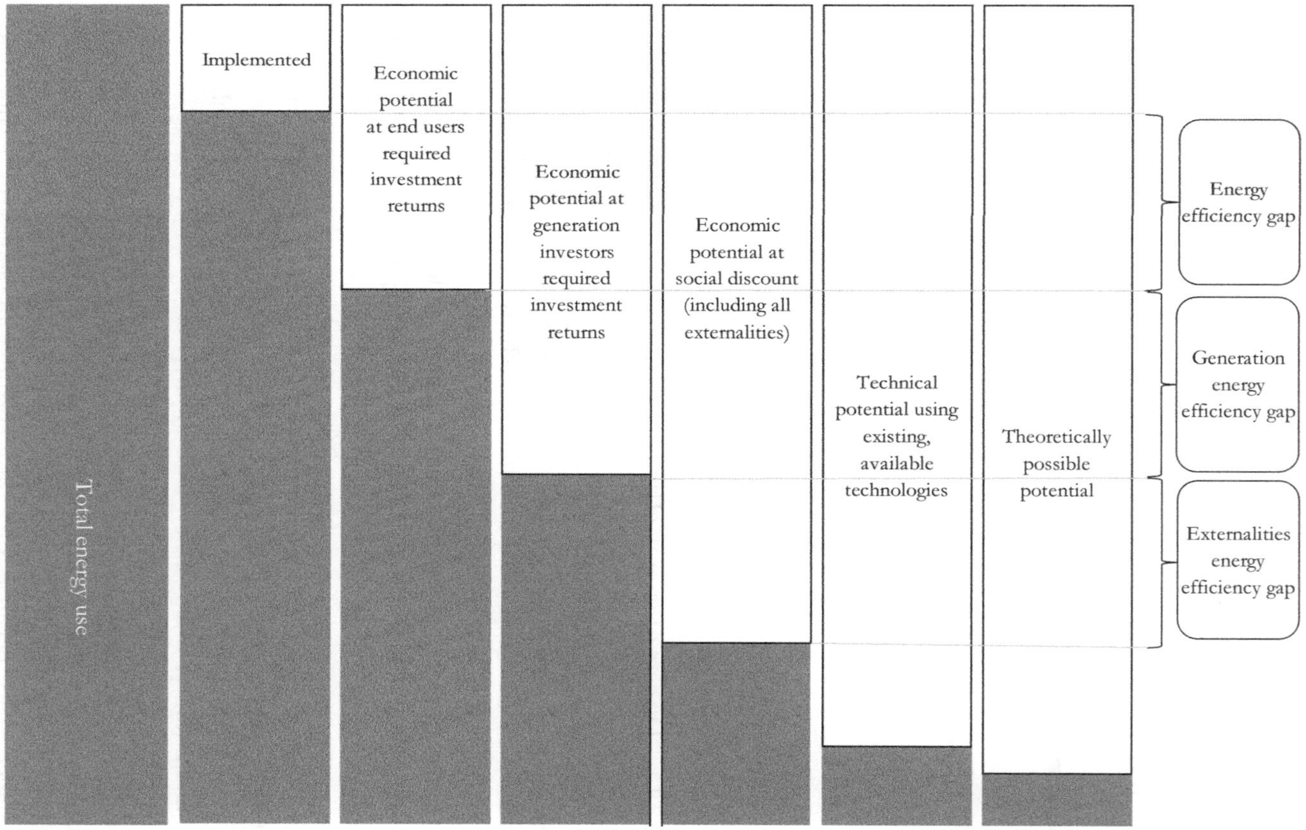

Energy efficiency gap

Generation energy efficiency gap

Externalities energy efficiency gap

Theoretically possible potential

Technical potential using existing, available technologies

Economic potential at social discount (including all externalities)

Economic potential at generation investors required investment returns

Economic potential at end users required investment returns

Implemented

Total energy use

Not to scale

**Figure 3.2  Energy efficiency potentials**

For example, the introduction of light-emitting diode (LED) lighting technologies increased the technological potential for energy efficiency in lighting significantly. The next energy efficiency gap can be labelled the 'technological energy efficiency gap'.

The next level of potential is the difference between the level of performance being achieved now and what could be achieved if all technologies that were economic including externalities in any given situation were applied. The assessment of the economic case would include external factors such as pollution and health benefits, etc., as well as considerations of energy security which is, of course, a theoretical exercise. It is driven by the value ascribed to these external benefits and is separated from the next level of potential by an 'externality energy efficiency gap'. To assess this potential we would effectively be using a social discount rate to assess the economics of the investment case.

The next level is the potential for energy efficiency that would be economic, applying the same definition of economic that is used in the energy supply industry. This is an important gap that policy makers in particular need to consider more carefully. The energy supply industry makes investment decisions on new energy supply facilities, generating plant and transmission and distribution capacity, with long-term horizons and typically fairly low economic returns: 10 to 15 per cent 10-year IRRs and five- to eight-year payback periods. Energy efficiency investments, in contrast, are usually subject to much stricter investment criteria, typically two- to five-year maximum payback periods (30 to 50 per cent 10-year IRRs). This means we have a basic mismatch in investment criteria that works against energy efficiency and results in the economy operating at a lower overall productivity of capital than it could if the same investment criteria were applied to both energy supply and demand. If we could ensure investment happened in all energy efficiency opportunities with the same investment criteria as energy supply investment opportunities we would see a marked increase in overall energy efficiency. Policies can, and should be, devised to support this aim (see Chapter 11).

The 'generation energy efficiency gap' defines the difference between the potential that is economic by using the same investment criteria as generation and that which is economic to the end user, i.e. economic using the end users' investment criteria.

Finally, the 'energy efficiency gap' that is most often discussed, because it is the most useful in the real world, separates the economic potential according to the investor's criteria from what is actually invested in and implemented. The level of implementation is driven by factors such as energy management capacity and the attention paid to the issue by management. In organizations with excellent energy management programmes you would expect this gap to be small because all, or nearly all, economic opportunities are exploited as they occur. One of the factors that governments seeking to improve energy efficiency can affect is the design and delivery of programmes to help organizations improve the quality of energy management. Chapter 6 considers energy management processes.

Of the economic potential for energy efficiency, a proportion is potential that can be achieved with investment and a proportion is potential that can be improved without investment. The later can be achieved through better operations, maintenance or 'good housekeeping'. This is the 'low-hanging fruit', or as US Secretary of Energy Stephen Chu described it, 'the fruit lying on the floor', that all organizations should exploit before moving on to measures with capital expenditure.

Any macro study of potentials for energy cost savings, energy reductions, or any other of the benefits outlined below needs to be explicit about what level of potential is being investigated. Micro-level studies of potential at the level of individual organizations are usually much more concerned with the potential that is economic using the investor's criteria.

## Studies of Potentials

The starting point for quantifying any of the benefits is to look at the amount of energy that could be saved through improved energy efficiency. Many people, over many years, including the author, have studied the potential for improved energy efficiency at corporate, national and international levels, with studies covering all sectors of the economy or selected sectors, for all technologies or a limited selection of technologies, as well as technical potential or economic potentials. Table 3.1 summarizes just a few of those studies for different sectors and different geographies. The results can only be briefly summarized here. As well as macro studies there are many, many case studies covering all kinds of situations that show energy savings that have been achieved and the financial returns resulting from those investments.

## A NOTE ON ENERGY UNITS

One of the realities of studying energy is that there are many different types of energy units of measurement. There are both metric and imperial units, with specific units for different types of energy driven by local or regional historical usage. Any energy analyst has to become used to converting from one unit of energy (and power) to another. In this book we have avoided converting units when reporting both macro- and micro-level studies. The main units of energy used in estimates of potential shown in Table 3.1 are:

QBTU    quadrillion British Thermal Units ('Quad')
TWh     terawatt hours
GWh     gigawatt hours
Mtoe    million tonnes oil equivalent
BOE     Barrels of oil equivalent
EJ      Exajoules (1018 Joules)

A conversion table is included in Appendix 2.

From all these studies and many others in different countries and sectors it is clear that there is a very large potential for improved energy efficiency in all sectors globally. The economic potential alone represents a massive potential prize that, if we can exploit it, will make us wealthier, help us to reduce the stresses and strains in the global energy system, and create jobs.

## Is There a Limit to Energy Efficiency?

It is worth briefly considering the question: is there a limit to how far we can improve energy efficiency and to the size of the energy efficiency resource? Obviously, for any individual process there is a fundamental limit set by the laws of thermodynamics, and in practice no real-life technology can achieve that. Cullen (2009) points out that it is only sensible to talk about a theoretical ultimate energy efficiency target for conversion devices rather than passive systems such as buildings. For instance, a super-insulated house which requires no external heat input created by the use of fuel or electricity has an infinite efficiency (level of service divided by zero), which is nonsensical. The efficiency limits of passive devices depend solely on the practical engineering design constraints rather than the underlying physics of energy conversion.

**Table 3.1      Summary of studies of potential**

| Title and Authors | Publication date | Sector(s) | Geographical scope | Summary of conclusions |
|---|---|---|---|---|
| *Curbing Global Energy Demand Growth: The Energy Productivity Opportunity* McKinsey Global Institute | 2007 | All | Global | 135 QBTU by 2020 (64m bbl oil per day) Reduced growth in energy demand from 2.2% p.a. Business As Usual (BAU) to 0.6% p.a. $170bn p.a. investment at >10% IRR at $70/bbl oil |
| *Energy Efficiency in Buildings. Transforming the Market.* World Council for Sustainable Development | 2009 | Buildings | Global | Building energy use could be cut by 60% by 2050 |
| *Reducing Energy Demand: What Are the Practical Limits?* J. Cullen, J. Allwood and E. Borgstein | 2011 | All | Global | 73% savings potential. Technical potential. |
| *World Energy Outlook 2012* IEA | 2012 | All | Global | Efficient World Scenario compared to New Policies Scenario results in: Boost to cumulative economic output through 2035 of $18 trillion – equivalent to current sizes of the economies of the US, Canada, Mexico and Chile combined Additional investment of $11.8 trillion needed Reduces fuel expenditures by $17.5 trillion and supply-side investment by $5.9 trillion Growth in primary energy demand 2010–2035 is halved Oil demand peaks at 91 million barrels per day before 2020 and declines to 87 million barrels per day in 2035 Energy-related $CO_2$ emissions peak before 2020 and decline to 30.5 Gt in 2035 |
| *U.S. Building-Sector Energy Efficiency Potential* Rich Brown, Sam Borgeson, Jon Koomey and Peter Biermayer Lawrence Berkeley National Laboratory | 2008 | Residential and commercial buildings | USA | Residential: Electricity: 567 TWh (30% of BAU) Gas: 1.51 QBTU (28% of BAU) Commercial: Electricity: 705 TWh (34% of BAU) Gas: 1.51 QBTU (35% of BAU) |

**Table 3.1    Summary of studies of potential** *continued*

| Title and Authors | Publication date | Sector(s) | Geographical scope | Summary of conclusions |
|---|---|---|---|---|
| *Unlocking Energy Efficiency in the US Economy* McKinsey Global Institute | 2009 | All | USA | 9.1 QBTU end use (18.4 QBTU primary), 23% projected end use by 2020, 1.1 Gtonnes/a reduction in GHG emissions 35% of potential in residential 40% in industry 25% in commercial |
| *Assessment of Achievable Potential from Energy Efficiency and Demand Response Programs in the US (2010–2030)* Electric Power Research Institute (EPRI) | 2009 | All | USA | 'Achievable potential' of 5% to 8% Potential to reduce growth rate of electricity demand in US Energy Information Administration (EIA) 2008 Annual Energy Outlook Reference Case forecast from 1.07% per annum to 0.83% per annum Ideally this could be improved to 0.68% Peak demand could be cut by 14 to 20% by reducing growth rate in peak demand from base case of 1.5% to between 0.83% and 0.53% |
| *Real Prospects for Energy Efficiency in the United States* US National Academy of Science, National Academy of Engineering, National Research Council | 2010 | All | USA | Conservative scenario: 2020: 28.6 QBTU (17% of EIA baseline projections) 2030: 30.5 QBTU (26% of EIA baseline) Optimistic scenario: 2020: 22.1 QBTU (19% of EIA baseline) 2030: 35.8 QBTU (30% of EIA baseline) |
| *Energy Saving Potential of Solid-State Lighting in General Illumination Applications 2010–2030* Lighting Research and Development Building Technologies Program Office of Energy Efficiency and Renewable Energy U.S. Department of Energy | 2010 | General illumination | USA | 2.05 QBTU (190 TWh) by 2030, 25% of reference scenario for general illumination energy use |

**Table 3.1     Summary of studies of potential** *continued*

| Title and Author | Publication date | Sector(s) | Geographical scope | Summary of conclusions |
|---|---|---|---|---|
| *Reinventing Fire* A. Lovins and The Rocky Mountain Institute | 2011 | All | USA | 2050 consumption of 71 QBTU compared to 117 QBTU in BAU scenario (40%) $CO_2$ emissions reduced by 82–86% |
| *The Long-Term Energy Efficiency Potential: What the Evidence Suggests* John A. 'Skip' Laitner, Steven Nadel, R. Neal Elliott, Harvey Sachs and A. Siddiq Khan American Council for an Energy Efficient Economy | 2012 | All | USA | Advanced scenario: 42% by 2050 Phoenix scenario: 59% by 2050 Savings relative to projections in EIA Annual Energy Outlook (122 QBTU by 2050 in Annual Energy Outlook) |
| *United States Building Energy Efficiency Retrofits. Market Sizing and Financing Models.* Rockefeller Foundation and Deutsche Bank | 2012 | Buildings (residential, commercial and institutional) | USA | BTU: 3,033 trillion Investment ($bn): 279 Cumulative job years: 3.3m Greenhouse gas (GHG) reduction (million tonnes per year): 616 |
| *Capturing the European Energy Productivity Opportunity* McKinsey Global Institute | 2008 | All | EU-25 | Energy savings 17.4 QBTUs by 2020 (20%) Reduce GHG emissions by 1 bn tonnes p.a. (check) IRR > 10% Would cap energy use at current level compared to 1.2% p.a. growth in base case |
| *Study on the Energy Savings Potentials in EU Member States, Candidate Countries and EEA Countries* European Commission | 2009 | All | EU and EEA countries | 4 scenarios, $61/barrel oil price in 2020 and $63/barrel in 2035 at 2005 prices. Savings relative to Primes EU27 Final energy scenario September 2007 Technical potential: 44% savings High policy intensity scenario: 32% savings Low policy intensity scenario: 21% savings |
| *A Low Energy Strategy for the UK* G. Leach et al., International Institute for the Environment and Development | 1979 | All | UK | UK could use 7% less primary energy by 2000 and 22% less by 2025 compared to 1976 while maintaining economic growth |

**Table 3.1     Summary of studies of potential** *continued*

| Title and Authors | Publication date | Sector(s) | Geographical scope | Summary of conclusions |
|---|---|---|---|---|
| *The Potential for Energy Conserving Capital Equipment in UK Industries* S.D. Fawkes | 1985 | Brewing, malting, distilleries and dairies | UK | Critique of Leach et al. concluded that a 'low energy future' as defined by Leach was achievable in these sectors despite some failings in Leach's approach |
| *Capturing the full electricity efficiency potential of the UK* McKinsey for DECC | 2012 | Electricity in residential, services and industry | UK | Savings potential of 155 TWh (c.40% of demand) |
| *Market Potential in Energy Efficiency in Southeast Asia* Sustainability Committee of the European Chamber of Commerce, Singapore and Roland Berger Strategy Consultants | 2011 | All | Indonesia, Malaysia, Singapore, Thailand, Vietnam (86% GDP of SE Asia) | 12–30% energy savings 119–297 TWh $15bn–$43bn p.a. savings |
| *Estimating Technical Energy Saving Potential from Improved Appliance Efficiency in Indian Households* Alexander Boegle, Daljit Singh and Girish Sant | 2010 | Appliances: Incandescent lamp Tube lamp Refrigerator Standby power Fan Television Air conditioning Water heater Air cooler | India | Saving of 57 TWh by 2013 compared to 2008 consumption of 138 TWh (41%) |
| *India's Energy Efficiency Potential* Jayant Sayethe Lawrence Berkeley National Laboratory | 2011 | All | India | Total benefit to economy of Rs2.4 million crores ($500bn) Removal of electricity shortage to consumers (358 TWh) and producers (246 TWh) Reduction of 312 million tonnes $CO_2$ 2009–2020 Reduced import of coal and gas of 42.3 thousand crores ($9.6bn) |
| *Energy Efficiency in Russia: Untapped Reserves* IFC/The World Bank | 2008 | All | Russia | Estimate 45% savings: 240bn $m^3$ of gas 340bn kWh of electricity 89m tonnes coal 43m tonnes oil and refined products Worth $80–90bn a year (2007 prices) in additional energy exports that would be possible |

**Table 3.1    Summary of studies of potential** *concluded*

| Title and Authors | Publication date | Sector(s) | Geographical scope | Summary of conclusions |
|---|---|---|---|---|
| *Energy Efficiency Potential Study* KEMA Inc. for Kauai Island Utility Cooperative, Lihue, Hawaii | 2005 | Residential and commercial (all) | Kauai Island, Hawaii | Economic potential of 142 GWh/y (24%) and reduction in peak demand of 17 MW (23%) |
| *Potential of Drastic Improvement of Energy Efficiency in Japan* Seiji Ikkatai and Haruki Tsuchiya | 2011 | All | Japan | Potential through using existing technology is 31.6% |

In the case of buildings, for example, we have been able to use the technologies needed to achieve very high levels of performance for many years, such as houses that require no heating energy in cold climates. The issue from a policy point of view is how to roll out those technologies to ensure all buildings are built to a similar level of performance.

Cullen et al. (2011) conclude that the existing economy could run on 73 per cent less energy supply by applying known engineering best practice to passive systems that transform useful energy to services. Furthermore, they estimate the reduction potential in conversion devices to be 85 per cent without any reduction in service levels. They conclude that overall we use 475 EJ of primary energy resources (oil, coal, gas, biomass, renewables and nuclear) to provide 55 EJ of useful energy services (motion, heat, cooling, light and sound). This means that, even with all our advanced technologies, we have achieved an overall energy efficiency of only 11 per cent. Although these analyses do not take into account economic considerations, they serve to highlight the huge potential for energy efficiency and should give all consumers, managers and policy makers pause for thought. We still have a long way to go but the evidence from the last thirty years is that we can continue to improve energy efficiency profitably year after year, and even decade after decade.

## Barriers to Achieving the Potential Benefits

The barriers to improved energy efficiency have been researched and written about for the last 30 years and more. Even Oliver Lyle, in his classic 1947 text *The Efficient Use of Steam*, discussed technical and management barriers to achieving greater levels of efficiency.

There are various schemas for categorizing the barriers, but they can largely be divided into the categories discussed below.

### INFORMATION

Energy consumers, senior management, designers such as engineers and architects, financiers and policy makers often do not have adequate information about the potential for energy efficiency, the technologies for energy efficiency, or the management and financial techniques that can be used to significantly improve energy efficiency. Even though many private and government agencies have tried to address this issue over many years, and it does sometimes appear that some agencies have flooded the market with information, 'lack of information' remains a problem. One issue with information, particularly relating to case studies on costs and benefits, is uncertainty over whether that information is correct or whether it applies to the decision maker's particular situation. However close a case study is to the decision maker's own situation there will be a degree of scepticism and the barrier of the decision maker thinking 'my situation is different'. Also, very few case studies are independently verified. As with all information-related topics, the recipient's perceptions, education and motivations affect the way that information is received and processed. The power of paradigms and beliefs should not be underestimated; remember the old view (not heard so much nowadays) that it was more efficient to leave fluorescent tubes on rather than switch them off for short periods? This may have been true for the earliest generations of the technology but the belief hung around for many decades after it was proven to be incorrect.

To be effective, information has to be presented to decision makers in the right form, the right language and at the right time. Different aspects of the information problem require specific approaches. For instance, training architects and engineers in the potential and techniques of integrated design techniques is a different type of informational problem than persuading property developers and investors that insisting on a holistic design approach is both feasible and profitable.

Another informational problem is that many organizations still do not have accurate, timely and disaggregated information on their energy use, i.e. monitoring and targeting systems, of a standard that allows them to make sensible management or investment decisions.

## ENERGY PRICING

In many markets around the world energy is still subsidized, and in most markets it is priced below the full economic cost of all the externalities associated with energy production, processing, transportation and use. In addition, because of the nature of energy markets, energy prices do not generally reflect the real-time or marginal costs of production to consumers. As we will discuss in the chapter on policy, this is one of the elephants in the room around energy efficiency.

## FINANCIAL

A number of significant financial barriers exist. First, most decision makers looking at energy efficiency investments in firms, the public sector and households typically seek short payback periods, of the order of two to three years. These payback periods are much shorter than those required by investors in new energy generation or supply facilities.

Upfront capital costs are a barrier to many decision makers. In order to exploit the benefits of energy efficiency, investments do have to be made, and unless these are made by a third party in some sort of shared saving deal (see Chapter 10 on financing), the end user has to find the upfront capital. In many cases capital is either not available or there are competing demands for investment capital which are deemed more attractive, such as investing in marketing to increase sales, as opposed to investing in energy efficiency to cut costs – so-called 'offensive' spending versus 'defensive' spending.

Energy efficiency investments can carry high transaction costs which are not always considered in simple analyses.

Typically, energy efficiency investments are quite small. In the well-known case of the Empire State Building, the total additional cost of energy efficiency measures as part of a much larger refurbishment investment was only $13 million (Shaw 2012). The small scale of energy efficiency investments, particularly when compared to the large scale of energy supply investments, is a major barrier for attracting third-party financing from institutional investors who have minimum investment ticket sizes of tens, or even hundreds, of millions of pounds, euros or dollars.

## INSTITUTIONAL/MANAGERIAL

There are a number of institutional and managerial barriers to energy efficiency. First, there can be a lack of leadership on the subject. As we highlight in Chapter 6, all successful energy efficiency programmes, whether they are corporate, local, regional, national or international, require clear and strong leadership.

Another institutional barrier is lack of capacity in many aspects of energy management, meaning lack of human capacity. In the UK of the 1980s, for instance, a lot of capacity and skills were built up in energy management but, when prices fell after the privatization of the electricity and gas industries and the collapse of the oil price, much of this capacity was lost as energy managers were redeployed or moved onto other things. Any organization or country considering positive action on energy efficiency has to address issues of capacity building in several areas including, amongst others, technical capacity (engineers and architects), clients, institutional investors, financiers and, last but not least, policy makers. In the UK and US, as well as other markets around the world, demand for suitably qualified and experienced energy efficiency professionals is currently high.

Finally, in some markets, particularly the commercial office world, there is the problem of the split incentive: energy costs are largely passed on to the tenant, but the investment has to be made by the landlord.

## REGULATORY BARRIERS

A number of regulatory barriers also exist in different markets. These include the general and almost universal point that energy suppliers are incentivized to sell more energy, not to reduce consumption. In the UK, for example, DNOs (Distribution Network Operators) are rewarded according to capital spent on new capacity, and even if they were to identify very profitable energy efficiency investment opportunities, they have no incentive to invest in them.

In addition, even building codes and specification standards can work against energy efficiency, an example being a National Health Service requirement to have $n+2$ redundancy in boilers (for obvious security of supply reasons), which works against achieving the optimum holistic design.

## What Can We Do About the Barriers?

The barriers to improving energy efficiency are well known and cannot be ignored. If we are to achieve the massive potential for improving energy efficiency globally, policy makers and designers of energy management programmes of all kinds must understand them and address them. Rather than thinking about barriers, it is perhaps best to consider the enabling conditions which, if they are in place, can enable an increase in the rate of improvement of energy efficiency. These enabling conditions are sector and segment specific. For example, even within the public sector, which is often lumped into one group, there will be differences between the health sector, schools and local authority buildings. Even within the health sector there may be different enabling conditions between acute hospitals and specialist hospitals, for instance. The energy efficiency industry and energy efficiency analysts have not traditionally been very good at market segmentation and really understanding the conditions in each segment that lead to decisions to invest in energy efficiency.

For any segment, the enabling conditions will be a combination of things that are best addressed by government (regulations, for example), and things that are best addressed by the industry but which can be encouraged, catalysed or supported by the government. As well as sector/segment-specific conditions there will be some cross-sector actions that can be taken, including the elephant in the room of opening up the electricity market to encourage the use of the demand-side resource. We will discuss some of these issues in later chapters.

## References and Bibliography

Allwood, J.M. 2009. *Industrial Carbon Emissions: A 50% Reduction While Demand Doubles?* Presentation at Smith School, Oxford. [Online]. Available at: http://www.lcmp.eng.cam.ac.uk/wp-content/uploads/jma-smith-school-8-jun-09.pdf [accessed 26 January 2013].

Allwood, J.M. 2011. *The Physical Basis for a Low Carbon Economy*. Presentation at Imperial College. [Online]. Available at: https://workspace.imperial. ac.uk/energyfutureslab/Public/Events/JMA%20Feb%202011.pdf [accessed 19 April 2013].

American Physical Society. 2008. *Energy Future. Think Efficiency. How America Can Look Within to Achieve Energy Security and Reduce Global Warming.* [Online]. Available at: http://www.aps.org/energyefficiencyreport/report/ aps-energyreport.pdf [accessed 26 January 2013].

Boegle, A., Singh, D. and Sant, G. 2010. *Estimating Technical Energy Saving Potential from Improved Appliance Efficiency in Indian Households.* [Online]. Available at: http://www.aceee.org/files/proceedings/2010/data/papers/2093. pdf [accessed 26 January 2013].

Brown, R., Borgeson, S., Koomey, J. and Biermayer, P. 2008. *U.S. Building-Sector Energy Efficiency Potential.* [Online]. Available at: http://enduse.lbl.gov/info/ LBNL-1096E.pdf [accessed 26 January 2013].

Cullen, J.M. 2009. 'Engineering Fundamentals of Energy Efficiency'. PhD Thesis. University of Cambridge.

Cullen, J.M. and Allwood, J.M. 2010a. 'Theoretical Efficiency Limits for Energy Conversion Devices'. *Energy* 35 (2010): 2059–69.

Cullen, J.M. and Allwood, J.M. 2010b. 'The Efficient Use of Energy: Tracing the Global Flow of Energy from Fuel to Service'. *Energy Policy* 38 (2010): 75–81.

Cullen, J.M., Allwood, J.M and Borgstein, E.H. 2011. 'Reducing Energy Demand: What Are the Practical Limits?' *Environmental Science & Technology*, 45(4): 1711–18.

Energy Research Partnership. 2011. *Industrial Energy Efficiency Key Messages.* [Online]. Available at: http://www.energyresearchpartnership.org.uk/tiki-read_article.php?articleId=27 [accessed 26 January 2013].

EPRI. 2009. *Assessment of Achievable Potential from Energy Efficiency and Demand Response Programs in the U.S. (2010–2030).* [Online]. Available at: http:// www.edisonfoundation.net/IEE/Documents/EPRI_SummaryAssessment AchievableEEPotential0109.pdf [accessed 26 January 2013].

European Commission. 2009. *Study on the Energy Savings Potentials in EU Member States, Candidate Countries and EEA Countries. Final Report.* [Online]. Available at: http://ec.europa.eu/energy/efficiency/studies/doc/2009_03_15_ esd_efficiency_potentials_final_report.pdf [accessed 26 January 2013].

Fawkes, S.D. 1985. 'The Potential for Energy Conserving Capital Equipment in UK Industries'. PhD thesis, University of Stirling.

Gillingham, K., Newell, R.G. and Palmer, K. 2009. *Energy Efficiency Economics and Policy.* [Online]. Available at: http://www.rff.org/rff/Documents/RFF-DP-09-13.pdf [accessed 26 January 2013].

IEA. 2012. *World Energy Outlook 2012, Executive Summary*. [Online]. Available at: http://www.iea.org/publications/freepublications/publication/English. pdf [accessed 28 April 2013].

IFC/The World Bank. 2008. *Energy Efficiency in Russia: Untapped Resources*. [Online]. Available at: http://www1.ifc.org/wps/wcm/connect/400e2400 4b5f69148d21bd6eac26e1c2/Final_EE_report_engl.pdf?MOD=AJPERES [accessed 26 January 2013].

Ikkatai, S. and Tsuchiya, H. 2011. 'Potential of Drastic Improvement of Energy Efficiency in Japan', in *Zero-Carbon Energy Kyoto 2011*. Green Energy and Technology 2012, pp. 5–13.

Laitner, J.A. Nadel, S., Elliott, N.R., Sachs, H. and Khan, A.S. 2012. *The Long-Term Energy Efficiency Potential: What the Evidence Suggests*. American Council for an Energy Efficient Economy. [Online]. Available at: http://aceee.org/ research-report/e121 [accessed 26 January 2013].

Leach, G., Lewis, C., Romig, F., van Buren, A. and Foley, G. 1979. *A Low Energy Strategy for the United Kingdom*. The International Institute for the Environment and Development. London, Science Reviews.

Lovins, A. and Rocky Mountain Institute. 2011. *Reinventing Fire*. White River Junction VT, Chelsea Green Publishing Company.

Lyle, O. 1947. *The Efficient Use of Steam*. Ministry of Fuel and Power. London, HM Stationery Office.

Martinez, S., Ettenson, L., Long, N. and Wang, D. 2011. *Public Power's Energy Efficiency Progress: An Evaluation of California's Publicly Owned Utility Energy Efficiency Achievements and Targets*. [Online]. Available at: http://switchboard. nrdc.org/blogs/lettenson/NRDC%20Assessment%20of%20POU%20EE%20 Achievements%20and%20Targets_August%202011.pdf [accessed 26 January 2013].

McKinsey & Company. 2007. *Curbing Global Energy-Demand Growth: The Energy Productivity Opportunity*. [Online]. Available at: http://www.mckinsey.com/ insights/mgi/research/natural_resources/curbing_global_energy_demand_ growth [accessed 26 January 2013].

McKinsey & Company. 2008. *Capturing the European Energy Productivity Opportunity*. [Online]. Available at: http://www.mckinsey.com/insights/ mgi/research/natural_resources/capturing_european_energy_productivity [accessed 26 January 2013].

McKinsey & Company. 2009. *Unlocking Energy Efficiency in the US Economy*. [Online]. Available at: http://www.mckinsey.com/client_service/electric_ power_and_natural_gas/latest_thinking/unlocking_energy_efficiency_in_ the_us_economy [accessed 26 January 2013].

McKinsey & Company. 2012. *Capturing the Full Electricity Efficiency Potential of the UK*. Report commissioned by the Department of Energy and Climate Change. [Online]. Available at: https://www.gov.uk/government/uploads/system/uploads/attachment_data/file/48456/5776-capturing-the-full-electricity-efficiency-potentia.pdf [accessed 26 January 2013].

Rockefeller Foundation and Deutsche Bank Climate Change Advisers. 2012. *United States Building Energy Efficiency Retrofits. Market Sizing and Financing Models*. [Online]. Available at: http://www.rockefellerfoundation.org/uploads/files/791d15ac-90e1-4998-8932-5379bcd654c9-building.pdf [accessed 26 January 2013].

Roland Berger Strategy Consultants. 2011. *Market Potential in Energy Efficiency in South East Asia*. [Online]. Available at: http://www.rolandberger.com/media/publications/2011-11-03-rbsc-pub-Market_potential_in_energy_efficiency_in_SE_Asia.html [accessed 26 January 2013].

Sayathe, J. 2011. *India's Energy Efficiency Potential*. [Online]. Available at: http://igov.berkeley.edu/content/india's-energy-efficiency-potential [accessed 16 January 2013].

Shaw, J. 2012. 'A Green Empire', *Harvard Magazine*. [Online]. Available at: http://harvardmagazine.com/2012/03/a-green-empire [accessed 26 January 2013].

US Department of Energy. 2010. *Energy Saving Potential of Solid-State Lighting in General Illumination Applications 2010–2030*. [Online]. Available at: http://apps1.eere.energy.gov/buildings/publications/pdfs/ssl/ssl_energy-savings-report_10-30.pdf [accessed 26 January 2013].

US National Academy of Science, National Academy of Engineering and National Research Council. 2010. *Real Prospects for Energy Efficiency in the United States*. Washington DC, The National Academies Press.

World Business Council for Sustainable Development. 2009. *Transforming the Market: Energy Efficiency in Buildings*. [Online]. Available at: http://www.wbcsd.org/transformingthemarketeeb.aspx [accessed 26 January 2013].

# 4

# A Systematic View of the Benefits of Efficiency

*The overall name of these interrelated structures is system. The motorcycle is a system. A real system. ... There's so much talk about the system. And so little understanding. That's all a motorcycle is, a system of concepts worked out in steel. There's no part in it, no shape in it that is not in someone's mind. I've noticed that people who have never worked with steel have trouble seeing this – that the motorcycle is primarily a mental phenomenon.*

Robert Pirsig, Zen and the Art of Motorcycle Maintenance

*All models are wrong. Some models are useful.*

George E.P. Box, Statistician, 1919–2013

As with all complex subjects, the study of energy efficiency is most effective when we take a systems-based view. This is particularly true when looking at the benefits of improving energy efficiency as those benefits arise at different system levels. Some benefits of improving energy efficiency fall into the domain of the energy user, whether they are a homeowner, company or government department. Others fall outside this and into wider society, whether at the level of an individual country or the entire global population. When considering energy efficiency, all decision makers, including householders, managers of organizations and heads of governments, need to consider and properly value all the benefits. One of the generic problems of energy policy is failure to recognize all the benefits and the difficulties of designing mechanisms that capture the value from all of the benefits of energy efficiency.

## Benefits to the Energy User or System Host

### REDUCED OPERATING COSTS

Reducing operating costs remains the number one reason for improving energy efficiency for most end users. This is despite a recent period – at least in Europe – where reducing carbon emissions was as, or more, important to some organizations and individuals. There is no doubt that improving energy efficiency brings with it reduced operating costs when compared to the alternative situation of no action to improve efficiency.

### REDUCED EXPOSURE TO ENERGY PRICE VOLATILITY

By reducing energy spend through energy efficiency, organizations and individuals reduce their exposure to the effects of energy price volatility on profits or budgets. Reducing energy consumption by 20 per cent over a period in which energy prices go up 30 per cent results in only a 4 per cent increase in costs as opposed to a 30 per cent increase. Reducing cost volatility by improved energy management is valuable for organizations trying to predict financial performance and is increasingly seen as a major factor in driving corporate energy efficiency programmes (Curwin 2011).

### REDUCED EMISSIONS OF CARBON DIOXIDE (REDUCED CARBON FOOTPRINT)

Reducing energy use reduces carbon emissions. In the case of fuel burnt there is a direct reduction at the point of combustion, and in the case of electricity there is a reduction at the generating station. The value of this benefit depends on your view on climate change and whether or not it is primarily caused by man-made emissions of carbon dioxide. In some regulatory systems, reducing emissions for some entities is mandatory and may have a value through some form of carbon pricing or market, e.g. through the EU Emissions Trading Scheme (ETS) or California's cap and trade scheme. In other jurisdictions, reducing carbon emissions carries no direct financial benefit but some individuals and organizations still value this benefit because of perceived sense of purpose or reputational effects.

Other, lesser-known, benefits within the energy users' system boundary may include those discussed below.

## REDUCED NEED TO INVEST IN ENERGY SUPPLY INFRASTRUCTURE

An example would be a situation where increasing production in a factory requires investing in a larger electrical grid connection due to increased peak electricity demand. Implementing energy efficiency measures can reduce, or even totally remove, the need for this investment. A good example is the Costa Coffee bean roasting plant in south London (Hockaday 2012). By implementing ISO 50001 and systematically examining all aspects of the energy performance of the site, management and staff were able to reduce energy use by 16 per cent. Without these measures the company would have needed to build a completely new site to overcome capacity constraints in the system.

## IMPROVED QUALITY OF PRODUCTION

Improving energy efficiency can also bring with it improved quality control. Examples include:

- better temperature control of furnaces and ovens;

- better temperature controls in refrigeration in brewing (Galitsky et al. 2003) and other processes;

- better control of compressed air pressure leading to less downtime and the associated loss of quality due to plant stoppages, as well as reduced equipment lifetime;

- new welding techniques that reduce sputter and improve weld quality (Shih 2010);

- air drying of paper compared to infra-red drying.

## HIGHER PRODUCTIVITY, HEALTH AND WELL-BEING OF EMPLOYEES

Many studies have shown that lighting upgrades, which bring with them an improvement in energy efficiency, also result in higher employee productivity (Philips 2008). Improved control of space temperatures have also been shown to bring higher productivity (Seppänen, Fisk and Faulkner 2004). A number of studies have shown that energy-efficient offices are more productive (Institute for Building Efficiency 2012), perhaps by as much as 15 to 25 per cent, and that they can also improve worker morale, reduce sickness, reduce employee turnover and ease recruitment. Other studies have shown that green, energy-efficient schools can reduce levels of asthma, colds, flu and absenteeism (Kats 2006).

## IMPROVED COMFORT AND ASSOCIATED HEALTH EFFECTS

Improving energy efficiency, notably through the application of additional insulation to buildings in cold climates, brings with it improved comfort for the occupants. Thermal comfort, whether we feel cold or warm, is determined by the interaction of four environmental factors: air temperature, radiant temperature, air movements and humidity; plus the personal factors of metabolic rate and clothing insulation levels. Improving thermal insulation of a building improves comfort through a combination of increased internal air temperatures, increased internal wall, floor and ceiling temperatures (reducing thermal losses from radiation) and reduction of draughts. Improved comfort conditions can bring with them improved health, particularly in the case of the very young and the elderly.

## INCREASED PROPERTY VALUES

There is evidence that, in some markets at least, energy-efficient offices and homes can command a higher value and sell faster than equivalent, less efficient properties, although this has not yet been widely accepted. The Appraisal Institute in the USA has done a great deal of work on how to value the effect of energy efficiency, notably with the Institute for Market Transformation (2012). In one case cited by the Appraisal Institute, a reduction in energy costs of 45 per cent resulting from an energy efficiency retrofit led to an 8.5 per cent increase in the calculated value of the building through reducing operating expenses.

Research projects in Oregon, Washington and California suggest that newly constructed houses with third-party certification of energy efficiency and sustainability sell for higher prices, as much as 18 per cent higher in some areas (Earth Advantage Institute 2012). A study conducted by the Institute in Seattle and Portland showed that houses sold with energy efficiency certifications appeared to sell faster than those that didn't.

Some analysts remain unconvinced about the value enhancement of green buildings. Property industry experts question the idea by pointing out that green buildings tend to be high quality buildings and so the additional value may be more to do with the overall quality level rather than the specific green characteristics. Further research is required on the specific value enhancement that can come from energy efficiency. Building occupiers assign value to many different characteristics of buildings, including location, a sense of well-being, health and employee productivity. Energy is very low on the priority list when organizations are looking to move to a new building, and in many cases is not on the list at all.

The power of regulations around building energy performance to drive investment decisions to improve energy efficiency is clearly an important factor in determining whether or not buildings are efficient. In the UK, the Energy Act of 2011 prohibits selling or leasing a residential or commercial building with an energy rating of less than 'F' after 2018. This kind of regulation will clearly affect property values directly if fully implemented and enforced.

## REDUCED LOCAL POLLUTION

An improvement in energy efficiency can reduce local air pollution, both indoors and outdoors. In Ulaanbaatar, Mongolia, 'the coldest city in the world', coal-fired heaters and cooking stoves contribute to terrible air pollution in winter. A project supported by the Millennium Challenge Corporation is promoting energy-efficient solutions to the problem of winter-time pollution. The Millennium Challenge Account (MCA) Mongolia Energy and Environment Project (EEP) provides financial incentives to encourage consumers to switch to more efficient appliances (Millennium Challenge Corporation 2012).

In another example, a long way from Mongolia, the potential for 'cool roofs' is being explored. Cool roofs absorb less radiation and hence lead to a reduction in building air conditioning to reduce energy use, emissions and smog in US cities. These innovations have been extensively studied by the Heat Island Group at the Lawrence Berkeley Laboratory. Akbari, Pomerantz and Taha (2001) reported that simulations showed that raising the albedo of roofs in the Los Angeles basin by 0.3 during normal refurbishment could reduce smog (ozone) by 10–20 per cent, as well as significantly reducing energy use and peak loads for air conditioning.

## Benefits Outside the System Boundary of the Host

At the wider level, outside the domain of individual energy users, improving energy efficiency helps us address the macro energy stresses and strains described in Chapter 2.

The International Energy Agency's World Energy Outlook 2012 feature on energy efficiency highlighted the macro benefits that could result from improved efficiency. Its Efficient World Scenario, in which all economic efficiency measures are realized, would, when compared to its central New Policies Scenario:

- reduce world primary energy demand in 2035 by 14 per cent;

- reduce the rate of demand growth from 1.2 per cent to 0.6 per cent per annum;

- increase the rate of reduction of energy intensity from 0.8 per cent per annum to 2.4 per cent per annum;

- boost global GDP by $18 trillion in the period up to 2035;

- result in global carbon dioxide emissions peaking in 2020 at 32.4 gigatonnes with a reduction to 30.5 gigatonnes by 2035;

- this reduction in carbon dioxide emissions is consistent with stabilizing atmospheric carbon dioxide at 550 ppm, which is consistent with a 50 per cent probability of staying below a temperature increase of 3°C.

## JOB CREATION

An additional benefit to the economy of improving energy efficiency is job creation. Some controversy about the impact of energy efficiency programmes on job creation still lingers on, but on the whole the case seems to have been proven.

Energy efficiency creates jobs in three ways: direct, indirect and induced. Direct jobs are those resulting directly from the investment, which tend to be in construction-related areas. Indirect jobs are those manufacturing and supplying energy efficiency products, as well as associated services such as consulting or measurement and verification. Induced jobs are those that result from the spending of the savings in the economy.

There are numerous estimates for the number of jobs that can be, and have been, created by energy efficiency, including:

- The UNEP 2011 Green Economy Report (UNEP 2011) states that 'investments in improved energy efficiency in buildings could generate an additional 2–3.5 million jobs in Europe and the United States alone'.

- The French Ministry for Ecology, Energy, Sustainable Development and Spatial Planning estimates that for every one million euros of investment in property-related thermal renovation, 14.2 jobs are created in energy-related work. Using the estimated investment requirement of 60 billion euros suggests 850,000 jobs in the EU (L'Union Sociale Pour L' Habitat 2011).

- The American Council for an Energy Efficient Economy (ACEEE 2012) report that energy efficiency produces 20 jobs per million dollars spent compared to 17 jobs per million dollars on average in the economy and 10 jobs per million in the energy sector. The ACEEE give an example of a city spending 15 million dollars on energy efficiency. This expenditure will result in a net gain of 45 jobs in the first year $((20 \times 15) - (17 \times 15))$. Over the lifetime of the investment, assuming a five-year payback period, there will be an additional three million dollars per annum in the economy which, in the business-as-usual case, would have been spent on energy. This will create an additional seven jobs per year $((3 \times 17) - (3 \times 10))$ for the lifetime of the investment.

- In an October 2012 report, Consumer Focus (2012) estimated that spending the circa £4 billion per year that UK energy consumers will have to pay in carbon floor price and EU ETS-related charges on retrofitting homes would create 71,000 jobs by 2015 and boost GDP by 0.2 per cent.

Given the urgent need to create growth and jobs, particularly in developed countries affected by the global financial crisis, this aspect of energy efficiency policy still has not received the attention it deserves in most countries.

## References and Bibliography

ACEEE. 2012. *How Does Energy Efficiency Create Jobs?* [Online]. Available at: http://www.aceee.org/files/pdf/fact-sheet/ee-job-creation.pdf [accessed 26 January 2013].

Akbari, H., Pomerantz, M. and Taha, H. 2001. 'Cool Surfaces and Shade Trees to Reduce Energy Use and Improve Air Quality in Urban Areas', *Solar Energy* 70: 295–310. [Online]. Available at: http://www.sciencedirect.com/science/article/pii/S0038092X0000089X [accessed 28 December 2012].

Bell, C.J. 2012. *Energy Efficiency Job Creation: Real World Experiences.* [Online]. Available at: http://www.aceee.org/files/pdf/white-paper/energy-efficiency-job-creation.pdf [accessed 26 January 2013].

Consumer Focus. 2012. *Jobs, Growth and Warmer Homes: Evaluating the Economic Stimulus of Investing in Energy Efficiency Measures in Fuel Poor Homes.* [Online]. Available at: http://www.consumerfocus.org.uk/files/2012/11/Jobs-growth-and-warmer-homes-November-2012.pdf [accessed 3 January 2013].

Curwin, T. 2011. 'Energy Price Volatility Now A Major Factor in Corporate Efficiency Drive'. *CNBC*, 23 August 2011. [Online]. Available at: http://www.cnbc.com/id/44072900/Energy_Price_Volatility_Now_A_Major_Factor_In_Corporate_Efficiency_Drive [accessed 28 December 2012].

Earth Advantage Institute. 2012. *Economic Benefits.* [Online]. Available at: http://www.earthadvantage.org/building-green/value-of-building-green/economic-benefits/ [accessed 28 December 2012].

Fawkes, S. 2013. 'Setting the Stage for Energy Efficiency Investment'. *Environmental Finance*, 9 January 2013. [Online]. Available at: http://www.environmental-finance.com/features/view/818 [accessed 26 January 2013].

Galitsky, C., Martin, N., Worrell, E. and Lehman, B. 2003. *Energy Efficiency Improvement and Cost Saving Opportunities for Breweries. An ENERGY STAR® Guide for Energy and Plant Managers.* Lawrence Berkeley National Laboratory. [Online]. Available at: http://ies.lbl.gov/iespubs/50934.pdf [accessed 28 December 2012].

Hockaday, M. 2012. 'Costa Increases Production with Eco Measures', *Green Build News*, 16 July 2012. [Online]. Available at: http://www.greenbuildnews.co.uk/projects-details/Costa-increases-production-with-eco-measures/645 [accessed 26 April 2013].

Institute for Building Efficiency 2012. *Productivity Gains from Energy Efficiency.* [Online]. Available at: http://www.institutebe.com/Existing-Building-Retrofits/Productivity-Gains-from-Energy-Efficiency.aspx [accessed 28 December 2012].

Institute for Market Transformation and Appraisal Institute. 2012. *Recognition of Energy Costs and Energy Performance in Real Property Valuation*. [Online]. Available at: http://www.imt.org/uploads/resources/files/Energy_Reporting_in_Appraisal.pdf [accessed 28 December 2012].

Kats, G. 2003. *The Costs and Benefits of Green Buildings: A Report to California's Sustainable Building Task Force*. Capital E Analytics. [Online]. Available at: http://www.calrecycle.ca.gov/greenbuilding/design/costbenefit/report.pdf [accessed 26 January 2013].

Kats, G. 2006. *Greening America's SchoolsL: Costs and Benefits*. Capital E Analytics. [Online]. Available at: http://www.usgbc.org/ShowFile. aspx?DocumentID=2908 [accessed 29 December 2012].

Loftness, V., Hartkopf, V., Gurtekin, B., Hansen, D. and Hitchcock, R. 2003. *Linking Energy to Health and Productivity in the Built Environment*. Center for Building Performance and Diagnostics, Carnegie Mellon. [Online]. Available at: http://www.usgbc.org/Docs/Archive/MediaArchive/207_Loftness_PA876 .pdf [accessed 26 January 2013].

Lomonaco, C. and Miller, D. 1997. *Environmental Satisfaction, Personal Control and the Positive Correlation to Increased Productivity*. Johnson Controls.

L'Union Social pour l'Habitat. 2011. *Plan européen pour la relance économique COM(2008) 800 final Mesure n°6: Améliorer l'efficacité énergétique dans les bâtiments. Reprogrammation des programmes opérationnels régionaux des Fonds structurels en faveur des logements sociaux*. [Online]. Available at: http://union-habitat.eu/IMG/pdf/Plan_de_relance_evaluation_FEDER_logement_social_ FR_synthese.pdf [accessed 26 January 2013].

McGraw Hill Construction. 2009. *Green Building Retrofit & Renovation*. [Online]. Available at: http://mts.sustainableproducts.com/Capital_Markets_ Partnership/BusinessCase/MHC%20Green%20Building%20Retrofit%20 %26%20Renovation%20SMR%20(2009).pdf [accessed 26 January 2013].

McGraw Hill Construction. 2012. *2012 World Green Building Trends*. [Online]. Available at: http://analyticsstore.construction.com/index.php/2012-world-green-building-trends-key-facts.html [accessed 26 January 2013].

Millennium Challenge Corporation. *Promoting Energy-Efficient Solutions to Address Wintertime Pollution in Mongolia*. [Online]. Available at: http://www. mcc.gov/pages/povertyreductionblog/entry/promoting-energy-efficient-solutions-to-address-wintertime-pollution-in-mon [accessed 28 December 2012].

Newsham, G.R., Veitch, J.A., Arsenault, C. and Duval, C. 2004. 'Effect of Dimming Control on Office Worker Satisfaction and Performance', in *Proceedings of the Annual Conference of the Illuminating Engineering Society of North America*, Tampa, Florida.

Philips Lighting. 2008. *Lighting Upgrades Boost Workplace Productivity*. Philips. [Online]. Available at: http://www.graybar.com/documents/philips-wp-lighting-upgrades.pdf [accessed 28 December 2012].

Ries, R., Bilec, M., Gokhan, N. and Needy, K. 2006. 'The Economic Benefits of Green Buildings: A Comprehensive Case Study', *The Engineering Economist* 51(3): 259–95.

Seppänen, O., Fisk, W.J. and Faulkner, D. 2004. *Control of Temperature for Health and Productivity in Offices*. Lawrence Berkeley National Laboratory. [Online]. Available at: http://www.escholarship.org/uc/item/39s1m92c#page-1 [accessed 29 December 2012].

Seppänen, O., Fisk, W.J. and Lei, Q.H. 2006. *Effect of Temperature on Task Performance in Office Environment*. [Online]. Available at: http://www.osti. gov/bridge/servlets/purl/903490-F5SQYA/903490.pdf [accessed 26 January 2013].

Shih, K. 2010. *Improve Energy Efficiency and Weld Quality by Eliminating Expulsion Welds on Automobile Assembly Line*. [Online]. Available at: http://www. autosteel.org/~/media/Files/Autosteel/Great%20Designs%20in%20Steel/ GDIS%202011/25%20-%20Kelvin%20Shih%20-%20Improve%20Energy%20 Efficiency%20and%20Weld%20Quality.pdf [accessed 29 December 2012].

Singh, A., Syat, M., Grady, S.G. and Korkmaz, S. 2010. 'Effects of Green Buildings on Employee Health and Productivity'. *American Journal of Public Health*, 15 July 2010. [Online]. Available at: http://news.msu.edu/media/ documents/2010/08/840514e8-0b32-4aa4-9fc8-276b688dfed4.pdf [accessed 26 January 2013].

UNEP. 2011. *Towards a Green Economy: Pathways to Sustainable Development and Poverty Eradication*. [Online]. Available at: http://www.unep.org/ greeneconomy/Portals/88/documents/ger/ger_final_dec_2011/Green%20 EconomyReport_Final_Dec2011.pdf [accessed 26 January 2013].

US Department of Energy, Office of Electricity Delivery and Energy Reliability. 2012. *Infrastructure Security and Energy Restoration*. [Online]. Available at: http://energy.gov/sites/prod/files/Large%20Power%20Transformer%20 Study%20-%20June%202012_0.pdf [accessed 28 December 2012].

Williamson, T., Grant. E., Hansen, A., Pisaniello, D. and Andamon, M. 2009. *An Investigation of Potential Health Benefits from Increasing Energy Efficiency Stringency Requirements. Building Code of Australia Volumes One & Two*. The University of Adelaide. [Online]. Available at: http://www.abcb. gov.au/~/media/Files/Download%20Documents/Archived/Major%20 Initiatives/Energy%20Efficiency/Residential%20Housing/31114%20An%20 Investigation%20of%20Potential%20Health%20Benefits%20from%20 Increasing%20Energy%20Efficiency%20Stringency%20Requirements.pdf [accessed 28 December 2012].

Wyon, D.P. 2004. 'The Effects of Indoor Air Quality on Performance and Productivity'. *Indoor Air* 14: 92–101.

# 5

# Jevons, Rebound and Backfire

*Day by day it becomes more evident that the Coal we happily possess in excellent quantity and abundance is the Mainspring of Modern Material Civilization … Accordingly it is the chief agent in almost every improvement or discovery in the arts which the present age brings forth … Coal alone … commands this age … the Age of Coal.*

*William Stanley Jevons, Economist and Logician, 1835–1882*

## Introduction

This chapter examines the Jevons paradox or rebound effect – the proposition that technological progress that increases the efficiency with which energy is used tends to increase, rather than decrease, the rate of consumption of that resource. This 'paradox' is occasionally used to argue that increasing efforts to improve energy efficiency is futile. But examination of the actual debate shows that even when people are fully committed to the idea that rebound effects are larger than assumed by energy efficiency advocates, they still recognize the value of policies to improve efficiency.

The debate, which has been quite heated over the years, is actually about how large the rebound effect really is, and that depends strongly on the specific technologies, sectors and economies being studied. Another important proposition that would also merit further study is the possibility that the efficiency of energy use is actually a far more important determinant of economic growth than is assumed in classical economics.

## A Quick History Lesson

The Jevons paradox was first identified by William Stanley Jevons, who was specifically looking at the issue of improving efficiency of coal use in an age when the British Empire was powered by coal. His book *The Coal Question*, published in 1865, stated that greater efficiency in the use of coal would lead to greater national consumption of coal and not less (Jevons 1865). Jevons said:

> *It is wholly a confusion of ideas to suppose that the economical use of fuel is equivalent to a diminished consumption. The very contrary is the truth … Every improvement of the engine, when effected, does but accelerate anew the consumption of coal.*

The concept was picked up again seriously in the 1980s when the economists Daniel Khazzoom and Leonard Brookes both argued that increased energy efficiency leads to increased energy consumption. In 1992, Harry Saunders, a US economist, dubbed this hypothesis the Khazzoom–Brookes postulate and showed that it was true under neo-classical growth theory over a wide range of assumptions. In short, it suggests that although improving energy efficiency is justified at the micro level, at the macro level it leads to higher energy consumption. Put simply, individuals and firms make energy savings but then use the money saved to buy other energy-consuming services. Examples include:

- consumers install low energy lighting but then use the savings in energy costs to use more lighting and/or go out and buy more electricity consuming equipment;

- more efficient aircraft are introduced but the reduction in costs leads to more people flying leading to an increase in fuel use by aviation.

The sum total of the various effects is also known as 'rebound' or, in the extreme when the additional energy consumption is larger than the energy saved, as 'backfire'.

After several years of relative obscurity the issue was raised again in 2005 in a House of Lords Science and Technology Committee debate which was followed up by a 2007 UK Energy Research Council (UKERC) study, *The Rebound Effect: An Assessment of the Evidence for Economy-Wide Energy Savings* (UKERC 2007). There has also been research by the European Commission which resulted in the 2011 report, *Addressing the Rebound Effect* (Maxwell et al. 2011).

## An Argument Against Energy Efficiency?

In 2010, the rebound effect began to appear in the mainstream press, sometimes in a way that argued against programmes for improving energy efficiency. Some of the commentary came from an environmental point of view, arguing that energy efficiency programmes needed to be preceded by efforts to reduce energy use, i.e. reduce energy services by restraining economic output. Others used the rebound effect to effectively snipe at efforts to improve efficiency. In 2010, *The New Yorker* ran an article by David Owen called 'The Efficiency Dilemma' (Owen 2010), which was followed by his 2012 book, *The Conundrum* (Owen 2012a). Owen essentially says that improving energy efficiency is a waste of time and effort unless it is preceded by measures that force reduction in energy use: 'efficiency initiatives make no sense, as an environmental strategy, unless they're preceded – and more than negated – by measures that force major cuts in total energy use'. This story and book were widely reported and debated on the internet. This was picked up by elements of the US press and used as an argument against energy efficiency generally, and in particular the Obama administration's efforts to improve efficiency.

In 2011, The Breakthrough Institute published a series of useful articles and a report on the issue, as well as the output from an email correspondence between both sides of the argument; effectively, those who think the rebound effect is large (including Harry Saunders, Jesse Jenkins, et al.) and those who think the rebound effect is small (including leading energy efficiency advocates such as Amory Lovins, Skip Laitner, et al.). Although in places it is quite technical from an economics standpoint, the email exchange is well worth reading.

## Disentangling the Rebound Effect

Rebound is split into direct and indirect rebound.

### DIRECT REBOUND

Direct rebound applies to individual energy services such as driving a car or heating a house. For example, buying a more fuel-efficient car results in consumers driving more miles; or buying more efficient light bulbs leads consumers to leave lights on longer or use more lights. In economics terms there are two effects at play here: a substitution effect and an income effect. The substitution effect comes about because consumption of the energy service, made cheaper by energy efficiency, substitutes for the consumption of other goods and services. An example would be more efficient cars lowering the cost of driving leading to people using their car instead of the bus. The income effect comes about because the cheaper energy services effectively increases consumers' incomes, which allows them to increase consumption of the energy service. An example is that cheaper driving brought about by more efficient cars leads to an increase in the distance driven, i.e. new journeys are undertaken that would not otherwise have been undertaken.

For producers, the direct rebound effects come either as a substitution effect or an output effect which is analogous to those for consumers. The substitution effect is where the cheaper energy service is used to substitute for other inputs such as capital, labour or materials at a constant level of production. The output effect is where the cost savings resulting from improved energy efficiency allow production to increase – through higher demand – and therefore increase the quantity of energy service used as well as the use of other inputs such as capital, labour or materials. The latter also leads to indirect rebound.

## INDIRECT REBOUND

Indirect rebound effects are classified into the different categories described below.

Embodied energy: the investment in an energy efficiency technology, e.g. insulation or LED lighting, has a certain quantity of energy embodied in it through its manufacture. At one time in the 1970s and 1980s there was a great deal of analysis of embodied energy and occasionally you still see studies on it, for example attempting to answer the question whether a nuclear power station or a wind turbine produce more energy than it takes to make it.

Consumers, benefiting from the income effect, i.e. they have more disposable money because energy efficiency measures have reduced the amount they spend on energy, go out and purchase other services. For example, they save on their winter heating bill because their house has been insulated more effectively, but then go out and buy a winter holiday that requires flying to the Mediterranean.

Producers use the cost savings to increase output, as described above under direct rebound, and therefore increase their use of capital, labour and materials – all of which themselves require energy to be produced.

Implementation of cost-effective energy efficiency measures leads to improvements in overall productivity in the economy which leads to more economic growth, leading to more energy use.

A large-scale reduction in energy demand results in a decrease in energy prices which then leads to an increase in energy use.

The energy efficiency improvements and associated reductions in energy prices lead to a reduction in the price of energy-intensive goods and services relative to less energy-intensive goods and services, leading to an increase in demand for the more energy-intensive goods and services.

## Measuring Rebound

A number of methods are used to estimate rebound effects:

- evaluation studies of the effects of specific energy efficiency measures at the micro level;

- econometric studies of secondary data sources to estimate the elasticity of the demand for energy services;

- elasticity of substitution studies which look at the elasticity of substitution between energy and other inputs such as capital;

- Computable General Equilibrium (CGE) modelling which provide estimates of the rebound across the economy using CGE macro-economy models;

- energy productivity and economic growth studies which use a range of data, including economic historic studies, neoclassical growth and production studies, ecologic economics and others.

## So Just How High Is the Rebound?

Many studies have tried to calculate the rebound effect in different sectors and different countries, and it seems that everyone who studies it is agreed that measurement of rebound is difficult and full of uncertainties. The UKERC study stated that measurement of rebound is 'problematic at best and impossible at worst'. One important observation seems to be that the rebound effect diminishes through the stages of a country's development.

Table 5.1 shows estimates of the long-run direct rebound effect for consumer energy services in the OECD.

**Table 5.1     Estimates of rebound**

| End use | Range of values in evidence base | 'Best guess' | Number of studies | Degree of confidence |
|---|---|---|---|---|
| Personal automotive transport | 5–87 per cent | 10–30 per cent | 17 | High |
| Space heating | 1.4–60 per cent | 10–30 per cent | 9 | Medium |
| Space cooling | 1–26 per cent | 1–26 per cent | 2 | Low |
| Other consumer energy services | 0–49 per cent | <20 per cent | 3 | Low |
| Space cooling | 0–50 per cent | 1–26 per cent | n/a | Low |
| Water heating | <10–40 per cent | n/a | n/a | Very low |

*Source*: UKERC (first four rows) and The Breakthrough Institute (last two rows).

These numbers suggest that rebound effects can be significant.

## Is There a Backfire?

In their study of the Jevons paradox, Khazzoom–Brookes postulate that backfire is defined as when improving energy efficiency leads to an increase in energy use, i.e. the rebound effect is greater than unity. The Khazzoom–Brookes postulate essentially says that the rebound effect is always greater than unity.

## Commentary

Having read and re-read many of the studies and the sometimes heated debates over many years, it seems clear that there are rebound effects, both within the system boundary of the end user who is making the improvement in energy efficiency, and throughout the economy as a whole. The real questions are how big they are, and therefore how important are they for energy scenarios?

There are many issues surrounding at least one of the methods used to estimate rebound, namely CGE models. These models assume purely rational behaviour (a favourite economist's assumption that is rarely, if ever, seen in the real world). Many examples over the last few years, not the least of which is the global financial crisis, strongly suggest that the reliance on large computer models when applied to complex economic and social problems – let alone technical problems like global warming – is fraught with difficulty. Economic models need to be treated with extreme care.

Much of the debate around the rebound effect comes in reaction to energy consumption scenarios in which energy efficiency is expected to produce much of the reduction in greenhouse gas emissions which are believed to be required to stabilize atmospheric levels of carbon dioxide. These scenarios, such as the International Energy Agency (IEA) study *World Energy Outlook* in 2010 (IEA 2010) and the Intergovernmental Panel on Climate Change (IPCC) 2007 study *Contribution of Working Group III to the Fourth Assessment Report* (IPCC 2007), implicitly contain an assumption that a certain level of energy efficiency achievement within individual firms or households results in the same level of macro-economic improvement, i.e. an assumption that there is no rebound at all.

The size of the rebound effect will depend on the structure and stage of development of the economy under examination. In the economy of a developing country the demand for energy services is clearly farther away from any saturation than in more advanced economies, and so the income effects of an increase in energy efficiency does lead to consumers buying more energy-using equipment.

Coming from a background of implementing large-scale energy efficiency programmes in a wide range of building types and industry, it does seem that the debate sometimes misses some important points. First, as Amory Lovins has pointed out (Lovins 2011), a unit of energy saved at the site of the end user, be it a factory or a home, results in a greater saving as you pass back up the energy supply chain. For example, if a more efficient electric pumping system is installed, using more efficient motors, every kilowatt hour (kWh) of power saved within the factory results in a $1.0x$ kWh saving at the input level to the power system ($x$ is due to small but measurable losses within the transmission and distribution system – say 5 per cent). A saving of $1.0x$ kWh of power will result in a primary fuel saving of $(1.0x) \times (1/e_{system})$, where $e_{system}$ is the overall efficiency of the generation system, somewhere between 30 and 40 per cent in most countries. With an $x$ factor of 5 per cent for the transmission and distribution losses and an $e_{system}$ of 33 per cent, the net effect of saving 1 kWh at the factory level will be $(1.05) \times (1/33)$ per cent = 3.15 kWh of fuel input at the power station level.

Some analyses of individual energy efficiency technologies show little or no evidence of direct rebound effects. Some of the anecdotal reports on the rebound effect referred to domestic refrigeration, a sector where the efficiency of individual appliances has increased over the years, partly driven by appliance energy standards. Some analysts have said that these gains are taken up by an increase in average refrigerator size, plus the phenomenon where many people, on replacing their old fridge or freezer with a more efficient (although possibly larger) appliance, keep the old one in operation in the garage or the basement. Afsah et al. (2012) looked at the domestic refrigeration energy using data from the US Energy Information Agency. Between 2001 and 2005 the data showed that the share of households with two or more refrigerators increased from 16.9 per cent to 22.1 per cent. In the same time, the total electricity used in refrigeration went down 3.3 per cent, refrigerator electricity per household fell by 7 per cent and refrigerator electricity per capita fell by 6.7 per cent.

In a similar way, energy per square foot of residential floor area in both the USA and Canada has declined, in the case of Canada by an average of 1.36 per cent per annum between 1990 and 2008. If residential energy efficiency had remained stagnant at the 1990 level, Canada would have needed an additional 111 million megawatt hours (MWh) of energy, equivalent to the output of four large power stations. Despite this consistent increase in efficiency, the total residential energy used in Canada grew 0.7 per cent per annum between 1990 and 2008. This is partly driven by growth in GDP of one per cent per annum on average, and partly by a growth in population of two per cent per annum.

Next, it should be noted that the rebound effect only applies to energy efficiency measures that are below cost, i.e. cost effective. There are many other options for energy efficiency that are not below cost for the host, and the question is, cost-effective to whom (i.e. at what system level)? Energy efficiency measures are typically subject to strict investment-return criteria, typically three-year simple payback or less, whereas most energy supply options typically have much longer payback periods (in excess of seven to ten years). Applying the same economic criteria to energy efficiency as are applied to energy supply would lead to an increase in investment in energy efficiency, a reduction in energy use and, according to the economists, no rebound effect.

In recent years the large-scale benefits of improving energy efficiency have been recognized in sectors such as building. There is increasing evidence – see, for example, New Buildings Institute (2011) – that using holistic, integrative design techniques can result in large-scale retrofits in commercial offices and other buildings that produce energy savings of 30 to 50 per cent, plus rapid payback periods. This goes against conventional wisdom based on traditional design techniques that only identify incremental savings. If an economy were to launch a major programme of deep-energy retrofits in the built environment there would undoubtedly be rebound effects, but there would also be significant impact on disposable incomes – profits – that no longer have to be spent on energy, and also on employment.

Even if the rebound effect across the whole economy is 52 per cent, as some analysts maintain, it means there will still be a net saving from any specific energy efficiency measure. Even the advocates of a strong rebound effect still believe in the validity of improving energy efficiency as a policy option. The Breakthrough Institute, which has been one of the strongest voices for the existence of large rebound effects, states that 'efficiency is still good economic policy, and there are plenty of reasons to continue to pursue truly cost-effective efficiency'. As is often the way, many of the shorter, press versions of a story simplify a complex issue too much and result in headline conclusions which don't reflect the real conclusions of the original study.

In Victorian England, when Jevons was writing, and in today's rapidly-developing countries, the rebound effect is large and probably over unity. This makes intuitive sense. In rapidly developing economies the demands for goods and services are rising steeply. As economies mature, however, there is a degree of saturation. However wealthy someone becomes they can only drive so many miles in a year – yes, they may buy a bigger, faster, less fuel-efficient car but the number of miles they can physically drive in one year is limited by time. With lighting, the cost of lighting has fallen consistently over the decades and centuries and the quantity of lighting has consistently increased faster. But even with lighting, there is a natural saturation limit that eventually we have to reach, the ultimate (and extremely unlikely) scenario being one in which every building is lit to a very high level of brightness, 24 hours a day, and every building, city and road has outside lighting on 24 hours a day. There has to be a limit at which lighting demand slows and stops. It is true, of course, that we then invent new ways of using energy, my favourite example (because of my lifelong interest in space travel) is space tourism. We are witnessing the emergence of a whole new space tourism industry in which thousands, and ultimately millions of people, will be able to take a sub-orbital space flight and ultimately one day an orbital space trip. This represents a completely new demand for fuel (probably kerosene or hydrogen or solid rocket fuels), plus all the associated energy demand of building the vehicles, operating and maintaining them, building and operating the facilities (terminals, hangers, etc.), as well as the energy used to transport passengers to and from the spaceport. This is what economists call a frontier effect – strangely appropriate for the space tourism example – and this means an expansion in the production frontier.

Many environmentalists, who want to limit consumption, would decry new activities such as space tourism that expand the production frontier. I would argue strongly that such development is inevitable; it is part of human nature – the drive to innovate, the drive to do new things, and the drive to travel and explore are built into our species, those are the characteristics that make us human. Such development drives the economy forward and increases overall wealth. Stopping or banning such activities is impossible and wrong – it is 'making do with less' or 'conservation'. The issue is about making all new economic developments and fields of activity as energy efficient as possible, as well as minimizing their other environmental impacts.

In any event, to a decision maker, whether they be an industrialist or a householder, looking at making an energy efficiency investment decision, the rebound effect really is irrelevant. They will make the decision by weighing up the costs and the benefits in some way and applying some decision-making technique and criteria to the decision. In the case of the industrialist this is likely to be a normal investment decision technique such as Internal Rate of Return (IRR) or Net Present Value (NPV); for a householder it is likely to be more complicated. Consideration of rebound, however, will not come into the decision, and should not.

Another issue with the whole Jevons paradox debate is that, as the economists clearly recognize, the same phenomenon applies to all resources. If we improve the efficiency (productivity) of an input into a process, for example reducing the amount of steel going into a car by using better design techniques such as finite element analysis to achieve the same (or better) crash resistance, or if a retailer redesigns packaging to use less cardboard or plastic, we do not worry about the rebound effects. There will, of course, be rebound effects in exactly the same way as there are energy rebound effects from improving energy efficiency. In these examples the car producer and the retailer will make more profit. Improving productivity is a major driver of economic wealth creation.

There is a view that the importance of energy efficiency in determining economic growth has been seriously underestimated, and it may be that rapid improvements in efficiency can help drive economic growth. This is an area that needs further research.

## Conclusions

To conclude, there is no doubt that improving energy efficiency frees up resources which are then spent on other things, and those things have an energy consumption, so of course there is a rebound. It would appear from a literature review that all of the analysts that have studied the rebound effect have measured rebound effects below unity, and they all maintain that promoting improved energy efficiency is still a worthwhile policy aim. They are simply saying that there is not a one-to-one equivalence. A unit of energy saved at the end use will not necessarily result in a unit of energy saved at the level of the whole economy. There may well be policy options such as energy or carbon taxes that help to reduce rebound effects.

The policy implications of the rebound effect are that we do need more research to understand it better; it needs to be taken into account when undertaking energy scenarios, as there is not a one-to-one equivalence between energy saved at the level of an individual energy efficiency measure; ways to mitigate the rebound effect need to be considered, such as energy or carbon taxes; and we need more research on the links between improvements in energy productivity and economic growth.

## References and Bibliography

Afsah, S., Sakcito, K., and Wielga, C. 2012. *Energy Efficiency is for Real, Energy Rebound a Distraction*. [Online]. Available at: http://co2scorecard.org/Content/uploads/Energy_Efficiency_is_for_Real_CO2_Scorecard_Research_Jan_11_12.pdf [accessed 27 January 2013].

Alcot, B. 2009. *The Rebound Effect: Introduction and Historical Perspective.* Presentation at the University of Cambridge 14 May 2009. [Online]. Available at: http://www.cambridgeenergy.com/archive/2009-05-14/Blake%20Alcott%20to%20send%20to%20participants.pdf [accessed 27 January 2013].

Barker, T. and Foxon, T. 2008. 'The Macroeconomic Rebound Effect and the UK Economy'. UK Energy Research Centre. [Online]. Available at: http://www.sciencedirect.com/science/article/pii/S0301421507001565 [accessed 26 January 2013].

Barker, T. and Dagoumas, A. 2009. *The Global Macroeconomic Rebound Effect of Energy Efficiency Policies: An Analysis 2012–2030 using E3MG.* Presentation made at Cambridge University, 14 May 2009. [Online]. Available at: http://www.cambridgeenergy.com/archive/2009-05-14/Barker%20&%20Dagoumas_Rebound_14052009V3.pdf [accessed 27 January 2013].

Barrett, J. 2011a. *Rebounds and Jevons: Nobody Goes There Anymore. It's Too Crowded.* [Online]. Available at: http://realclimateeconomics.org/wp/archives/654 [accessed 27 January 2013].

Barrett, J. 2011b. *Rebounds Gone Wild.* [Online]. Available at: http://realclimateeconomics.org/wp/archives/647 [accessed 27 January 2013].

Bosshard, P. 2010. *Energy Efficiency: Paid Lunch or False Shortcut?* [Online]. Available at: http://www.huffingtonpost.com/peter-bosshard/paid-lunch-or-false-short_b_802532.html [accessed 27 January 2013].

Brookes, L. 1990. 'Energy Efficiency and Economic Fallacies'. *Energy Policy* (March): 783–5.

Butler, K. 2011. *Do Green Cars Just Make People Drive More?* [Online]. Available at: http://www.motherjones.com/blue-marble/2011/03/green-cars-jevons-paradox [accessed 27 January 2013].

Chameides, B. 2011. *Energy Efficiency on the Rebound.* [Online]. Available at: http://www.huffingtonpost.com/bill-chameides/energy-efficiency-on-the_b_831127.html [accessed 27 January 2013].

Goldstein, D. 2010. *Some Dilemma: Efficient Appliances Use Less Energy, Produce the Same Level of Service with Less Pollution and Provide Consumers with Greater Savings. What's Not to Like?* [Online]. Available at: http://switchboard.nrdc.org/blogs/dgoldstein/some_dilemma_efficient_applian_1.html [accessed 21 April 2013].

Herring, H. 2006. 'Energy Efficiency—A Critical View'. *Energy* 31 (2006): 10–20. [Online]. Available at: http://www.fraw.org.uk/files/economics/herring_2006.pdf [accessed 27 January 2013].

Herring, H. and Roy, R. 2007. 'Technological Innovation, Energy Efficient Design and the Rebound Effect'. *Technovation* 27(4): 194–203.

IEA. 2010. *World Energy Outlook 2010*. [Online]. Available at: http://www.worldenergyoutlook.org/media/weo2010.pdf [accessed 26 April 2013].

Jenkins, J. and Saunders, H. 2011. *Hot Topic: Does Energy Efficiency Lead to Increased Energy Consumption*. [Online]. Available at: http://www.makingitmagazine.net/?p=3460 [accessed 27 January 2013].

IPCC. 2007. *Climate Change 2007. Mitigation of Climate Change*. Contribution of Working Group III to the Fourth Assessment Report. [Online]. Available at: http://www.ipcc.ch/pdf/assessment-report/ar4/wg3/ar4_wg3_full_report.pdf [accessed 26 April 2013].

Jenkins, J., Norhaus, T. and Shellenberger, M. 2011. *Energy Emergence. Rebound and Backfire as Emergent Phenomena*. The Breakthrough Institute. [Online]. Available at: http://thebreakthrough.org/blog/Energy_Emergence.pdf [accessed 26 January 2013].

Jevons, W.S. 1865. *The Coal Question; An Inquiry Concerning the Progress of the Nation, and the Probable Exhaustion of Our Coal Mines*. [Online]. Available at: http://www.econlib.org/library/YPDBooks/Jevons/jvnCQ1.html [accessed 28 April 2013].

Kemp, R. 2009. *Responses to Increased Energy Efficiency in the Real World*. Presentation at Cambridge University, 14 May 2009. [Online]. Available at: http://www.cambridgeenergy.com/archive/2009-05-14/On%20the%20rebound%20-%20Kemp-1.pdf [accessed 27 January 2013].

Khazzoom, J.D. 1980. 'Economic Implications of Mandated Efficiency Standards for Household Appliances', *The Energy Journal* 11(2): 21–40.

Khazzoom, J.D. 1987. 'Energy Saving Resulting from the Adoption of More Efficient Appliances', *The Energy Journal* 8(4): 85–9.

Khazzoom, J.D. 1989. 'Energy Savings from More Efficient Appliances: A Rejoinder', *The Energy Journal* 10(1): 157–66.

Koerth-Baker, M., Turner, K., De Fence, J. and Xin Cui, C. 2011. *The Rebound Effect: Some Questions Answered*. Strathclyde Discussion Papers in Economics. [Online]. Available at: http://www.strath.ac.uk/media/departments/economics/researchdiscussionpapers/2011/11-07_final.pdf [accessed 27 January 2013].

Komanoff, C. 2010. *If Efficiency Hasn't Cut Energy Use, Then What?* [Online]. Available at: http://grist.org/politics/2010-12-15-if-efficiency-hasnt-cut-energy-use-then-what/ [accessed 27 January 2013].

Koomey, J.G. 2011. *A Fascinating Encounter with Advocates of Large Rebound Effects*. [Online]. Available at: http://www.koomey.com/post/3286897788 [accessed 27 January 2013].

Kotchen, M. 'Beware of the Rebound Effect', *The New York Times*, 20 March 2012. [Online]. Available at: http://www.nytimes.com/roomfordebate/2012/03/19/the-siren-song-of-energy-efficiency/reduce-energy-use-and-beware-of-the-rebound-effect [accessed 27 January 2013].

Lee, R. and Wagner, G. *The Rebound Effect in a More Fuel Efficient Transportation Centre*. The Institute for Policy Integrity, New York University School of Law. [Online]. Available at: http://policyintegrity.org/files/publications/The_Rebound_Effect.pdf [accessed 27 January 2013].

Levi, M. 2010. *Mangling Energy Efficiency Economics*. [Online]. Available at: http://blogs.cfr.org/levi/2010/12/14/mangling-energy-efficiency-economics/ [accessed 27 January 2013].

Lomberg, B. 2011. *If You Think Efficiency Reduces Our Energy Use, Think Again*. [Online]. Available at: http://www.thenational.ae/thenationalconversation/news-comment/if-you-think-efficiency-reduces-our-energy-use-think-again [accessed 27 January 2013].

Lovins, A. 2011. *Reply to 'The Efficiency Dilemma'*. [Online]. Available at: http://www.rmi.org/Knowledge-Center/Library/2011-01_ReplyToNewYorker [accessed 27 January 2013].

Maxwell, D., Owen, P., McAndrew, L., Muehmel, K. and Neubauer, A. 2011. *Addressing the Rebound Effect*. A report for the European Commission DG Environment. [Online]. Available at: http://ec.europa.eu/environment/eussd/pdf/rebound_effect_report.pdf [accessed 27 January 2013].

New Buildings Institute. 2011. *Examples of Deep Energy Savings in Existing Buildings*. [Online]. Available at: http://newbuildings.org/sites/default/files/NBI_NEEA_DeepSavingsSearchPhase1_FinalR2_June2011.pdf [accessed 26 April 2013].

Owen, D. 2010. 'The Efficiency Dilemma'. *The New Yorker*, 20 December 2010, p. 78. [Online]. Available at: http://www.newyorker.com/reporting/2010/12/20/101220fa_fact_owen [accessed 27 January 2013].

Owen, D. 2012a. *The Conundrum: How Scientific Innovation, Increased Efficiency, and Good Intentions Can Make Our Energy and Climate Problems Worse*. New York, Riverhead Trade.

Owen, D. 2012b. 'Efficiency's Promise: Too Good to Be True'. *The New York Times*, 4 April 2012. [Online]. Available at: http://www.nytimes.com/roomfordebate/2012/03/19/the-siren-song-of-energy-efficiency/efficiencys-promise-is-too-good-to-be-true [accessed 27 January 2013].

Polimeni, J.M., Mayumi, K., Giampietro, M. and Alcott, B. 2008. *The Myth of Resource Efficiency. The Jevons Paradox*. London, Earthscan.

Powell, B.A. 2010. *Brother, Can You Spare a Fridge?* [Online]. Available at: http://grist.org/food/food-2010-12-22-brother-can-you-spare-a-fridge/ [accessed 27 January 2013].

Roberts, D. 2012. *What's the Deal with the Rebound Effect?* [Online]. Available at: http://grist.org/energy-efficiency/whats-the-deal-with-the-rebound-effect/ [accessed 29 December 2012].

Sorrell, S. 2009. 'Jevons' Paradox Revisited: The Evidence for Backfire from Improved Energy Efficiency', *Energy Policy* 3(4): 1456–569.

Sorrell, S. 2009. *The Rebound Effect. Mechanisms, Evidence and Implications*. Presentation made at Cambridge University, 14 May 2009. [Online]. Available at: http://www.cambridgeenergy.com/archive/2009-05-14/Steve%20Sorrell.pdf [accessed 27 January 2013].

Sorrel, S. 2010. 'Energy, Economic Growth and Environmental Sustainability: Five Propositions', *Sustainability* 2: 1784–809.

Sorrell, S., Dimitropoulos, J. and Sommerville, M. 2009. 'Empirical Estimates of the Direct Rebound Effect: A Review', *Energy Policy* 37(4): 1356–71.

Stavins, R.N., Jaffe, J. and Schatzki, T. 2007. *Too Good to Be True? An Examination of Three Economic Assessments of California Climate Change Policy*. AEI-Brookings Joint Center for Regulatory Affairs. [Online]. Available at: http://www.nber.org/papers/w13587.pdf [accessed 27 January 2013].

Street, K. 2011. *Does Improving Efficiency Do Any Good?* [Online]. Available at: http://theenergycollective.com/karenstreet/49288/new-yorker-article-jevons-paradox-does-improving-efficiency-do-any-good [accessed 27 January 2013].

Thompson, C. 2012. 'Clive Thompson on Unsaving the Planet', *Wired* (March 2012). [Online]. Available at: http://www.wired.com/magazine/2012/02/st_thompson_energy/ [accessed 27 January 2013].

Tiernery, J. 2011. 'When Energy Efficiency Sullies the Environment', *The New York Times*, 7 March 2011. [Online]. Available at: http://www.nytimes.com/2011/03/08/science/08tier.html?_r=2&hp [accessed 27 January 2013].

Tlhalefang, J.B. 2009. 'The Impact of Increased Efficiency in the Transport Sectors' Energy Use: A Computable General Equilibrium Analysis for the Botswana Economy', *Botswana Journal of Economics*. [Online]. Available at: http://www.ajol.info/index.php/boje/article/view/72975/61866 [accessed 27 January 2013].

Tsao, J.Y., Saunders, H.D., Creighton, J.R., Coltrin, M.E. and Simmons, J.A. 2010. 'Solid-State Lighting: An Energy-Economics Perspective', *J.Phys. D: Appl. Phys.* 43: 354001.

UKERC. 2007. *The Rebound Effect: An Assessment of the Evidence for Economy-Wide Energy Savings from Improved Energy Efficiency*. [Online]. Available at: http://www.blakealcott.org/pdf/Rebound_Report_UKERC.pdf [accessed 27 January 2013].

Vaughn, K. 2012. *Jevons Paradox: The Debate That Just Won't Die*. [Online]. Available at: http://blog.rmi.org/blog_Jevons_Paradox [accessed 27 January 2013].

Vienneau, R. 2011. *Blah, Blah, Jevon's Paradox, Blah, Blah, Backfire*. [Online]. Available at: http://robertvienneau.blogspot.co.uk/2011/01/blah-blah-jevons-paradox-blah-blah.html [accessed 27 January 2013].

# 6

# Management Techniques

*Management is doing things right; leadership is doing the right things.*
*What is measured improves.*
*The best way to predict your future is to create it.*

> Peter F. Drucker,
> *Management Consultant, Educator and Author, 1909–2005*

## It Is About Management, Not Technology

The process of improving energy productivity is a not a technical problem. It is a management problem. Many technologies already exist that can radically improve the energy efficiency of almost all fuel- and electricity-using processes in buildings, industry and transport. In fact, even if no further technologies were developed or discovered, and we just applied all the existing technologies that are economically viable right now, we would close the 'energy efficiency gap' and achieve far higher levels of efficiency than we see today. Clearly, new and improved technologies and techniques are emerging constantly as part of what Joseph Schumpeter called the 'gale of creative destruction', and in Chapter 8 we will look at just a few of the existing and emerging technologies.

Over the years, many researchers and practitioners, myself included, have developed tools and models of the energy management process designed to make it easier to understand and manage. Some of these draw heavily on wider models of managing technical change. All of them have been developed, applied and refined as part of real projects. They are therefore proven and practical rather than mere theory. In the words of the old adage, 'theory without practice is useless, practice without theory is impossible'.

## Management Techniques

### ENABLING CONDITIONS FOR ENERGY MANAGEMENT

In order for any private or public sector organization to achieve the optimal level of energy efficiency there are certain enabling conditions that have to be in place. We start by looking at these, and how they can be implemented.

The first enabling condition, and the most important, is explicit and strong leadership from top management. Efficiency, like other resources, is only really there when someone looks for it. Many energy managers and engineers work in organizations where they are well aware of the profitable energy efficiency opportunities that exist, but they are unable to persuade senior management to take action. In other organizations, no one is actually looking for the opportunities. Without the explicit support of the leadership of the organization, and appropriate resources being dedicated to energy efficiency, these significant opportunities will remain an underexploited source of profit, reduced emissions and potential employee engagement.

Therefore, the first challenge for agents of change is how to truly engage top management. In order to persuade senior management of the importance of energy efficiency it is important to talk about the energy efficiency opportunity in the right language and to frame the conversation in the right way. In the case of private sector organizations this will most likely be profit and productivity. A commonly heard comment on energy efficiency in many organizations with low or medium energy intensity is that energy is only a small fraction of total costs, and this view often inhibits effective action. Potential energy savings should be compared to profit rather than total costs, and in many cases achievable energy savings will be a significant proportion of profit. Given that energy savings go straight to the bottom line, the potential savings, and the relative ease of achieving them, should be compared to the increase in revenue that would be necessary to achieve the same increase in profit and the difficulties of doing that, particularly in the current economic climate. In October 2011, for instance, the British Plastics Federation released a report stating that energy costs at plastics processing sites were approaching the cost of direct labour, and energy costs were almost always higher than actual profits (BPF 2011). Energy costs should also be thought of as a controllable cost, far more controllable than some other costs such as labour.

The views of an organization's leaders, whether they accept or understand the risks presented by existing energy supply arrangements and potential benefits from improving energy efficiency, will always determine their motivation to take action. These views are not always an accurate reflection of the real situation within their organization and, for many people, energy efficiency will always be low on their priority list. For some top managers it will be purely a risk/reward-type calculation, but for others it will be driven by a belief in the need for action to improve sustainability in order to combat environmental problems. A number of 'conversions' to an environmental or sustainability driven perspective have been documented in the mass of sustainability literature, including the case of the late Ray Anderson of Interface, an early convert and great leader on the sustainability agenda, and Lee Scott, the CEO of Walmart from 2000 to 2009 who started the company on its highly effective sustainability journey. But we should not forget that for most leaders saving money is likely to remain the main objective. The challenge for agents of change, whether they be internal employees or external consultants, is to find the winning arguments that catalyse top management into taking serious action to improve energy efficiency. Once that is done, the processes and tools to do the job can be put in place.

The next enabling condition of energy management which is often forgotten is that responsibility and accountability for energy use has to be given to those that can do something about it, and this really means production-facility managers or profit-centre managers at an appropriate level. In the early days of energy management, responsibility for reducing energy use was often given to an energy manager. The problem with giving an 'energy manager' responsibility for energy use is that he or she does not, and cannot, control the activities within profit centres which lead to energy being used. The energy manager, who may be energy specialist, can only ever be a service provider, an internal consultant and provider of information and advice – he or she cannot manage energy in profit centres. Only by giving explicit responsibility and accountability to profit-centre managers, and in particular by adding energy efficiency improvement to the managers' targets, preferably linked to reward structures, can you really achieve the best results. The flip side of giving responsibility for energy use to a manager is that the manager must be able to control the variables that affect energy use and he or she must also have timely and accurate information on energy use as well as appropriate benchmarks. Giving responsibility without both the ability to act and performance information, just like giving responsibility to the wrong person, cannot work.

As with other resources and important management issues such as quality control, the responsibility for energy efficiency should be passed as far down the organization and as close to the point of energy use as possible. Doing this helps to engage employees and can bring out their responsibility and inspire creative new ways of reducing energy use. How far devolved responsibility can be taken will depend on the corporate culture, the ability to provide regular information and the costs of providing data by sub-metering. Using energy as a spearhead can in some cases help to drive wider efforts to improve employee engagement, as it is a subject that all people have some interest in. Energy efficiency motivation programmes at work can also help employees save energy at home.

## Energy Management as a Process of Technical Change

Energy management is at least partly a process of technical change, and students of energy management can learn a lot from the literature on managing technical change. Langrish (1979) proposed that there are three necessary conditions before a technical change of any sort can occur. These are:

- a *technical concept* must exist, capable of being developed to the stage of achieving;

- an *advantage* over alternative technical concepts (and the status quo); and

- the *capability* of developing the concept to the stage of achieving the advantage must exist.

All three conditions have to occur in the same place at the same time. An important modification to this model would be that it is the perception of advantage and capability, rather than any absolute values, that motivate an actor to bring all three together and force a technical change. The actor fulfils an entrepreneurial role even though, in most cases of technical change associated with improving energy efficiency, he or she is unlikely to be a classic independent entrepreneur, but rather an employee of an established organization.

## THE TECHNICAL CONCEPT

The technical concept may be a brand new idea, a new combination of ideas (old and/or new) or an old idea not previously developed. The degree of capability needed to turn the concept into a commercial, implemented project will depend on the nature of the concept and the extent to which it is already embodied in existing hardware and systems.

## THE ADVANTAGE

The advantage in the case of energy efficiency is usually a financial one, although other non-economic, or at least harder-to-measure, advantages such as improved quality of working environment may occur. A major exception to a purely economic advantage would be a situation where investment in a certain energy efficiency technology is required by law or regulation, irrespective of economics.

An important factor when considering energy efficiency investments is the issue of adoption costs over and above the basic equipment cost. The technical concept may be embodied in easily available commercial hardware, e.g. low-energy lamps or heat exchangers, but to make a viable system some level of engineering design work is usually required, however simple the technology. The system has to be engineered and the total costs will be affected by very site-specific factors. For example, boiler economizers are a mature technology (first patented in 1845) which in principle can be applied to any gas-fired boiler, or dual-fuel boiler if a bypass is used during oil firing. However, numerous site-specific factors affect the financial viability of proposals to install boiler economizers, including: physical space available for the hardware; load-bearing supports; quantity and quality of demand for hot water; flue gas temperature and composition; boiler utilization and load pattern. Total system costs can be two to three times the hardware costs for heat recovery and other technologies.

## THE CAPABILITY

The host organization, its consultants or advisers, and/or the supplier of the equipment must have the capability to deliver a concept. For most energy efficiency measures the degree of development work is small and in the form of relatively routine engineering rather than the full-blown product development needed for new technologies. The importance of this type of work and its quality, however, should not be underestimated.

## A Soft-Systems Model of Energy Management

The model of energy management presented here is a soft-systems model developed in the 1980s by the author and used successfully as a context and background for many successful energy management programmes. Here we are talking about management systems, i.e. systems for managing energy, rather than technical energy management systems such as those provided by control technologies like Building Management Systems (BMS).

The soft-systems methodology was developed by Peter Checkland and others at the University of Lancaster in the UK and was based on action research (Checkland 1981). It is a framework for dealing with the kind of messy problems that often occur in real life and which are difficult to model using conventional, 'hard' systems engineering. It has been applied to many diverse situations, including the development of a military information operations capability for the Australian Defence Force and a methodology to enhance creativity. Soft systems is a powerful tool for intervening in many complex situations that managers, politicians and civil servants find themselves facing, and should be better known and more widely applied.

The soft-systems methodology is a seven step process:

1.  Identifying the problem situation.

2.  Researching the situation and building a 'rich picture' of it.

3.  Selecting perspectives and building 'root definitions' (key processes that need to take place within the desired system).

4.  Developing a conceptual model of the change system.

5.  Comparing the model to the real-world situation.

6.  Defining the changes to be implemented.

7.  Taking action.

The Root Definition used to design the model of energy management was:

> *To design a management system for an organization that results in staff and other agents of change creating, identifying and exploiting opportunities to improve energy efficiency that are profitable to the organization (using its own definition of profitable).*

The energy management system has three levels which interact with each other and with other systems within the organization.

## FIRST LEVEL – GOOD HOUSEKEEPING

The first level is about managing energy use within the constraints of existing equipment with no investment. This level has often been called 'good housekeeping' or 'no-cost' and relies on Monitoring and Targeting (M&T) and employee engagement. To be effective, M&T should answer the question 'where is cost being incurred?' As Drucker (1964) said, 'it is impossible to manage an aggregate'. M&T must also correct or normalize for factors outside the control of the manager, such as weather, and provide comparisons with expected energy consumptions in a timely manner so that variances can be spotted and corrected. This level of energy management can also involve employee training. Evidence from many years of case studies shows that savings from implementing this level of energy management alone can produce savings of 5 to 30 per cent, and in some cases more. It is primarily designed to prevent waste through change of behaviours.

## SECOND LEVEL – RETROFITTING

The second level of energy management activity is concerned with retrofitting measures onto existing buildings or processes. Many of the energy management case studies are concerned with retrofitting work to improve efficiency.

## THIRD LEVEL – NEW BUILDINGS, FACILITIES OR PROCESSES

The third level is concerned with investment in new buildings, industrial facilities or processes. Often these are not undertaken for energy efficiency reasons alone, and the challenge for agents of change is to ensure that the opportunities for improved efficiency presented by such major investments are fully exploited. In many organizations these opportunities to incorporate energy efficiency into new facilities, which only come about infrequently, are often missed – partly because the energy management process is not adequately integrated into the capital expenditure process.

## IDENTIFYING AND APPRAISING OPPORTUNITIES

To identify or create investment opportunities requires information about energy costs (from M&T) coupled with knowledge of relevant technical concepts. Basically, a creative synthesis of internal and external information is required. Creativity can always redefine what is relevant. When considering technical measures an explicit decision on the appropriate level of innovation or technical risk is needed. Some organizations may be willing to take on the risk of using a prototype or early version of a new piece of technology. But for most organizations, the simple adoption of existing technologies is the more appropriate response for energy efficiency investments – usually, there is no desire or need to take risks with technology.

Once opportunities to reduce energy use are identified they must be appraised technically, economically and contextually. These appraisals can interact in an iterative process that itself leads to new idea. This is essentially a process of project development. Contextual appraisal covers interactions with other management decisions being considered or made, such as possible closure of a facility or relocation. Failure to undertake adequate contextual appraisal often leads to wasted investment, for example, where recently retrofitted equipment has to be removed during a relocation or due to a planned closure of a plant that was not properly considered in the investment decision. Project development also has to take into account operation and maintenance factors. In addition, technical staff developing projects, who may be outside the organization, need to ensure good communications are in place with the relevant operations and maintenance staff. External factors such as noise, vibrations and emissions also need to be properly assessed during project development.

Energy efficiency projects can, and in the real world often do, interact with each other, as well as interacting with other process or operational changes. These interactions can be either positively or negatively synergistic. Assembling a portfolio of potential projects, maintaining them in a database, and regularly re-evaluating them independently, as well as together, are useful techniques.

## The Importance of Looking at Total Costs

When considering energy it is important to look at all costs associated with energy usage including operations and maintenance costs, committed capital costs and planned capital costs. By undertaking a proper audit of the full costs of energy use, and then addressing total costs rather than just energy costs, both capital expenditure and energy costs can be optimized.

## Interactions of the Energy Management System with Other Management Functions

Energy management is, of course, only one facet of running an organization and will never, and should never, be the be all and end all of management attention. As well as ensuring that a proper energy management process and organization is put in place along with appropriate reporting procedures, senior management need to ensure that the interfaces between the energy management process and other parts of the business or organization are defined and appropriate linkages put in place.

In particular energy efficiency processes need to be explicitly linked into the following systems.

### PROPERTY PORTFOLIO MANAGEMENT

For large property portfolio holders in all sectors it is essential that the energy efficiency process is properly integrated into the overall portfolio management processes. For instance, when examining a portfolio from an energy efficiency perspective it is important that any plans to redevelop or sell properties are fully considered and factored into the energy management programme. There is no point spending time and money in improving the efficiency of a building that is scheduled to be sold – unless the retrofit is perceived to increase its value enough to justify the investment.

### SUSTAINABILITY PROCESSES

Many organizations have adopted sustainability objectives and processes. In many cases these are still based on a compliance mentality but increasingly, leading-edge companies are viewing sustainability as a source of value creation. When reviewing all aspects of sustainability the one that can create most value is usually energy efficiency. Other sustainability initiatives, such as reducing packaging, can also have an impact on overall energy efficiency both in transportation and in the supply chain. Some 'greening' efforts, e.g. adding bicycle racks in a building to achieve a certain green rating, will not produce direct economic effects, whereas energy efficiency always produces immediate, measureable direct economic benefits in the form of reduced costs.

## ENVIRONMENTAL SYSTEMS, E.G. ISO 14000

Prior to the introduction of ISO 50001 (ISO 2012), the environmental quality standard ISO 14000 (ISO 2009) was sometimes applied to energy management systems, and it can still have a role to play in energy management.

## QUALITY CONTROL SYSTEMS

Quality control systems such as ISO 9001 and Six Sigma can be used to help energy management processes (EPA 2012). Improving quality control is about reducing statistical variations in quality and reducing waste. This is analogous to energy management which is, in part, trying to reduce statistical variation through the use of M&T systems. Furthermore, if a quality assurance programme reduces waste, or the reject rate from an industrial manufacturing process, it will improve energy efficiency by eliminating the energy used to make a rejected product. Quality assurance should, of course, also be applied to the energy management processes themselves.

## RESOURCE EFFICIENCY

All efforts to improve resource efficiencies will interact with energy use. A particular example is water usage. Reducing water usage, as well as having the direct benefit of lower water costs, will cut energy use by reducing water pumping requirements, both within the factory or building itself, as well as upstream in the water distribution system. By improving the efficiency of raw material usage there will be reductions in energy use in materials handling, transportation and logistics – both within the immediate subsystem of the firm making the improvement and upstream in the supplier chain.

## DESIGN OR ACQUISITION OF NEW BUILDINGS OR MAJOR EQUIPMENT

The acquisition of new equipment or a new building is a major opportunity to incorporate energy efficiency, but even in some organizations that generally have effective energy management systems these opportunities are still being missed. Tight time pressures to design or acquire a new piece of equipment or a new building sometimes lead to failure to include energy efficiency in the design and acquisition criteria. This leads to energy efficiency opportunities being missed and excessive energy use being 'locked in' for many years, or even decades.

## PROCUREMENT

Everyday decisions by procurement departments to purchase energy-using items such as computers, refrigerators, cars or photocopiers affect energy use and overall energy efficiency. Failure of procurement departments to take energy efficiency into account in procurement decisions can have a negative effect on individual employees' motivation levels. When employees are making efforts to reduce energy use it is frustrating and demotivating to see procurement decisions that work against energy efficiency. All too often, even today, procurement is largely based on best first price rather than whole life-cycle costs. Energy efficiency and its impact on life cycle costs needs to be fully incorporated into procurement policies and evaluation procedures.

## OVERALL CORPORATE STRATEGY

The management tools and processes we describe later in this chapter apply to managing existing assets. Strategic decisions taken to meet other objectives may radically transform energy use and improve energy efficiency far more than the incremental changes that normal energy management typically produces. An example is the idea of developing multi-use buildings in the UK public sector where NHS clinics, schools and other groups share a building. In this kind of example energy use can be reduced significantly by closing redundant buildings, and then the remaining buildings can be deep retrofitted, which could reduce energy use by 50 per cent.

## SUPPLY CHAIN MANAGEMENT

Large companies have extensive supply chains and considerable purchasing power that can be used to achieve environmental or energy objectives. Analysis of the carbon footprint of retailers, for example, shows that the majority of carbon emissions are a result of supply chain operations rather than internal operations. McKinsey (2007) reported that

> *Analysis suggests that for consumer-goods makers, high-tech players, and other manufacturers, between 40 and 60 per cent of a company's carbon footprint resides upstream in its supply chain – from raw materials, transport, and packaging to the energy consumed in manufacturing processes. For retailers, the figure can be 80 per cent.*

According to McKinsey (2009), there are six levers to increase energy efficiency in supply chains:

- increase value density, i.e. reduce weight per economic value;

- reduce average distance travelled, change the mix of transportation modes (i.e. substitute low energy modes such as rail for higher energy modes, e.g. road);

- improve the energy performance of the transportation mode(s) being used;

- assess the usage of individual transportation assets;

- assess the usage of collective assets.

Large companies constantly exert pressure on their supply chain to improve performance and reduce costs, and improving energy efficiency can help these objectives. Simply demanding greater energy efficiency from suppliers, however, is unlikely to be effective as suppliers often lack the technical capabilities and the capital to invest in energy efficiency. Therefore it is important to address these constraints. Large companies can help suppliers by providing technical assistance, utilizing the buying power of the supply chain for energy efficiency technologies such as variable speed drives and lighting upgrades, and facilitating access to credit lines to fund energy efficiency investment, as well as possibly facilitating third-party investment.

In order to do this successfully it is important that the initiative is seen as collaborative rather than imposed by the large company.

## Energy Management Tools

There are a number of effective tools that should be used within the energy management system. Here we summarize the most common and useful.

### THE PARETO PRINCIPLE

The Pareto Principle, or 80/20 rule, when applied to energy management, says that 20 per cent of any portfolio of buildings, or 20 per cent of the equipment or processes within a facility, will account for 80 per cent of the energy usage, and therefore it is better to focus attention on that 20 per cent. In any particular situation the exact numbers are unlikely to be 80/20, but the principle still holds: focus on those areas that are likely to yield the biggest result. This is particularly true in large property portfolios.

### ISO 50001

ISO 50001 is the first internationally recognized standard to set out an integrated set of processes and tools to help organizations to implement an energy management system. By choosing to adopt ISO 50001, senior management can make a clear and visible commitment to improving energy efficiency through a systematic energy management programme, and ensure that appropriate systems and standards are in place. The standard goes from high-level strategy to operational actions such as monitoring and targeting energy use. ISO 50001 uses the Plan-Do-Check-Act (PDCA) approach to encourage energy savings.

The introduction of ISO 50001 is a very welcome step forward in energy management and even though it has only been in place since 2011 it is gaining significant traction globally. The adoption of previous ISOs such as 9001 in 1987 and 14001 in 1996, both of which are now widely used across industry and commerce, is encouraging, and adoption of ISO 50001 will formalize and improve energy management in most organizations. We would expect to see large companies starting to require their suppliers to have ISO 50001 just as they do for ISOs 9001 and 140001.

## MONITORING AND TARGETING

Monitoring and Targeting (M&T) is the process of collecting energy usage data, setting a consumption target, and then comparing usage to the target figure. This process enables ongoing management of energy as well as identification of high-spending areas that may provide investment opportunities. Energy usage data can be collected at a facility or building level but is ideally collected at a disaggregated level related to individual departments or profit centres through sub-metres. Targets can be based on a theoretical calculation of optimum consumption, an arbitrary target such as 10 per cent saving compared to a previous period, or the best performance achieved within a set period. M&T systems should always normalize to take out the effect of factors that are not controllable by management such as the weather, i.e. average temperature. Information from an M&T system should always be passed to the manager(s) with responsibility for energy use. For the best description of M&T systems see Vesma (2012).

## NORMALIZED PERFORMANCE INDICATORS OR BENCHMARKS

Normalized Performance Indicators (NPIs), also known as benchmarks, can be useful for comparing energy performance of large numbers of buildings or similar facilities. Examples of NPIs include energy per square metre for buildings, corrected for weather and hours of use; energy per hectolitre of beer, corrected for product mix, packaging mix and size of brewery; or energy per connection for mobile phone operators, corrected for variables such as cell sites per connection, voice traffic per cell station and cooling degree days (the number of days that ambient temperature is above a defined value – air conditioning energy use is generally proportional to cooling degree days). NPIs or benchmarks are useful for comparing performance between facilities or companies. Several industries have implemented benchmarking schemes, notably the UK brewing industry which has been reporting specific energy consumption per hectolitre since 1976, giving a consistent dataset for more than thirty years. Between 1976 and 2004 the UK brewing industry reduced its specific energy consumption by 47 per cent. In addition, between 2000 and 2010 it exceeded its target under the Climate Change Agreement. The target agreed with the UK government was 20 per cent improvement; the industry achieved a 25 per cent improvement in energy efficiency, with 4.3 per cent being achieved in 2010 (British Beer and Pub Association 2011). Although they can be useful at industry level NPIs need to be used with care as of course, like any other single number, they can only convey part of the story. A building with a high NPI, i.e. high efficiency, for example may have more potential for savings than a building with a low NPI, i.e. low efficiency, due to site specific factors that constrain the practical potential in the low NPI building. Combined with total spend per building they can be a first, high-level indicator of where maximum potential may exist.

## MEASUREMENT AND VERIFICATION

Measurement and Verification (M&V) is a systematic way of assessing actual energy savings from energy efficiency projects. It grew out of the International Performance and Measurement Protocol (IPMVP) originally supported by the US Department of Energy in the 1990s and now operated by EVO, an international not-for-profit organization. IPMVP provides a standardized way of establishing energy savings from any particular measure. There are significant differences between M&V and M&T. As described above, M&T is the process of collecting information on energy usage, setting an energy consumption target and comparing actual usage to the target. It should be ongoing and cover total energy use, broken down when possible. M&V is usually related to specific investment measures and is often, although not always, limited to a certain period of time. In most cases M&V will use the output from an M&T system and there is a move towards real-time M&T and M&V.

## THE ENERGY MANAGEMENT MATRIX

The energy management matrix was developed in the 1990s and is a tool used to assess the status of an organization's energy management efforts. It covers energy policy, organization, information systems, marketing and communications, and investment. The matrix can help management and external agents to assess the current state of play and to monitor progress over time. For a description of the matrix, see Fawkes (2007).

## MARGINAL ABATEMENT COST CURVES

The Marginal Abatement Cost Curve (MACC) presentation of energy-saving opportunities gained prominence in 2007 when it was used by McKinsey in its study of energy efficiency potential (McKinsey 2007). The MACC shows the cost of avoiding a tonne of $CO_2$ emissions using different technologies and graphically illustrated the cost effectiveness of most energy efficiency measures compared to renewable energy sources, with many efficiency measures having negative costs, implying that they are profitable without subsidy. Like all presentation and management tools, MACCs have to be used with caution and users should be careful to consider the assumptions behind the analysis. Ekins et al. (2011) produced a useful critique of the technique. Combining the MACC presentation with Internal Rates of Return, as proposed by Lavery (2011), is a useful technique for making the financial case for investment in energy efficiency to top management in individual firms.

## Summary

Energy efficiency is a management problem and not a technical problem. The management tools needed for organizations of every type to manage their energy usage and achieve significant improvements in energy efficiency are well known and are proven to work across all sectors, as shown by our case studies (see Chapter 7) and many other examples. The management tools are starting to be codified within standards such as ISO 50001, which will help their wider application. One of the major factors in the success of any energy management programme is leadership, and leaders of all organizations need to ensure that their organization is appropriately organized and managed to exploit the full potential. That alone will go a long way to closing the 'energy efficiency gap'.

## References and Bibliography

BPF. 2011. *Energy Management in Plastics Processing. A Signposting Guide by the British Plastics Federation.* [Online]. Available at: http://www.tangram.co.uk/TI-Energy%20Management%20in%20Plastics%20Processing%20-%20BPF.pdf [accessed 26 April 2013].

British Beer and Pub Association. 2005. *The UK Brewing Industry: Reducing Emissions.* [Online]. Available at: http://www.fcrn.org.uk/sites/default/files/BBPA.pdf [accessed 27 January 2013].

British Beer and Pub Association. 2006. *The British Brewing Industry. Thirty Years of Environmental Improvement 1976–2006.* [Online]. Available at: https://www.ibd.org.uk/cms/file/338 [accessed 31 January 2013].

British Beer and Pub Association. 2011. *Great British Pint Keeps Getting Greener – 25 per cent Rise in Energy Efficiency Adds to Great Record for UK Brewers.* [Online]. Available at: http://www.beerandpub.com/news/great-british-pint-keeps-getting-greener-25-per-cent-rise-in-energy-efficiency-adds-to-great-record-for-uk-brewers?from_search=1 [accessed 31 January 2013].

Broad, L. 2012. *How to Engage Your Employees on Energy Management: Dos and Don'ts.* [Online]. Available at: http://www.2degreesnetwork.com/groups/employee-engagement/resources/how-engage-your-employees-energy-management-dos-and-donts/ [accessed 27 January 2013].

Checkland, P.B. 1981. *Systems Thinking, Systems Practice.* Chichester, John Wiley & Sons.

Drucker, P.F. 1964. *Managing for Results.* New York, Harper & Row.

Ekins, P., Kesicki, F. and Smith, A.Z.P. 2011. *Marginal Abatement Cost Curves: A Call for Caution.* [Online]. Available at: http://www.bartlett.ucl.ac.uk/energy/news/documents/ei-news-290611-macc.pdf [accessed 27 January 2013].

EPA (United States Environmental Protection Agency). 2012. *3M Lean Six Sigma and Sustainability.* [Online]. Available at: http://www.epa.gov/lean/environment/studies/3m.htm [accessed 28 December 2012].

Fawkes, S. 2007. *Outsourcing Energy Management.* Aldershot, Gower Publishing.

IMO (International Maritime Organization). 2012. *Energy Efficiency and the Reduction of GHG Emissions from Ships.* [Online]. Available at: http://www.imo.org/MediaCentre/HotTopics/GHG/Pages/default.aspx [accessed 27 January 2013].

ISO. 2009. *Environmental Management. The ISO 14000 Family of International Standards.* [Online]. Available at: http://www.iso.org/iso/theiso14000family_2009.pdf [accessed 26 April 2013].

ISO. 2012. *ISO 50001 – Energy Management.* [Online]. Available at: http://www.iso.org/iso/home/standards/management-standards/iso50001.htm [accessed 27 January 2013].

Langrish, J. 1979. 'The Effects of Technological Change', in Baker, M. (ed.) *Industrial Innovation: Technology, Policy and Diffusion.* London, Macmillan.

Lavery, G. 2011. *ERICs Replacing Marginal Abatement Cost Curves (MACCs).* [Online]. Available at: http://drgreglavery.wordpress.com/erics-replacing-maccs/ [accessed 27 January 2013].

McKinsey and Company. 2007. *Reducing U.S. Greenhouse Gas Emissions: How Much at What Cost?* [Online]. Available at: http://www.mckinsey.com/client_service/sustainability/latest_thinking/reducing_us_greenhouse_gas_emissions [accessed 26 April 2013].

McKinsey and Company. 2009. *Increasing the Energy Efficiency of Supply Chains.* [Online]. Available at: http://www.mckinseyquarterly.com/Increasing_the_energy_efficiency_of_supply_chains_2414 [accessed 27 January 2013].

McLean-Conner, P. 2009. *Energy Efficiency. Principles and Practice.* Tulsa OK, PennWell.

Oung, K. 2013. *Energy Management in Business.* Farnham, Gower Publishing.

Schultz, S. 2010. *Implementing a Corporate Energy Management System*. Presented at the US Department of Energy Industrial Technologies Program, 3 June 2010 Webcast. [Online]. Available at http://www1.eere.enery.gov/manufacturing/pdfs/20100603_webcast_implementing_a_corporate_energy_management_system.pdf [accessed 29 June 2013].

Vesma, V. 2012. *Energy Management Principles and Practice*. London, British Standards Institute. [Online]. Available at: http://shop.bsigroup.com/upload/Standards%20&%20Publications/Environment/BIPS/Sample%20pages_BIP%202187.pdf [accessed 27 January 2013].

# 7

# Energy Management Examples

*Transforming the discussion about energy from 'What can we save?' to*
*'What is actually required?' has enabled many of Toyota's manufacturing*
*plants in the U.S. to be among the most energy-efficient in the nation.*
*Josephine S. Cooper, Group Vice President,*
*Government and Industry Affairs, Toyota Motor North America*

There are many fine case studies and examples of successful energy management programmes in the energy efficiency literature, and several of these cover multi-decade energy management programmes (notably 3M and Dow Chemical). Highlighted here are only three examples from many more that could have been used: Owens Corning (industrial), Stena (shipping) and Telstra (telecoms). All three demonstrate the right way to implement energy management programmes, as well as great results. The information in these case studies is taken from publicly available material.

## Owens Corning – Energy Saving in Processes As Well As Products

Owens Corning, with $5.3 billion revenue in 2011, produces glass and insulation products and has a long-established commitment to energy efficiency, as well as to making products that help customers save energy. In 1999 it declared a target of reducing energy costs by 20 per cent. Reactions within the company included the often-heard objections:

- our energy buyers have got the best deals;

- our engineering is 100 per cent perfect and here are the reams of data to prove it;

- it's been OK for 50 years – why change?

- the leadership isn't serious about this;

- someone tries this about every five years;

- we know what needs to be done but the investment is always rejected.

Having implemented an innovative $2.4 billion energy services deal with Enron Energy Services in 1999, which was to be paid for from productivity improvements and covered the supply of energy and investment in energy efficiency projects, Owens Corning was left high and dry by the collapse of Enron in 2001. At that point the company formed an internal Energy Service Company (ESCO). Simple measurements such as energy use/unit of saleable production were introduced to each business unit. Ideas for improvements were encouraged through competitions and awards.

In 2003 the company reduced annual energy costs from $260m to $220m and invested less than $20m in energy efficiency, i.e. many of the measures were no or low cost. Over the period, production increased by 18 per cent and energy prices rose by 10 per cent – meaning that the total energy productivity gain was $80m, split equally between capital projects identified by the internal ESCO, capital projects driven by employees, improved procurement and low-cost/no-cost measures identified and implemented by employees – three-quarters of the gain was from employee teams. Interestingly enough, the energy productivity champion plants also had the highest quality and safety and the lowest waste levels – reflecting the fact that good energy management usually reflects good general management.

After this period the company continued to ruthlessly pursue energy productivity with a series of measures including 'plant of the future' pilot plants which could achieve a further increase in productivity of 30 per cent. One of the major changes achieved at Owens Corning, and one that should be replicated in all organizations, is that the questions being asked about energy changed. Instead of 'how can I get the energy supply capacity I need?' people began to ask 'how much energy do I need for that application?' and 'what is the optimum investment in fuel, conversion and distribution mix to supply it?' Asking different questions about energy leads to different answers; radically different in many cases. The results were:

- optimized manufacturing processes;

- fuel-efficient supply processes;

- new management models;

- dramatically reduced GHG and other emissions;

- enhanced competiveness through:
  - reduced operating costs,
  - improved environmental performance and credits,
  - increased energy supply security.

Owens Corning have gone on to further improve energy efficiency and set even more ambitious targets. Between 2002 and 2011 energy intensity reduced by 20 per cent and absolute energy use was reduced from about 11 million MWh to about 8.5 million MWh. The company is targeting a further 20 per cent reduction in energy intensity by 2020 relative to the 2010 achievement.

The Owens Corning case study illustrates the long-term improvements that can be achieved year after year – and in the case of other companies such as Dow and 3M, decade after decade. It also shows the importance of leadership in overcoming initial internal reactions, which are often sceptical and negative, and asking different questions when considering energy use. Because it starts with the actual demand side rather than the supply side, 'how much energy do I need for that application?' is a more valuable question than 'how do I get the energy supply I need?'

## Stena – Marine Energy Management

The Stena group consists of three wholly owned companies: Stena AB, Stena Sessan AB and Stena Metall AB. The group's businesses cover ferry lines, shipping, offshore drilling, property, finance, venture capital, renewable energy and recycling. Stena is one of Sweden's biggest family-owned businesses with a turnover of 48 billion SEK, (c. £4.4bn) and 18,500 employees. Although it is a diversified group it is best known for its shipping activities, which sit within Stena AB.

The shipping industry, driven by cost pressures as well as environmental concerns, has taken several steps to improve energy efficiency. Global shipping is a major energy user and, although it receives less publicity than aviation, is a larger emitter of carbon dioxide than aviation. According to the International Maritime Organization (IMO), global shipping was responsible for 870 million tonnes of carbon dioxide emissions, about 2.7 per cent of the global man-made emissions in 2007 (IMO 2013), compared to 670 million tonnes, about 2.1 per cent, for aviation according to the International Air Transport Association (IATA 2009). Because ships traditionally use heavy grades of fuel oil (bunker fuel) they are also major emitters of particulates, sulphur dioxide and vanadium, as well as carbon dioxide.

In response to these pressures the IMO has introduced several measures to help improve energy efficiency in the industry, including voting in July 2011 to implement an Energy Efficient Design Index (EEDI) from 2013 as well as a Ship Energy Efficiency Management Plan (SEEMP) for existing ships. The EEDI design standards apply to new ships built from 2013 and give designers flexibility on the measures they implement. There has also been a move by the IMO to reduce sulphur emissions from shipping in certain regions which necessitates the use of higher-cost, low-sulphur fuel. There have also been signs of customer demand for greater efficiency: in October 2012 it was announced that three large multinationals, who between them ship 350 million tonnes of commodities per annum, have agreed only to charter the most efficient ships (Shippingefficiency.org 2012).

Stena has been, and continues to be, a leader in energy management within the shipping industry. Stena has succeeded in reducing its fuel consumption by 2.5 per cent every year since 2005 when the company started its Energy Saving Programme, ESP. In 2005 the company implemented Shipboard Energy Management Plans on its vessels. Staff were encouraged to identify and implement no-cost and low-cost measures, and more than 200 separate measures were implemented. In early 2012 Northern Marine Management Ltd, the ship management division of Stena, was certified under the newly introduced BS ISO 50001-2011, making it one of the first five organizations in the UK to achieve the ISO standard.

A central feature of Stena's energy management programme is its use of employee suggestions, which are encouraged within the Stena corporate culture. Stena has a suggestion page on its intranet – for all ideas, not just energy saving – and once employees make a suggestion other employees can comment on it and they can follow its progress through a review process to either implementation or rejection. If ideas are rejected the reasons are fed back to the employee making the suggestion. The company reports that 20 per cent (out of a total reduction of 30 per cent) of the fuel savings achieved since 2007 were achieved from the employee suggestions, and the other 10 per cent was saved from speed reductions.

Changes that have been introduced include 'eco-driving', solar control films on cabin windows, electrical connections when in port, new propeller designs and more efficient designs for new ferries. Eco-driving is assisted by a display on the bridge of ships which displays fuel consumption and how it has been influenced by factors such as currents, depth and ship's speed, effectively a form of real-time M&T. Solar films added to cabin and public space windows reduce solar gain, reducing the load on the ship's air conditioning systems. Traditionally when ships are in port they use auxiliary engines to drive generators to supply electricity for onboard systems. Stena has introduced in-port electrical connections for a number of its ships and contracted for green electricity supply for these connections, which are estimated to have reduced the energy costs while in port by 50 per cent. Stena has reviewed the design of propellers and the potential savings from changing propeller designs. In one case fuel consumption was reduced by 16 per cent. Algae and other plants that have fastened onto the propeller and hull are washed away at regular intervals to reduce drag.

Two new ferries have been designed with improved hull design, more efficient engines and improved ventilation systems that adjust to demand. Fuel consumption has been reduced by 15 per cent despite the ferries being larger than those they replaced. One of the two also has a new surface treatment that prevents algae growth. As the two ships are similar in design and have similar operations, this will allow the company to monitor the effect of this coating.

Stena Bulk, which operates tankers, introduced a range of energy-saving measures in a new 158,700 dwt (deadweight tonnes), 274-metre-long SuezMax vessel, the *Stena Superior*, which was launched in November 2011 and is the first of seven similar vessels. The technologies used include optimized hull lines, a propeller with increased diameter and winglets that reduce induced drag, a bulb rudder, energy-saving fins ahead of the propeller which optimize flow and reduce vibration, and an electronically controlled derated main engine. Fuel-saving and environmental equipment cost about $2.5 million out of the total cost of $67.4 million. The *Stena Superior*'s performance is judged to be 20 per cent better than the standard design of 2009, and 8–10 per cent better than conventional designs.

An average SuezMax tanker of similar size burns about 55 to 58 tonnes of fuel a day at 14 knots, 52 tonnes a day at 15 knots in ballast and 6 tonnes/day anchored or in port. Fuel costs obviously vary, but in July 2012 bunker fuel (IFO380 heavy fuel oil – used by most ships) was between $570 and $600 per tonne while low-sulphur fuel was between $650 and $750 per tonne, giving fuel costs of about $30,000 a day at current prices and an estimated payback on the additional capital of three to four years. This will be significantly reduced as fuel costs increase due to the regulatory requirement to use low-sulphur fuel.

Stena has also been active in developing innovative technology, most notably its AirMax design which uses an 'air cushion' under the vessel to reduce the wetted area, a major driver of drag. Air is bubbled into a cavity under the hull. Although simple in theory, in practice there are complications such as the effect of waves in the cavity and the nature of the trade-offs involving air pressure – the higher the pressure the lower the resistance, but the higher the loss of air and hence energy consumption in producing the air bubbles.

The company has developed the E-Max Air concept for a 15,000 dwt tanker which incorporates the following energy-saving features: optimized hull design for 13-knot cruising speed, slow-rotating propellers, the AirMax air cushion technology, use of Liquified Natural Gas (LNG) as a fuel, and a kite sail. Design estimates suggest that this vessel would use 32 per cent less fuel, reduce $CO_2$ emissions by 35 to 40 per cent, reduce nitrogen dioxide emissions by 90 per cent, eliminate sulphur dioxide emissions completely and reduce particulate emission by 99 per cent. Running on LNG would also reduce engine maintenance.

As well as its conventional ships, Stena has applied energy management to other types of vessel. On an advanced drilling rig, the *Stena Don*, a number of energy-efficient features were adopted including inverter control of low-voltage drilling motors and an intelligent power-management system which monitors the entire electrical system and starts and stops generators in an optimal way.

Stena AB is a great example of energy management in several ways. First of all it demonstrates how the principles of sound energy management can be applied in a specialized industry which does not often feature in energy management examples, showing the universality of both energy management principles and the potential for energy saving. It is also an example of leadership from the very top, as the energy efficiency programme has the full support of the company Chairman and board who take time to communicate the importance and success of the programme both internally and externally. It has implemented monitoring and targeting which gives relevant information to the appropriate decision makers who can affect energy use, engaged staff in a meaningful way through its suggestion scheme, implemented a range of simple existing technologies and continues to invest in radical innovation.

## Telstra – Leading Energy Management in Telecoms

Telstra is Australia's largest provider of fixed telephone line services, and also provides mobile telephone services with more than 13 million mobile connections. In 2011/12 revenues were A$25.4 billion, with earnings before interest, taxes, depreciation and amortization of A$10.2 billion. According to their website, in 2011/12 the company handled three billion local calls, 4.7 billion national long distance calls, 12 billion text messages and 16 billion mobile voice minutes. The company operates more than 11,000 telephone exchanges and completes around 23,000 customer service jobs a day. Like most telecoms companies around the world Telstra is experiencing rapidly growing demand for its data services, with data usage nearly doubling every year.

The company has been measuring and reporting carbon emissions since 2000 and set aggressive targets to reduce energy consumption and carbon emissions. In 2011 the company's board approved a new carbon intensity measure, tonnes of $CO_2$ ($tCO_2$) per terabyte of data, and set a target of reducing it by 15 per cent, and approved a A$41.3 million, five-year energy-efficiency investment programme.

In 2011/12 Telstra used 1.37 TWh of electricity (for comparison, BT, the UK telecoms operator, uses about 2.3 TWh) and had carbon emissions of 1.68 million tonnes $CO_2$.

In a typical Telstra network facility electricity consumption is split as follows: 44 per cent telecoms and IT equipment; 43 per cent cooling; 7 per cent power conversion and 6 per cent lighting and general power.

Telstra implemented an energy management database which includes all relevant site parameters, as well as inspection and audit data and ongoing energy usage compared to previous consumption. The system allows comparison of a site's profile before and after optimization projects are completed, uses dynamic charting and is able to detect subtle changes in energy usage resulting from small changes of set points.

Since July 2011 more than 600 sites have been audited and optimized. As an example, adjusting the set points and upgrading the air conditioning controls to enable controls to be locked resulted in annual energy savings of 30,500 kWh.

The energy efficiency measures identified as being most useful include small, on-site fresh-air cooling fans; electronic fan control; improved air conditioning controls; high-efficiency chillers and air conditioning systems; lighting controls and Variable Speed Drives (VSDs) on pumps and fans.

Of these, four have been developed as standard packages across many sites:

- 'Free cooling', i.e. using external air for cooling when it is cooler than the required room temperature, allowing the air conditioning to be switched off. This involved installing an economy cycle fan in the same opening as the existing room air conditioner. This measure typically provides a reduction of up to 57 per cent. On sites where the full package of measures have been implemented a reduction in running costs of approximately 60 per cent has been achieved.

- Use of higher-temperature batteries. Like all telecoms operators Telstra used Valve Regulated Lead Acid Batteries (VRLAs) as backup power at their mobile base station sites. These batteries are designed to operate optimally at a temperature of about 25°C and therefore require cooling. Telstra has started to deploy batteries that operate optimally at 30°C without affecting expected lifetime. This enables the cooling set point to be put at 30°C instead of 25°C, resulting in a significant reduction in cooling energy in the hot climates of Australia.

- Modification of air conditioning controls and increasing the mobile equipment operational temperatures from 25°C to 32°C.

- Installing purpose-built 'process coolers' to replace the standard room air conditioning units that were originally installed. In a typical mobile base station which has no economy cooling, the average air conditioning power consumption at 25°C is about 12,500 kWh per year. A mobile base station which is equipped with economy fans and high temperature VRLAs and is maintained at 29°C has a typical air conditioning load of 6,890 kWh a year, a saving of 44 per cent. With the addition of process coolers the average air conditioning load is reduced to 5,190 kWh per year.

Over a two-year period Telstra has implemented this suite of measures across 1,200 mobile base stations and achieved energy savings of 6,700 MWh, financial savings of A\$1.5 million and a reduction in carbon emissions of 6,700 tonnes $CO_2$.

As well as retrofitting these projects onto existing base stations the measures have been incorporated into the design standards for new-build sites.

To address the electricity used by telecoms equipment, effectively 'process' energy for a telecoms company, Telstra has introduced new Base Transmitter Station (BTS) technologies that have less radio frequency (RF) losses and are passively cooled, resulting in reductions in power use of more than 30 per cent, as well as reduced construction costs of 10 per cent. In another move to reduce process electricity use, Telstra have introduced a strategy of putting some equipment into standby mode during periods of low GSM traffic levels. This has reduced energy consumption in the 2G mobile network by about 2.5 per cent.

As well as technical measures, Telstra implemented a training programme for employees which built understanding of energy use within the business as well as detailed understanding of where energy is consumed in a typical site. Telstra is also looking at more innovative techniques including trigeneration (simultaneously producing power, heat and cooling), fuel cells and renewable (wind and solar) power.

To summarize, Telstra have established a clear target and a clear measure of success. It has obtained CEO and senior leadership approval for the energy and carbon reduction plan, as well as a significant investment budget. The company has asked powerful questions about where energy is being used and how consumption can be reduced simply and cost effectively. It has implemented a number of standardized high-return measures quickly across its portfolio of facilities, also ensuring that the measures are incorporated in new-build facilities, and is now evaluating more radical measures to reduce long-term energy use. It has also engaged employees through its training programmes.

In addition to improving its own energy efficiency, Telstra is actively participating in major industry-wide initiatives such as the GSMA's Mobile Energy Efficiency (MEE) programme. The GSMA represents nearly 800 of the world's mobile operators in more than 220 countries. The MEE programme offers benchmarking and optimization services which have led to startling improvements in energy efficiency and correspondingly high savings for participants.

Benchmarking provides detailed analysis of the relative performance of networks against a large anonymous dataset covering some 35 operators with more than 200 networks. Consumption data is normalized for factors that are outside the operator's control, such as temperature and population density, to allow like-for-like comparison between networks, and is reported annually to map improvements over time.

The optimization service is a follow-on service that helps operators develop action plans to reduce energy costs and carbon emissions. The service was launched in October 2011 and its first project, with Telefonica Germany and Nokia Siemens Networks' Energy Solutions, identified €1.8 million in savings with paybacks in less than three years.

Telefonica Germany had participated in the GSMA benchmarking programme since it was launched in 2010 and had already improved its network energy efficiency by 14 per cent per connection over three years. The additional measures identified by the optimization service included smart controls (€400,000 per annum savings with a nine-month payback period) and switching to more efficient rectifiers (which was planned to be implemented in 3,000 sites in 2012).

The GSMA's energy efficiency programme is an excellent example of how industry associations, either nationally or internationally, can work to improve energy efficiency throughout an industry.

## Conclusions

These brief case studies, and many others in the literature, demonstrate that the principles of systematic energy management can be applied in all industries and sectors with significant benefits. Most organizations, even those that have energy management programmes and have achieved some improvements in energy efficiency, have not yet implemented truly systematic programmes with the full support and commitment of senior leadership and appropriate resources and systems. In order to accelerate the uptake of economic energy efficiency we need to work to build human capacity in systematic energy management.


## References and Bibliography

Abe, A., Taguchi, E., Karakai, M., Kato, M. and Fujie, Y. 2012. *Energy Efficiency Measures in Japan: Case Studies*. [Online]. Available at: http://www.thegreengrid.org/~/media/WhitePapers/WP40%20%20 JapanCaseStudyWP0711Final_en.pdf?lang=en [accessed 27 January 2013].

Dow. 2012. *2011 Annual Sustainability Report*. [Online]. Available at: http:// www.dow.com/sustainability/pdf/23489-Sustainability-Report-interactive. pdf [accessed 3 January 2013].

Ecopare. 2012. *Lean Energy Management Case Study*. [Online]. Available at: http://www.ecopare.co.uk/portfolio/casestudy/Ecopare-case-study-001.pdf [accessed 27 January 2013].

EPA (United States Environmental Protection Agency). 2012. *3M Lean Six Sigma and Sustainability*. [Online]. Available at: http://www.epa.gov/lean/ environment/studies/3m.htm [accessed 28 December 2012].

Garforth, P. 2005a. *Corporate Energy Productivity and GHG Reduction Strategy. 'The Owens Corning Experience'*. Presented at Competing in a Carbon Constrained World, Berkeley CA, 19 April 2005.

Garforth, P. 2005b. *Managing Energy Productivity. 'A Competitive Prerequisite'*. [Online]. Available at: http://aceee.org/files/pdf/conferences/ ssi/2005/05ssgarforth.pdf [accessed 27 January 2013].

Garforth, P. 2008. *Energy in a Carbon Constrained World. Connecting the Dots of Opportunity*. [Online]. Available at: http://w3.usa.siemens.com/us/internet-dms/Internet/Glass/General/Docs/GlassDay2008_080812_%20Garforth_ Distribute.pdf [accessed 27 January 2013].

GSMA. 2012. *Mobile Energy Efficiency*. [Online]. Available at: http://www.gsma. com/publicpolicy/mobile-energy-efficiency [accessed 27 January 2013].

IATA (International Air Transport Association). 2009. 'A Global Approach to Reducing Aviation Emissions'. [Online]. Available at: http://www.iata. org/SiteCollectionDocuments/Documents/Global_Approach_Reducing_ Emissions_251109web.pdf [accessed 26 April 2013].

IMO (International Maritime Organization). 2012. *Energy Efficiency and the Reduction of GHG Emissions from Ships*. [Online]. Available at: http://www.imo. org/MediaCentre/HotTopics/GHG/Pages/default.aspx [accessed 27 January 2013].

IMO. 2013. 'Work on Updating Greenhouse Gas Emissions Estimate for International Shipping Moves Forward at Expert Workshop'. [Online]. Available at: http://www.imo.org/MediaCentre/PressBriefings/Pages/07-ghg-workshop-outcome.aspx [accessed 26 April 2013].

Kuse, C. 2012. *Challenges for Shipping Industry. Could New Fuels and Scrubbers be the Answer?* [Online]. Available at: http://www.markis.eu/fileadmin/Arkiv/Dokumenter/MARCOD/CarstenKruse-StenaLine.pdf [accessed 27 January 2013].

Motegi, N., Piette, M., Kinney, S. and Dewey, J. 2003. *Case Studies of Energy Information Systems and Related Technology: Operational Practices, Costs and Benefits.* [Online]. Available at: http://gaia.lbl.gov/btech/papers/53406.pdf [accessed 27 January 2013].

O'Brien-Bernini, F. 2011. *Sustainability at Owens Corning.* [Online]. Available at: http://ita.doc.gov/td/energy/Frank%20O%27Brien%20Bernini.pdf [accessed 27 January 2013].

Prindle, W.R. 2010. *From Shop Floor to Top Floor: Best Business Practices in Energy Efficiency.* Pew Center on Global Climate Change. [Online]. Available at: http://www.c2es.org/docUploads/PEW_EnergyEfficiency_FullReport.pdf [accessed 29 January 2013].

Public Sector Sustainability Association. 2012. *Case Studies – Energy Management.* [Online]. Available at: http://pssa.info/category/case-studies/case-studies-products-and-services/case-studies-energy-management/ [accessed 27 January 2013].

Shippingefficiency.org. 2012. 'Major Charterers Opt for More Efficient Vessels', *Tanker Operator*, 5 October 2012. [Online]. Available at: http://shippingefficiency.org/userfiles/files/0510-TankerOperator.pdf [accessed 26 April 2013].

United Nations Industrial Development Organization. 2010. *Global Industrial Energy Efficiency Benchmarking. An Energy Policy Tool.* [Online]. Available at: http://www.unido.org/fileadmin/user_media/Services/Energy_and_Climate_Change/Energy_Efficiency/Benchmarking_%20Energy_%20Policy_Tool.pdf [accessed 27 January 2013].

United States Department of Energy Advanced Manufacturing Office. 2012. *Case Studies.* [Online]. Available at: http://www1.eere.energy.gov/manufacturing/tech_deployment/case_studies.html [accessed 27 January 2013].

Urlaub, J. 2010. *Energy Efficiency: A Gateway to Employee Engagement.* [Online]. Available at: http://blog.taigacompany.com/blog/sustainability-business-life-environment/energy-efficiency-a-gateway-to-employee-engagement- [accessed 27 January 2013].

US Department of Energy Industrial Technologies Program, June 3 2010. [Online]. Available at: http://www1.eere.energy.gov/manufacturing/pdfs/20100603_webcast_implementing_a_corporate_energy_management_system.pdf [accessed 27 January 2013].

Wilkinson, L. 2012. *Energy Management in Practice: A Retail Case Study.* [Online]. Available at: http://www.esta.org.uk/EVENTS/2010_11_MSED/documents/2010_11_MSED_t-mac.pdf [accessed 27 January 2013].

# 8

# Technologies for Energy Efficiency

*Civilization advances by extending the number of important operations which we can perform without thinking of them.*
                                        *Alfred North Whitehead,*
                                        *Mathematician and Philosopher*

*Any sufficiently advanced technology is indistinguishable from magic.*
                                        *Arthur C. Clarke,*
                                        *Science fiction writer and Futurist*

*Any new technology has to go through a 25 year adoption cycle.*
                                        *Marc Andreesen,*
                                        *Entrepreneur, Software engineer and Investor*

*Prediction is very difficult, especially about the future.*
                                        *Niels Bohr, Physicist*

## Introduction

High energy prices coupled with stronger environmental and sustainability drivers have led to a surge of interest in applying existing energy efficiency technologies and an increase in investment in developing new technologies and techniques to improve efficiency. This field is now so wide that it is impossible to fully survey all of the energy efficiency technologies now in use or under development. Therefore, this chapter only looks at a small sample of technologies with large potentials.

As we have seen in Chapter 3, the energy efficiency gap is the gap that can be filled by the application of existing, economic technologies. The rate of technological change in all areas of technology is astounding and this also applies to energy efficiency technologies. Therefore, in this chapter we focus more on emerging technologies that have been commercialized recently or are in the process of commercialization. Many, many more examples, as well as detailed technical discussions of different technologies and their applications, can be found in the multitude of more specialized books and internet resources.

As well as pure demand-side technologies we have also included some distributed-generation technologies, namely small scale Combined Heat and Power (CHP or cogeneration) and Waste Heat to Power (WHP). These are part of the D3 resource (Demand Management, Demand Generation and Distributed Generation) referred to in Chapter 1 and can contribute to improvements in energy efficiency across the wider system by being more efficient than centralized generation and avoiding transmission and distribution losses.

Although this chapter looks at technologies, we should not forget the importance of the energy management process (see Chapter 6), the savings that can be achieved by better control over processes (using Monitoring and Targeting), behavioural change, or the savings that can be achieved by using a passive technique or piece of design such as using day lighting instead of artificial lighting, or eliminating a process or component altogether.

## A Note on Invention and Innovation

When considering technologies and their potential it is important to distinguish between technologies that have been invented but not yet commercially deployed, and those technologies that have already been innovated, i.e. commercially utilized.

The economic meaning of innovation was set out by Chris Freeman, one of the leading thinkers in the field, in his seminal 1974 work *The Economics of Industrial Innovation* (Freeman 1974):

> *An invention is an idea, a sketch or model for a new or improved device, product, process or system ... An innovation in the economic sense*

*is accompanied with the first commercial transaction involving the new product, process, system or device, although the word is used to describe the whole process.*

The OECD and Eurostat (OECD and Eurostat 2005) defined innovation as:

*Innovation is the implementation of a new or significantly improved product (good or service), process, new marketing method or a new organisational method in business practices, workplace organisation or external relation.*

The important point here is that innovation is a point in time marked by the first commercial use of a technology or technique. The technologies of most interest to energy users, organizations and policy makers should be those that have either had a first commercial use or, at best, are close to first commercial use. Most of the examples here are in those categories. Energy users will not, on the whole, want to take the risk of adopting technology that is not fully developed, and we do not need new technology to close the energy efficiency gap. Of course, this is not meant to imply we should reduce research and development on energy efficiency technologies or stop innovating – we need new cost-effective technologies that reduce the cost and hence expand the size of the economic energy efficiency resource.

## VC, PEs and EE

The economic boom that preceded the bust of the global financial crisis (GFC) coincided with a boom in interest in global warming and sustainability which, coupled with generous subsidies, led to a boom in investment in renewable energy and clean technology. Many venture capital (VC) and private equity (PE) funds were established around the world specifically to invest in this area, both by exploiting existing technologies, particularly wind and solar to take advantage of favourable tariffs, and to a lesser extent developing new technologies. Many existing funds, including large successful VC firms, also focused on the area and there has also been an increase in corporate venturing and product development with programmes such as GE's Ecomagination (Ecomagination 2013).

At the same time as the GFC was deepening and changes were being made in renewable energy feed-in tariffs in some jurisdictions, there was a growing realization that developing new energy technologies (particularly by small and sometimes under-capitalized firms) was very expensive and time consuming. This led some investors to switch away from renewables and towards energy efficiency (EE). As well as being less capital intensive, many energy efficiency technologies have more in common with the IT and software companies that the traditional VCs had successfully backed in Silicon Valley, Cambridge and Mumbai. These types of opportunities were much more appealing, and probably better understood by VCs, than the high-capital-cost energy generation technologies many VCs had backed in the first wave of enthusiasm for low-carbon technologies.

From the investors' point of view it is still too early to judge the success of this wave of investment as there have, as yet, been very few exits from most of the VC and PE funds. However, it is clear that many novel and interesting technologies are being developed. As well as technologies, some investors are developing new business models around energy services, transportation and building energy management. Innovation does not always benefit the early investors but it usually benefits society, and that will almost certainly apply in this case.

A range of possible future technologies are described in extensive literature covering all sectors. These works and this short summary also tend to focus on the 'known unknowns' rather than the 'unknown unknowns' – that is to say, the technologies that are generally understood and have had first commercial applications. Other potential game-changing innovations are undoubtedly being developed in laboratories, research centres, garages and garden sheds around the world but do not get reported, either by design or by accident. We cannot rule out big technological surprises, but the 'known knowns' combined with the 'known unknowns', i.e. things that are not yet commercial but may become so soon, are more than sufficient to meet and exceed any national or international energy efficiency target.

Whether any individual technology or technique will ultimately be successful depends on a host of factors including basic technology, the magnitude of the benefits resulting from adoption, market acceptance, quality of management and availability of sufficient finance during the innovation and business growth phases. Sometimes technologies are successfully deployed after the failure of the original innovating business. Prior to, and indeed even after, an innovation, i.e. first commercial application, there are significant technology risks, financial risks, market risks and execution risks.

## Building Technologies

Buildings account for about 40 per cent of total energy use in developed countries and so improving efficiency in the building stock, as well as new buildings, should be a major target for policy makers and entrepreneurs concerned with improving efficiency. The main building energy requirements are: heating, ventilating and air conditioning (HVAC); hot water for sanitary use; lighting and ancillary equipment use. In each of these areas there is a wide range of technologies that can improve energy efficiency.

### INSULATION MATERIALS

The building envelope serves to reduce the rate of energy leakage (heat in the case of cold climates) through heat conduction and air movement through gaps in the structure. Its energy performance can be improved by the addition of insulation to the solid elements – walls and roof, but also floors – and high-performance windows with lower rates of heat loss. Building insulation materials have generally remained unchanged for many years. With tightening building regulations requiring higher insulation values, the construction industry has generally responded by adding thicker layers of insulation. However, there is a need for thinner and smarter insulation materials and companies such as Dow are developing such using nanomaterials and composites.

Another example of innovative insulation that has a great deal of promise is dynamic insulation technology developed by EnergyFlo which 'uses the fabric of the building, with no need for costly additional heating or ventilation kit, to boost its insulation and energy performance' (EnergyFlo 2012). This has been trialled with several major builders and offers the potential to achieve higher levels of insulation at less thickness than conventional approaches, including the 'hard to treat' solid walls which are still common in some countries.

### ADAPTIVE MATERIALS FOR BUILDING FABRIC COMPONENTS

Advances in material science have enabled the development of materials that change thermal properties, opening up the possibility of adaptive buildings that respond to changing environmental conditions. One example is phase-change materials incorporated into building components such as ceiling tiles and wall boards developed by Datum Phase Change Ltd. These components store latent heat above a certain temperature which is then released when room temperatures cool, thus stabilizing temperatures and reducing air conditioning and/or heating loads. The products have been installed in a number of pilot projects and monitoring from trials suggests significant savings and improvements in thermal comfort (Datum Phase Change 2013).

## HIGH-PERFORMANCE WINDOWS

Traditionally, windows account for a significant percentage of heat loss in buildings and, as the insulation levels of other building elements has increased, this percentage is growing. However, modern high-performance windows, utilizing double or triple glazing, coated glass and/or films, inert gas layers, and low air leakage rates, now enable those losses to be cut significantly. In some cases windows can now lead to net positive energy gains rather than losses and, using new materials, the thermal and visual characteristics of glazing can be changed in response to changing ambient conditions.

A number of companies are commercializing adaptive glazing – glazing that changes its thermal and visual properties in response to changes in the environment. One company developing this technology is Soladigm – now renamed View Glass (View Glass 2013) – which reports that its products will be the same price as standard high emissivity glass and could reduce HVAC energy use by 25 per cent and peak loads by 30 per cent.

## HVAC TECHNOLOGIES

HVAC technologies (heating, air conditioning and ventilation systems) have traditionally been designed with little or no regard for energy efficiency. We are now seeing a flowering of innovation in these areas covering both incremental improvement of existing systems and more innovative technologies. Examples include incorporating efficient electric motors; improving fan efficiency; high-efficiency boilers and chillers; efficient, low leakage and low resistance ducting systems; and more radical technologies such as using carbon dioxide as a coolant.

### Efficient fans

Fan efficiency is a function of many variables including fan type, air flow, speed and impellor type. Like many devices the design of fans remained fairly constant over a long period because of lack of incentives to change, engineering conservatism and cost minimization. In the last few years we have seen significant improvements in fan design in some areas through the application of more advanced aerodynamics and computerized fluid analysis. In addition there have been more radical developments based on bio-mimicry by companies such as PAX Scientific Inc. which has developed fans based on nature's designs (PAX Scientific 2013). These systems look more like sea shells than conventional fans and, depending on their application, can produce savings of 10 to 85 per cent, as well as lower noise levels. Fans account for an estimated 14 per cent of industrial motor electrical use in the USA, and so improving fan efficiency can have a large effect on overall electricity demand.

## Domestic boiler heat recovery

Many, perhaps most, homes in Europe and elsewhere are heated by gas boilers feeding a wet central heating system using radiators. Even the most efficient condensing gas boilers still lose a significant amount of heat through the flue, and unlike in large commercial boilers, where it is possible to fit an economizer to recover some of this waste heat, in domestic boilers economizers have not existed until recently. British company Zenex has developed an economizer, the GasSaver, (Zenex 2013) which can be easily installed on the flue of a standard domestic gas boiler. Savings have been independently monitored at up to 40 per cent with average savings of 37 per cent. The system is now being incorporated into boilers from major manufacturers.

Zenex have also introduced the Blade range of scalable heating and hot water 'servers' that use Zenex's heat recovery technologies to produce heating and hot water more efficiently than traditional installations. The operational efficiency (over the year) of a Blade system is about 97 per cent compared to around 50 to 70 per cent for a typical system, depending on design and age. Zenex's work illustrates both the need to rethink mass-produced everyday technologies, and the difficulties of doing so.

## Micro-Combined Heat and Power

Micro-Combined Heat and Power (mCHP) is the concept of producing both heat and power simultaneously within an individual household or small commercial building. The concept has been around for a long time and offers potential benefits in terms of system-wide energy savings and carbon dioxide emission reduction. The energy savings result from displacement of power generated in a centralized power station produced at 35–40 per cent efficiency, and a further five per cent of the energy being lost in transmission and distribution. Gas coming into a home is converted by an mCHP unit, which replaces the conventional boiler, into both heat (hot water for space heating and domestic hot water (DHW)) and electricity with an overall efficiency of 80 per cent.

A number of companies around the world have developed mCHP units using different underlying technologies, including internal combustion engines, fuel cells – both Proton Exchange Membrane (PEMFC) and Solid Oxide (SOFC), Stirling engines and Organic Rankine Cycle (ORC) systems. Each technology has its own characteristics of heat-to-power ratio, ability to follow heat loads, output range and physical size. Internal combustion machines using engines based on automotive technology have been available commercially for several years with the largest market in the world being Japan, a market dominated by Honda's units.

In the UK, Energetix, an AIM-listed company (Energetix 2013), has developed an ORC system that utilizes scroll compressor technology that is similar to that used in automotive air conditioning. Heat from the boiler component, which is standard, is used to evaporate an organic fluid which then passes through a scroll expander which drives a generator. The fluid is then condensed in another heat exchanger cooled by the incoming water from the heating system.

Unlike some alternative technologies such as fuel cells which would require a complete technology change for boiler manufacturers, the ORC unit is designed to be integrated within existing designs of domestic boilers rather than replace them entirely. The entire package has the same dimensions as current wall-hung boilers, which is an essential characteristic as about 90 per cent of the Western European market is for wall-hung boilers. It is also lightweight, which eases installation, and can be wired straight into conventional domestic power circuits. Furthermore, the unit follows heat demand, which eliminates the need for supplementary heating or heat storage, and the economics are not dependent on exporting power to the grid. Energetix are now marketing its mCHP unit as 'Flow' using an innovative business model which involves giving the boiler away in return for benefiting from the electricity sales to the grid for a defined period, benefits which then pass to the house owner.

Stirling engines, closed-cycle external combustion reciprocating engines, and fuel cells are two technologies that were first invented in the nineteenth century (1816 and 1843 respectively) and which have been incorporated into mCHP units by several manufacturers. Stirling engines require a heat-up period which can restrict their application in replacing conventional boilers, and commercially available Stirling engine mCHP units tend to be relatively large and heavy, restricting their use to larger houses and small commercial buildings. Fuel cells for mCHP (and automotive applications) have been subject to several waves of enthusiasm in the last two decades and several companies around the world are still working to commercialize fuel cell mCHP systems. However, achieving real commerciality remains elusive.

The economics of mCHP are often presented on a single-household basis and to date the economic returns look marginal in many cases without support schemes such as Feed-in Tariffs (FiTs). However, if deployed widely, mCHP could bring other benefits to the electricity system as a whole including providing demand response (peak lopping), balancing services, frequency response, avoidance of network reinforcement costs and opportunities for trading. To be able to exploit these system benefits, an appropriate regulatory framework needs to be in place and new business models for energy suppliers have to be developed and successfully implemented.

## Innovative cooling systems

Conventional cooling systems use refrigerants such as R404A which has zero ozone depletion potential (ODP), as required under the Montreal Protocol, but has considerable global warming potential (GWP). A number of companies around the world are developing alternative refrigeration systems using carbon dioxide as a refrigerant and these systems can result in significant energy saving. Refrigeration is a major user of electricity, and in the food retailing sector refrigeration accounts for around 60 per cent of the total energy use. Novel systems such as using carbon dioxide as a refrigerant have potential for a step change in refrigeration energy use. The barriers to implementing this technology include higher first cost; understandable conservatism on the part of end users and original equipment manufacturers (OEMs) – continual, reliable and safe refrigeration is essential to the food retailers' business continuity and reputation; and maintenance staff and suppliers of maintenance services are used to working on existing systems. However, despite these barriers, innovative retailers are now adopting carbon-dioxide-based cooling systems.

## Natural ventilation

Natural ventilation, which allows the elimination of mechanical ventilation through ducts and fans, has long been viewed as an important strategy for reducing the energy consumption of buildings. However, many early attempts to implement natural ventilation were unsatisfactory. A five-year research programme at the University of Cambridge showed that natural ventilation resulted in lower electricity consumption – due, of course, to the absence of fans – but higher heating consumption than a conventional, mechanically ventilated building design, and higher heating consumption than intended at the design stage. The Cambridge team found that the 'traditional' approach to natural ventilation, which was based on upwards displacement, was flawed. They developed and patented new strategies and systems that introduce and mix cold fresh air with room air at high level. The intellectual property developed was licensed by the University to a spin-out company: Breathing Buildings (Breathing Buildings 2013). The company's systems have now been applied and further developed in several types of buildings, more than 80 in all, including those with atriums as well as retrofit solutions. Energy use per square meter of the buildings is typically less than half the corresponding benchmark for similar buildings.

## HOME ENERGY MANAGEMENT

As energy efficiency has risen up the agenda in the last decade or so, a large number of companies have entered what is called the 'home energy management' or home automation market. Home energy management is the modern manifestation of an old idea. In the 1970s and 1980s there were futuristic visions of automated homes where householders could control appliances remotely. The rapid development of internet and electronic technologies has made achieving those visions very possible and very affordable. More than one hundred systems are currently being sold commercially around the world (Delta Energy & Environment 2011a) with many large-scale trials being supported by energy suppliers, some of which have invested directly in companies offering home energy management solutions.

Home energy management products seem to come in three varieties: information only, information and automation, automation and control. Information-only services give users feedback on energy consumption, either through an in-home display (IHD) or through energy bills. Information being displayed on IHDs typically includes total energy use (often just electricity) but with some devices, e.g. Onzo's (Onzo 2013), providing disaggregated energy use by means of harmonic analysis or sub-metering.

Other suppliers sell devices that automate appliances, including heating and hot water boilers. 'Intelligent thermostats' gained much mainstream publicity on the launch of the Nest, which was designed by a former Apple product designer and was the first thermostat that looked 'cool', as well as probably the first one to sell out like a consumer product.

## A LIGHTING REVOLUTION

Lighting consumes about 20 per cent of our total electricity use and conventional lighting is shockingly inefficient. A typical tungsten lamp has a luminous efficacy of 12 lm/W, i.e. 12 lumens of visible light are emitted for every watt of power input, meaning that about 95 per cent of the energy supplied to the lamp is wasted. Even compact fluorescent lamps, so called 'low energy lamps', waste about 80 per cent of the energy supplied. Solid state lamps, LEDs, have an efficiency of about 50 per cent, and as well as high efficiency have a number of other advantages including extremely long life, tunable colour and they can work with dimmer circuits (unlike compact fluorescents). The problem with LEDs is currently one of cost, but as they are essentially solid-state electronic components, their cost is falling rapidly as production volumes increase and at the same time performance levels are improving rapidly – leading to dramatic improvements in cost per performance.

We are living in the midst of a global lighting revolution, with rapid growth in the use of LED lighting which brings with it about an 80 per cent reduction in energy use, as well as extended lamp life which reduces maintenance costs. Even at current prices the paybacks on LED lighting in some applications can be rapid when taking into account both energy savings and reduction in re-lamping costs. McKinseys' 2012 global lighting survey (McKinsey 2012) estimates that the LED share of the total market will reach 45 per cent in 2016 and almost 70 per cent in 2020, an increase from their estimates in 2011.

Technological advances have increased the range of colours available from LEDs, and they can also have health benefits such as reducing the incidence of Seasonal Affective Disorder. There is no doubt that LED lighting will become the norm in the next few decades, with significant electricity savings. It has been estimated that LEDs could, by 2030, save 300 TWh per annum, reduce lighting costs by $30 billion at today's energy prices and reduce carbon dioxide emissions by 210 million tonnes (US Department of Energy 2012).

## LIFTS/ELEVATORS AND ESCALATORS

Although relatively small in energy impact compared to lighting and HVAC, even the humble lift/elevator and escalator have been subject to innovation to improve energy efficiency. A study in Switzerland (Barney 2007) suggested that lifts use about 0.5 per cent of the country's electricity and about half of that is on standby power. Technological options to improve efficiency include the use of high-efficiency induction motors or permanent magnet motors; regeneration (generating electricity in certain modes, e.g. full lift going down); the use of more efficient gear boxes, e.g. helical gears rather than worm gears; improved traffic control strategies such that lifts move in the optimum pattern to meet traffic demands; use of lighter-weight sheaves (pulleys) using polyamides rather than cast iron; use of traction belts rather than ropes; use of LED lighting, and switching off lights and indicators when cars are not in use; efficient bearings; motor controllers for escalators and reduced speed mode when there are no passengers – which in practice can include stopping.

Combining these kinds of technologies can make modern lift systems at least 50 per cent more efficient than conventional systems, with the added benefits of lowering peak electrical loads and incidental heat gains from machinery.

## REDUCING PLUG LOAD

Plug load is the electrical load of appliances that are plugged into the electrical system of any type of building. Appliances include computers, displays, copiers and printers, TVs, set-top boxes, mobile phones and many others. Many of these devices now draw power from the system even when they are switched off or not functioning, using the standby or so called 'vampire' or 'phantom' power. Many are also unregulated by the building owner or operator as building users plug in their mobile phones, tablets, e-book readers and laptops to recharge them while at work. In a typical office, lighting consumes 40 per cent of total electricity, HVAC around 25 per cent and plug loads about 15 per cent (Kaneda et al. 2010). Integrated design techniques can reduce lighting and HVAC loads by 50 per cent or more, and once this happens, plug loads can reach 40 per cent or more of total energy use, making them harder to ignore.

Three emerging technologies can be used to reduce plug loads: plug load controls, DC microgrids and detailed monitoring. Plug load controls can take several forms, including using occupancy sensors to automatically shut off all power to the plug (either wall mounted or in a strip) when no one is present. Another approach is to use a power-sensing plug strip with a monitored master socket (outlet) and several slave sockets. A device such as a set-top box or a desktop computer CPU unit is plugged into the master socket and peripherals such as TV, DVD player, or display are plugged into the slave sockets.

When the master socket is not drawing any power because the device plugged into it is switched off, the strip switches off power to the slave sockets, thus eliminating phantom losses from the devices plugged into them. A third approach is to use the building security system, or building management system, to signal to circuit breakers to switch off devices such as printers when the building is unoccupied. These types of control system remove the unpredictable human behaviour factor.

Another promising concept to reduce plug load is the use of DC microgrids within the building. Most of the devices in use today actually run on DC power and require highly inefficient convertors to covert AC to DC – the conversion accounts for significant system losses. Plugging them into a DC microgrid would produce savings, and furthermore the DC microgrid could be powered by solar photovoltaic panels, which produce DC and produce most energy during the working day. DC microgrids are more suited to new buildings and major refurbishment projects than retrofits. Detailed monitoring of plug loads can produce energy savings by highlighting areas of waste, and several systems are now available to monitor individual plug circuits.

## BUILDING ENERGY ANALYTICS

Building energy analytics covers three areas: ongoing analytics to help users reduce energy use, e.g. Energy Deck and Green Pocket; building retrofit assessment and retro-commissioning tools, e.g. kWhOURS (kWhOURS 2013); and building design tools, e.g. Sefaira.

Energy Deck is a web-based platform that allows building owners to track energy use and asset performance (Energy Deck 2013). It allows sharing of data across portfolios or communities and is a powerful tool for assessing the success of individual investment projects, which is often neglected. Ongoing measurement and verification of projects can be done to IPMVP standards. Green Pocket is a German company that provides smart metering software for residential customers (Green Pocket 2013). Its web-based software provides a portal to allow consumers to monitor usage and budget their energy spend. Green Pocket is supplying 10 of the 20 largest utilities in Germany. Green Pocket was the first energy efficiency company in the world to launch a Facebook application.

kWhOURS is one of several (mainly US) firms that have developed IT tools to speed up the collection and analysis of building data for use in the process of developing energy efficiency retrofit projects. These packages are used through the initial energy audit data collection and analysis phase and then in the investment grade audit phase. Some packages, such as Retroficiency (Retroficiency 2013), utilize mapping software such as Google Earth along with data from utility bills to carry out a preliminary assessment without the expense of an auditor visiting the building. Packages such as kWhOURS reduce the cost and time of building assessments by 25 to 40 per cent, which in turn reduces the cost of developing retrofit projects, particularly in large multi-premise property portfolios. kWhOURS is also one of several tools that can be used for 'retro-commissioning' – the process of understanding how a building is operating (as opposed to how it was designed to operate) – and then continuously recommissioning the building to achieve optimum energy performance.

Sefaira has developed innovative, web-based building design software that allows designers to rapidly assess 'what-if' options during the design process and to work collaboratively (Sefaira 2013). This kind of software tool assists in the application of integrative design technologies (discussed in Chapter 9).

Many utility companies are in a phase of strategic uncertainty about their commitment to energy efficiency and although they have made commitments these have generally been driven by compliance with licence conditions such as the Carbon Emissions Reduction Target (CERT) programme and the Community Energy Saving Programme (CESP) in the UK, and are add-ons to their central business model. This uncertainty, along with a certain conservatism and slow decision making, is a major barrier to the wider use of software packages such as Green Pocket. Utilities are aware of the threats and the opportunities presented by energy efficiency but are as yet unable to make really major commitments to improving energy efficiency. This uncertainty, which is understandable given their heritage and skill sets in generation and retailing of energy, will continue until they develop and deploy new business models that truly encourage energy efficiency at scale. These business models, however, are only really likely to be adopted if the regulatory framework encourages it by decoupling financial returns from sales of electricity.

## LOCALIZED ENERGY HARVESTING

Energy harvesting from vibration (or heat or light) is a technology that produces power locally by turning this vibration directly into power. The power produced is at the micro scale and applications to date are concerned with powering sensors in systems such as Building Management Systems (BMS) and process control systems.

Application of this technology reduces energy use by displacing electricity from either the grid or batteries. By avoiding the requirement for wired systems there is both an ongoing energy saving as well as an energy saving associated with the production and installation of power cabling to sensors. By displacing battery systems there is a reduction in energy use associated with the production, transportation, installation, removal and disposal of batteries. This is a good example of the indirect effects of many energy-efficiency-related technologies. The energy saved throughout the energy system is considerably larger than just the amount of energy saved onsite in the project or installation itself. Barriers include conservatism in the sensor and BMS industry.

## INTEGRATION OF BUILDING TECHNOLOGIES AND MOVING TOWARDS NEAR ZERO ENERGY BUILDINGS

Overlaid above the individual building energy efficiency technologies there are benefits that can occur when components are integrated in a holistic way. The idea of near zero energy or near zero carbon buildings has emerged and a number of examples exist in different building sectors. Achieving near zero energy or carbon buildings requires a dedicated client and design team that can question the energy use of every building component or system and use integrated design techniques to ensure the gains are maximized, often at little, or no, or even reduced, capital cost (see Chapter 9 on design).

## Industry

Industrial energy efficiency technologies are very sector specific, but here we discuss some technologies with wide applicability.

## HIGH-EFFICIENCY ELECTRIC MOTORS

A variety of high-efficiency motors using different underlying technologies have been developed for a wide range of applications. For instance, Wellington Drives, a company based in New Zealand , uses electronically commutated motors (ECMs) for small power applications such as refrigerated display cases (Wellington 2013). ECMs are high efficiency, and retain high efficiency at part load, resulting in energy savings of 30 to 50 per cent compared to a conventional motor. They are also quieter, require less maintenance and have longer life. Paybacks can be as short as several months. The main barriers to the uptake of ECMs in the markets Wellington are addressing include higher upfront cost resulting from the fundamental technology and relatively small production volumes compared to conventional motors; conservatism on the part of the OEMs in terms of design; and reluctance of OEMs to place large-scale orders on small, specialized manufacturers.

Other types of high efficiency motors for wider industrial applications exist and several efficiency labelling schemes for motors are in operation around the world. Analysis has shown that higher efficiency motors are not necessarily more expensive to purchase than lower efficiency motors (Rocky Mountain Institute 2013) and therefore careful procurement is needed. Given the use of motors accounts for about 65 per cent of all electricity used in industry wider application of high efficiency motors would have significant effects on total usage.

## WASTE HEAT RECOVERY

The potential for waste heat recovery is still large in some industries in some markets, although energy-intensive industries in developed countries have implemented most cost-effective projects using a variety of technologies including heat pipes, heat wheels, run-around coils and waste heat boilers.

When considering the potential for heat recovery it is essential to consider the following critical factors.

First, the quantity and the quality of available heat, i.e. its temperature. In order to allow heat exchange to occur the heat source needs to be at a higher temperature than the heat sink. The difference in temperature is a measure of the quality of heat. The source and sink temperatures influence the rate of heat transfer for a given area of heat exchanger and the maximum theoretical efficiency of converting the waste heat into another form of energy, either mechanical or electrical. The temperature also directly affects the choice of materials for any heat recovery system. The composition of the heat-transfer medium also needs to be considered, including factors such as the presence of corrosive gases and the potential for fouling of heat exchanger surfaces. The minimum operating temperature is also an issue. Depending on the nature of the heat-transfer medium there will be a minimum operating temperature, which is usually defined by the need to prevent condensation of certain components of waste gas streams such as sulphur oxides and oxides of nitrogen within flue gases. If temperatures fall low enough to allow condensation of these components there is a high likelihood of corrosion, particularly if inadequate materials are selected.

Operating schedules are an additional factor. Heat is difficult to store economically and therefore the shorter the timeframe between the heat being generated, stored, transferred and used, the more energy and cost effective the process becomes. This is straightforward if the heat is being recovered into the same process but not when transferring heat from one source to another sink in a different process, or in a district heating application. Conversely, physical distance and layout between heat source and heat demand is also critical, particularly for low-temperature heat recovery. Also, even within industrial processes, space constraints may limit what is possible in practice.

## WASTE HEAT TO POWER

Waste Heat to Power (WHP) involves converting waste heat to power through generators using alternative cycles, as opposed to Rankine cycle steam turbines. The use of alternative fluids (organic compounds) or cycles allows the utilization of lower-temperature waste heat. The main barrier to wider application of waste heat to power systems utilizing Organic Rankine Cycle (ORC) or Wasabi Energy plc's Kalina cycle technology (Wasabi 2013), is high capital cost relative to savings, particularly in the UK market. This will be addressed by volume manufacturing but could also be encouraged by providing a renewable obligation credit (ROC) or FiT payment for electricity generated by waste heat, as is practiced in China where WHP has grown significantly. By the end of 2013 more than 700 Chinese cement plants had WHP plants (*Financial Times* 2013), many installed by third party Energy Service Companies. WHP remains a major under-utilized resource in most economies.

A different approach to WHP is using thermoelectric generators to generate power directly from heat. The thermoelectric effect is well known and has been used for many years in the space programme to generate power for spacecraft exploring the outer solar system using radioisotopes as a heat source, so called Radioisotope Thermal Generators (RTGs). One of the companies developing thermoelectric generators for earth-bound applications is the German company O-Flexx (O-Flexx 2013). O-Flexx is developing generators for various applications including automotive, transportation, sensors, geothermal, and process industries. If the technology can be developed to cost-effectively generate power from low-temperature heat sources, say below 100°C, the potential markets are huge.

## PROCESS INNOVATIONS

As well as the technologies whose main purpose is energy efficiency, overall efficiency is directly affected by major process innovations that happen for a multitude of reasons other than purely energy efficiency. In most industries process innovation only happens infrequently and slowly, but when it does happen it can have a step-change effect on energy use compared to the incremental changes that occur with retrofits and minor process improvements.

In the iron and steel industry for instance, a major energy consumer, a range of process innovations are being developed and commercialized, including 'near-net-shape casting'. Near-net-shape casting produces items close to their final shape rather than standard ingots which then have to be rolled and pressed, thus eliminating very energy-intensive processes using large amounts of heat and electricity. Four categories of near-net-shape casting are recognized: thin slab casting (40–80mm thickness); thin slab casting with liquid core reduction (10–25mm thickness); strip casting (1–10mm thickness) and spray casting (5–20mm thickness) (de Beer et al. 1998). The first two are evolutionary advances while the second two are major technology changes.

## AMAZING MATERIALS

Materials science, and our ability to selectively design new materials, is advancing rapidly, with 'wonder materials' such as graphene recently getting much media attention. Examples of materials advances affecting energy use include:

- Composites being used to reduce the weight of aircraft (Woodley 2012).

- Advanced aluminium-forming technologies for car bodies that enable significant weight reduction. In the case of the first generation Jaguar XJ, to switch to an aluminium body the weight saving was about 40 per cent, enabling significant gains in fuel efficiency, and the current Jaguar XJ body is about 136kg lighter compared to a steel body (UKTI 2012).

- Quantum dots, which enable more efficient LED TVs as well as lighting. Nanoco, a UK company, has developed low-cost, cadmium-free quantum dots that are now finding their way into TVs, displays and lighting. As well as energy efficiency they bring the advantages of greater colour purity and longer life (Nanoco 2013).

- Improved catalysts for chemical processes. Catalysts use functional surfaces to speed up or enable chemical reactions and therefore lower the amount of energy input required. Increasing the selectivity and conversion efficiency of catalysts can improve industrial processes and manufacturing by effectively boosting the yield of chemical production. Increasing yield for the same energy input is an increase in energy efficiency. Increasing the lifetime of catalysts reduces the need for replacement catalysts, and hence the energy required to manufacture them.

- Membrane–gas separation technologies, including composite membranes. Gas-separation membranes can be more energy efficient than other gas-separation methods including absorption/ adsorption, distillation and cryogenics.

- Advanced protective coatings, for example self-healing coatings such as those developed by Autonomic Materials Inc. (Autonomic Materials 2013), which extend product lifetime and hence reduce energy used for maintenance and replacement.

- Net-shape processing (as mentioned above) has several subsets. It can both reduce process energy use and significantly reduce waste, which in itself is an improvement in energy efficiency. *Solid state forming*, the shaping of wrought and worked materials into a net shape via processes such as stamping, forging and sheet/bulk forming, is another form of this processing. *Powder metallurgy* is the process of taking fine powders and bonding them into solid shapes via elevated temperatures and pressures. The energy efficiency of powder metallurgy has been relatively stable over the past 20 years and is expected to improve by about 20 per cent over the next 10 years due to decreases in the costs of new powder metallurgy technologies and high-performance powder materials, as well as the movement from batch to continuous processing (Committee on Integrated Computational Materials Engineering 2008).

- Additive manufacturing by which components are built up by adding layers of material which helps to reduce the need for energy-intensive heating and finishing processes.

- New materials for anodes and cathodes in aluminium production.

- Continuous production of titanium rather than batch production.

- Nanomaterials including nanocomposites (University of Leicester 2010).

- Materials that change thermal properties for building fabric components (both solid walls and glass).

It has been said that nearly all engineering problems ultimately come down to a materials problem. For example, in order to make more efficient jet engines, advances in materials were needed (so called superalloys) such that components of the engine can withstand higher temperatures and higher temperatures lead to higher efficiencies. New techniques in rapid discovery of materials have been pioneered by companies like Ilika plc (Ilika 2013) and these promise an acceleration in the development and commercialization of new materials.

## Information and Communications Technology

### EFFICIENT AC POWER CONVERSION

The conversion of AC power at either 110V or 220V to low voltage DC power has become ubiquitous with the massive growth of personal computers and mobile telephones. These convertors have typically been designed and built with the aim of reducing manufacturing costs and also with traditional technology that did not take energy use into consideration. A traditional linear converter can waste 1W when it is plugged into the mains socket, even if it is not charging anything (compared with 3 or 4W usage when charging a mobile phone, for example). Power conversion results in a massive waste of energy, with a device such as a cordless phone wasting about a third of the electricity it consumes and a mobile phone charger wasting even more, typically 50 per cent. The world market for chargers and power supplies is about two billion units a year, and that is without counting devices such as compact fluorescent lamps (CFLs) or LED lamps which all need power convertors.

A Cambridge-based high-tech company, CamSemi, has developed a range of high-efficiency power convertors for both chargers and, more recently, LED lighting (CamSemi 2013). CamSemi's products meet all the standards applied to power convertors and achieve five-star ratings under the voluntary standard introduced by the five largest mobile phone companies in 2008. The cheapest solution is to use linear converters with an efficiency of 50 per cent, while more expensive switched-mode power supply (SMPS) units have efficiencies of about 70 per cent. CamSemi's Resonant Discontinuous Forward Converter (RDFC) technology can achieve higher efficiencies than SMPS units at a similar cost to linear units. Power consumption can be cut from 1W to 0.1–0.2W, an 80 to 90 per cent reduction.

## MORE EFFICIENT WIRELESS AMPLIFIERS

The efficiency of wireless amplifiers in cell phone base stations and transmitters for radio and TV is not an area that receives much attention in energy circles. A UK company, Nujira, has developed a range of highly efficient power amplifiers for transmitters that improve efficiency through 'envelope tracking', where the power input is constantly adjusted to the load. Nujira's system can reduce network power consumption by 50 per cent (Nujira 2013).

## DATA CENTRE DESIGN

Data centres are major consumers of electricity and in recent years innovations have been introduced to make them more energy efficient, particularly around the area of integrative design. These have been widely covered in an extensive literature (some of which is referred to in the Bibliography section below). The issue for the data centre industry is now to ensure that new centres are built to the highest possible standards of energy efficiency and, wherever possible, existing centres are retrofitted to make them more efficient.

At a higher level there is the debate about whether cloud computing is more efficient than distributed storage. It seems clear that we are heading towards a 'cloud'-based IT infrastructure and this is another reason why the efficient design of data centres will become even more important.

## The Energy Sector

The energy sector itself has much potential to improve efficiency. Opportunities to improve efficiency exist in electrical generation, transmission and distribution. Delta Energy & Environment (2011b) estimate that the potential for supply-side efficiency could equal or exceed the potential for demand-side efficiency in the UK, Poland and France. There are a number of options for improving the efficiency of gas turbine generating plants, including optimizing cooling of gas turbine components; reducing leakage; use of heaters to improve the thermodynamic cycle; optimizing compressor washing; increasing part-load efficiency and fast start-ups.

Using these techniques, efficiency can be improved between 0.5 per cent and 2 per cent for a plant half way through its design lifetime, which may not sound much but has a big effect because of the scale of the plants and the lifetime of the generating plant. Overall efficiency is also driven strongly by the approach to despatching gas turbines. Delta estimate that in the UK something like 22 TWh of fuel savings could be made by implementing these measures as appropriate.

### COMBINED HEAT AND POWER

Greater use of CHP or cogeneration results in energy savings at the system level. Delta estimate that the application of economic potential for gas-fired CHP would result in primary energy savings of 48 TWh in the United Kingdom.

### NOVEL GENERATOR DESIGNS

Novel generator designs such as that being developed by Scottish firm NGenTec (NGenTec 2013) using technology spun out of the University of Edinburgh offer direct efficiency gains in the generation of renewable power, as well as indirect efficiency gains. Because these generator designs are lighter than conventional designs the wind turbine towers they are mounted on, and the foundations the towers sit on, can be lighter, with less steel and concrete, thus resulting in an indirect energy saving. In addition, transporting smaller and lighter generators results in a gain in transportation energy efficiency.

### HIGH-TEMPERATURE SUPERCONDUCTIVITY – A GLIMPSE INTO THE FUTURE?

Superconductivity, particularly high-temperature superconductivity (HTS), offers the prospect of zero-loss transmission of power, as well as lighter and more efficient generators. Companies such as American Superconductor Inc. (AMSC 2013) and, for a period, AIM-listed Zenergy Power plc (now out of HTS and renamed), as well as larger companies such as Sumitomo Electric (Sumitomo 2013) have been developing HTS products which offer much promise for energy efficiency. The commercialization of HTS technologies have, however, been extremely difficult and AMSC, having started in HTS technology soon after the discovery of the phenomenon in 1987, has sought other business areas such as wind power electronics. Despite the setbacks and difficulties for these individual innovative companies, HTS remains a technology with significant long-term potential to improve energy efficiency.

HTS is acknowledged by many observers as a technology that could revolutionize the electrical power industry, bringing with it step changes in energy and materials efficiency.

According to the US Department of Energy:

> At the heart of high-temperature superconductivity lies a promise for near- and long-term results that will ultimately lead to cost effectively transmitting and using electricity with near perfect efficiency and much higher capacity. High temperature superconductivity (HTS) has the potential to play an important role in the future of our nation's electricity grid. The aging of the nation's utility infrastructure has created an opportunity for the development of new transmission technologies, and there is an unprecedented opportunity in the coming years for rapid market penetration of HTS power equipment to replace existing transmission equipment to help expand grid capacity. Existing underground cables are becoming outdated and could be replaced with HTS lines that may carry two to five times the power within the same duct size.

All electrical conductors display resistance, which leads to electrical energy being converted to heat, and hence wasted. Superconductivity, the flow of electricity without any resistance, was first discovered in 1911. As temperatures fall, resistance falls, but with superconducting materials resistance completely disappears at a certain temperature. The first superconductors had to be cooled to 4K (−269°C – just above Absolute Zero) which made them prohibitively expensive and impractical to operate in commercial applications. In 1986, scientists discovered a family of materials (cuprate perovskite ceramics) which become superconducting at temperatures in excess of 90K (−183°C). These were the first high-temperature superconductors. The significance of 90K is that it is above the boiling point of liquid nitrogen (76K), a cryogenic fluid that is commonly available.

The potential applications of HTS were quickly recognized, including wires with no resistance (thus eliminating energy losses), transformers, motors, generators, fault current limiters and energy storage devices. A number of companies around the world were established to develop the technology, the highest-profile company being AMSC, and existing cable manufacturers and others started to invest in the technology.

When assessing the potential for HTS wires, it is important to remember that a typical HTS wire can carry 100 times the electrical current compared to a copper wire of the same dimensions. This means that machines such as motors can be physically smaller, and it could be particularly important for power transmission in urban areas where there is a need to transmit growing amounts of power down increasingly crowded utility ducts.

Although several companies are working on the commercialization of HTS technologies in wires, generators, motors and Fault Current Limiters (grid protection devices), the technology, however, remains in development and truly commercial installations remain elusive. The use of HTS motors in military ships, where the application brings benefits of size reduction as well as increased efficiency, has great potential and may be the first really commercial application. There remain many technical difficulties mainly centred on the problems of forming HTS conductors from what are essentially ceramics.

## Transport

### ROAD TRANSPORT

Road transport, and in particular passenger vehicles, have improved in energy efficiency over the years but most of this gain has been taken in growing average weight and increased performance. Increasingly tight fuel efficiency standards in the USA, Europe and Asia are now driving innovation in fuel efficiency. Technologies that are relevant include:

- light weighting;

- more efficient engines;

- hybrid power trains;

- more efficient tyres;

- aerodynamic devices (for example tabs for trucks);

- improved traffic information systems and dynamic traffic management.

There is an extensive literature on these areas, some of which is referenced in the Bibliography.

## AVIATION

The aircraft industry has consistently improved fuel efficiency over the decades, with fuel per passenger kilometre falling 40 per cent since the early jet airliners of the late 1950s and 1960s. This has been achieved mainly through improvements to jet engines, and the latest generation of engines can achieve further reductions of 10 to 20 per cent. With air passenger traffic expected to triple in the next 30 years, aviation emissions are a major concern and the drive towards low-cost air travel means that fuel costs need to be addressed. The fuel efficiency of aviation is now being addressed in two ways: more intelligent traffic management and technological changes to aircraft themselves. The former includes dynamic air traffic control that allows freer and more efficient routing, while the latter ranges from increased use of composites to save weight, as seen in the all-composite fuselage of the Boeing 787, through to more advanced concepts such as blended wing designs.

## SHIPPING

We have mentioned some technologies to improve shipping energy efficiency in the Stena energy management case study (Chapter 7). In an interesting policy move, Singapore, which is a major hub for the global shipping industry, has implemented innovative policies to promote improved energy efficiency in shipping. Singapore's port authority has invested SIN$100 million in the Maritime Green Initiative, a Green Ship Programme, a Green Port Programme and a Green Technology Programme. The Green Ship Programme encourages Singapore-flagged ships to achieve standards beyond the International Maritime Organization's Energy Efficiency Design Index. In return, the ships receive a 50 per cent rebate on their original registration fees (costs) and a 20 per cent rebate on annual tonnage tax.

The Green Port Programme offers a 15 per cent reduction in port duties for ships that use flue gas scrubbing technology or clean fuels with a sulphur content less than 1 per cent. The port uses energy-efficient cranes and has implemented other energy efficiency measures in its facilities. The Green Technology Programme will co-fund up to half the cost of developing or adopting new green technologies in local maritime industries. More than 40 international shipping companies have signed up for the Maritime Green Pledge.

### 'Intelligent Energy Efficiency'

The phrase 'intelligent energy efficiency' covers all those areas, across many different fundamental technology areas from buildings to transport to energy, where the application of 'intelligence', high levels of real-time data collection and processing at a system level, can result in improved energy efficiency. Examples include:

- using 'big data' to optimize the performance of buildings and groups of buildings across portfolios or cities;

- using traffic flow information and dynamic messaging to optimize routing;

- applying 'intelligence' to previously 'dumb' assets within the energy system to improve performance and reduce down times, thus reducing energy use within the system as well as energy used to provide maintenance.

The application of 'intelligence' to building, energy and transportation infrastructure will continue to grow as the general productivity drivers are strong. Often, an additional benefit will be increased energy efficiency. In 2012 the ACEEE reported that intelligent energy efficiency could reduce US energy consumption by nearly 25 per cent (Neal et al. 2012).

### Snake Oil and Scams – Caveat Emptor

Energy efficiency, particularly when energy prices are high, attracts its share of dubious technologies and dodgy sales techniques. Some of these use pseudo science/engineering to explain 'savings' that in practice are hard to measure and verify. Examples include some forms of electricity 'filtration' or 'power factor correction' – particularly around lighting and motors, plug-in 'energy savers', fuel additives and fuel treatment technologies using magnets which are particularly common for cars and lorries. Some of these have been remarkably long lived, based on powerful sales techniques, often promising very large savings, and target uninformed customers looking to reduce their energy costs. Some of these devices, particularly those sold to gullible householders, are potentially dangerous.

The adoption of more standardized measurement and verification techniques such as the use of the IPMVP in industry and commerce should make it harder to sell these kinds of technologies and equipment. As always, buyers should be careful and if in doubt ask for the results of independent M&V exercises. An example of testing various car fuel-saving devices is found in *Popular Mechanics* in 2005 (Allen 2005). It should be noted that voltage regulation, i.e. maintaining voltage at a level below its normal grid voltage, is a legitimate and cost-effective technique in many situations, in both commercial and residential applications – as pioneered by VPhase plc (VPhase 2013).

There is no substitute for sound understanding of the underlying science and independently measured and verified case studies.

## Barriers to Energy Efficiency Innovation

Innovators of energy efficiency products face some generic barriers, including:

- The higher upfront cost of energy-efficient products compared to a conventional solution (but with lower lifetime cost). Even when adoption of the technology would produce a rapid financial return, higher upfront cost often wins. As described in Chapter 6 this is a management issue, particularly around the procurement function which in most organizations is focused on lowest first cost rather than lifetime cost or financial returns. In the early stages of enthusiasm for the low-carbon economy there seemed to be a belief that customers would pay extra for environmental benefits but the onset of the financial crisis brought back some reality – consumers buy products for many reasons and, increasingly, environmental benefits are a 'hygiene factor', an added benefit for which consumers will not generally pay extra. Good product design should aim at beating competitive products on upfront cost as well as environmental advantages such as energy efficiency.

- Lack of energy management capacity within clients. In order to identify and assess proposed innovations (or to become an early adopter of new technologies) and then properly evaluate them and ultimately to adopt them by implementing a project, requires a certain level of energy management capacity. In organizations where energy management is relegated to lower-level technical staff, or in SMEs, there is typically insufficient capacity. Even in larger organizations energy efficiency capacity is insufficient.

- Uncertainty about savings. This barrier is related to lack of general energy management capacity as well as lack of knowledge of M&V techniques. If clients perceive there to be uncertainty around energy efficiency gains they are less likely to adopt new technologies.

- Conservatism in design techniques in all engineering disciplines. Most designers will tend to use a design and components they have used before. This is true across all design disciplines including building services, electrical engineering, mechanical engineering, chemical engineering and general industrial engineering.

- Understandable reluctance, on the part of purchasers, either end-users or OEMs incorporating the technologies into products or systems, to risk adopting new technology too early and to place reliance on a small manufacturer for a critical part of the supply chain. Small manufacturers are unable to provide the degree of confidence that comes with a large manufacturer/supplier.

These barriers are in addition to the normal barriers facing developers of all new technologies, especially small and usually under-funded businesses, such as insufficient technical resources, lack of finance and lack of marketing skills. Another critical barrier to widespread commercialization of *all* technologies, not just energy efficiency technologies, is described as 'crossing the chasm' (Moore 1991). This is the problem of moving from a small market of 'innovators', customers willing to take the risks of new technology adoption, to the slightly larger market of 'early adopters' and then on to the mass markets of 'early majority' and 'late majority' customers. *Crossing the Chasm* identifies that there are gaps, or chasms, in the usual marketing bell-curve diagram and big differences between these categories of customers that are often ignored in technology marketing. Many technology companies win early innovator customers, an initial 'beach head', but fail to cross the chasm and move beyond this point.

## Summary

From the multitude of studies discussed in Chapter 3 we know that applying just existing, economic technologies – closing the energy efficiency gap – would result in significant energy savings, reductions in emissions and job creation.

Practitioners and policy makers need to develop programmes and policies that work to drive the take-up of existing technologies. In a very real sense we don't need new technologies, but at the same time we are seeing a flowering of innovation across all sectors of the economy as more bright minds and more venture capital commit to developing new energy efficiency technologies and energy services. As these technologies and services are commercialized they will expand the frontier of the energy efficiency gap, possibly as fast as we work towards reducing it by applying existing technologies. I have little doubt that innovation in this area will continue to flourish, and even accelerate, and that we will be surprised by how much more energy inefficiency human ingenuity will allow us to drive out of our buildings, industrial processes, transport, energy systems and information technologies.

## References and Bibliography

Acker, B., Duarte, C. and Van Den Wymelenberg, K. 2012. *Office Space Plug Load Profiles and Energy Saving Interventions*. [Online]. Available at: http://www.aceee.org/files/proceedings/2012/data/papers/0193-000277.pdf [accessed 27 January 2013].

Air Movement and Control Association International Inc. 2010. *Inmotion*, Spring 2010. [Online]. Available at: http://www.amca.org/UserFiles/file/AMCA_Spring2010Revlores.pdf [accessed 22 April 2013].

Allen, M. 2005. 'Looking for a Miracle: We Test Automotive "Fuel Savers"', *Popular Mechanics*, 25 August 2005. [Online]. Available at: http://www.popularmechanics.com/cars/alternative-fuel/gas-mileage/1802932 [accessed 28 April 2013].

AMSC. 2013. *AMSC*. [Online]. Available at: http://www.amsc.com [accessed 28 April 2013].

Aspen Aerogels. 2013. *Case Studies*. [Online]. Available at: http://www.aerogel. com/markets/cases.html [accessed 27 January 2013].

Autonomic Materials. 2013. *Autonomic Materials*. [Online]. Available at: http:// www.autonomicmaterials.com [accessed 28 April 2013].

Barney, G. 2007. *Energy Efficiency of Lifts – Measurement, Conformance, Modelling, Prediction and Simulation*. [Online]. Available at: http://www.cibseliftsgroup. org/docs/Barney-on-energy%20efficiency%20of%20lifts.pdf [accessed 27 January 2013].

Boeing Research & Technology. 2010. *Subsonic Ultra Green Aircraft Research SUGAR Final Review*. [Online]. Available at: http://www.scribd.com/ doc/35315468/Boeing-Future-Airplanes-Sugar-Phase-i-Final-Review-v5 [accessed 27 January 2013].

Breathing Buildings. 2013. *Breathing Buildings*. [Online]. Available at: http:// www.breathingbuildings.com/home [accessed 28 April 2013].

Brendel, M. 2010. *The Role of Fan Efficiency in Reducing HVAC Energy Consumption*. [Online]. Available at: http://www.amca.org/UserFiles/file/ AMCA_Spring2010RoleOfFE.pdf [accessed 27 January 2013].

Buildings Performance Institute Europe. 2011a. *Principles for Nearly Zero-Energy Buildings*. [Online]. Available at: http://www.institutebe.com/InstituteBE/ media/Library/Resources/Existing%20Building%20Retrofits/BPIE-Report-Principles-for-Nearly-Zero-Energy-Buildings.pdf [accessed 27 January 2013].

Buildings Performance Institute Europe. 2011b. *Europe's Buildings Under the Microscope*. [Online]. Available at: http://www.europeanclimate.org/ documents/LR_%20CbC_study.pdf [accessed 27 January 2013].

CamSemi. 2013. *CamSemi. Controllers for Low Cost, Energy Efficient Power Conversion*. [Online]. Available at: http://www.camsemi.com [accessed 28 April 2013].

Carbon War Room. 2012. *Improving Building Performance. Reduce Energy Consumption by 20% with Little or No Cost*. [Online]. Available at: http://www. carbonwarroom.com/sites/default/files/reports/CWR2012_FinanceWhite_ E6.pdf [accessed 27 January 2013].

CDW-G. 2012. *Data Center Solutions that Deliver Energy Efficiency*. [Online]. Available at: http://www.cdwnewsroom.com/2012-energy-efficient-it-report/ [accessed 27 January 2013].

Cisco. 2007. *Cisco Energy Efficient Data Center Solutions and Best Practices*. [Online]. Available at: http://www.cisco.com/en/US/solutions/ns708/ networking_solutions_products_genericcontent0900aecd806fd32e.pdf [accessed 27 January 2013].

Commercial Buildings Consortium. 2011. *Next Generation Technologies Barriers & Industry Recommendations for Commercial Buildings*. [Online]. Available at: http://bloximages.newyork1.vip.townnews.com/sustainablecitynetwork. com/content/tncms/assets/v3/editorial/7/cf/7cf2fed4-3d66-11e0-bcc8-0017a4a78c22/4d61d52290e6a.pdf.pdf [accessed 27 January 2013].

Committee on Integrated Computational Materials Engineering, National Research Council. 2008. *Integrated Computational Materials Engineering: A Transformational Discipline for Improved Competitiveness and National Security*. Washington, DC, National Academies Press.

Council of Energy Ministers, Canada. 2009. *On the Road to a Fuel-Efficient Truck*. [Online]. Available at: http://fleetsmart.nrcan.gc.ca/documents/PDF/trucking.pdf [accessed 27 January 2013].

Datum Phase Change. 2013. *Datum Phase Change*. [Online]. Available at: http://www.datumphasechange.com/index.php?home [accessed 28 April 2013].

de Beer, J., Worrel, E. and Blok, K. 1998. 'Future Technologies for Energy-Efficient Iron and Steel Making, Annual Review', *Energy Environment* 23: 123–205.

Delta Energy & Environment. 2011a. *Home Energy Management in Europe: Lots of Solutions, but What's the Problem?* [Online]. Available at: http://www.delta-ee. com/images/downloads/pdfs/2011/Delta_Research_Paper_Home_Energy_Management_in_Europe_Autumn_2011.pdf [accessed 27 January 2013].

Delta Energy & Environment. 2011b. *Driving a Resource Efficiency Power Generation Sector in Europe*. [Online]. Available at: http://www.delta-ee. com/images/downloads/pdfs/2011/Delta%20Final%20Report%20-%20 Driving%20a%20Resource%20Efficient%20Power%20Generation%20 Sector%20in%20Europe.pdf [accessed 27 January 2013].

Ecomagination. 2013. *Ecomagination*. [Online]. Available at: www. ecomagination.com [accessed 28 April 2013].

Energetix. 2013. *Energetix*. [Online]. Available at: http://energetixgroup.com [accessed 28 April 2013].

Energy Deck. 2013. *Energy Deck*. [Online]. Available at: http://www.energydeck. com/home/ [accessed 28 April 2013].

EnergyFlo. 2012. *How Dynamic Insulation Works*. [Online]. Available at: http://www.energyflo.co.uk/technology/how-dynamic-insulation-works [accessed 28 April 2013].

Energy Savings Trust. 2011. *Lit Up: An LED Lighting Field Trial*. [Online]. Available at: http://www.energysavingtrust.org.uk/Publications2/Energy-efficiency/Lit-up-an-LED-lighting-field-trial [accessed 27 January 2013].

*Financial Times*. 2013. 'Entrepreneurship: Chinese Turn Attention to Waste Heat Recovery'. [Online]. Available at: http://www.ft.com/intl/cms/s/0/04d67220-66f2-11e2-a805-00144feab49a.html#axzz2UfnhGkMN [accessed 29 May 2013].

Fine, C. and Roth, R. 2010. *Lightweight Materials for Transport: Developing a Vehicle Technology Roadmap for the Use of Lightweight Materials.* [Online]. Available at: http://www.alum.mit.edu/sites/default/files/IC_assets/news/images/alumninews/Fine_Roth.pdf [accessed 27 January 2013].

Freeman, C. 1974. *The Economics of Industrial Innovation.* Harmondsworth, Penguin Modern Economic Texts.

Green Pocket. 2013. Green Pocket. [Online]. Available at: http://www.greenpocket.de [accessed 28 April 2013].

Ilika. 2013. *Ilika.* [Online]. Available at: http://www.ilika.com [accessed 28 April 2013].

International Aluminium Institute. 2012. *Improving Sustainability in the Transport Sector.* [Online]. Available at: http://www.world-aluminium.org/media/filer_public/2013/01/15/none_1 [accessed 27 January 2013].

International Energy Agency. 2010. *Guidebook on Energy Efficient Electric Lighting for Buildings.* [Online]. Available at: http://www.ecbcs.org/docs/ECBCS_Annex_45_Guidebook.pdf [accessed 27 January 2013].

Intelligent Energy Europe. 2010. *Energy Efficient Elevators and Escalators.* [Online]. Available at: http://www.e4project.eu/documenti/wp6/E4-WP6-Brochure.pdf [accessed 27 January 2013].

Jaguar Cars. 2012. *Innovation, Imagination, Intelligence.* [Online]. Available at: http://www.jaguar.com/gl/en/experience/jaguar_magazine/xj_special_edition/innov_imag_intellligence [accessed 27 January 2013].

Kaneda, D., Jacobson, B. and Rumsey, P. 2010. *Plug Load Reduction: The Next Big Hurdle for Net Zero Energy Building Design.* [Online]. Available at: http://www.institutebe.com/InstituteBE/media/Library/Resources/Green%20Buildings/Plug-Load-Reduction,-ACEEE.pdf [accessed 27 January 2013].

Knowledge Transfer Network. 2012. *UK Air Vehicle Technology. Emerging and Disruptive Technologies for Future Vehicles and Concepts.* [Online]. Available at: https://connect.innovateuk.org/c/document_library/get_file?uuid=25bcc502-0216-4761-89c5-79a1b63411de&groupId=176577 [accessed 27 January 2013].

Kroo, I. 2008. *Sustainable Aviation: Future Air Transportation and the Environment.* [Online]. Available at: http://aa.stanford.edu/events/50thAnniversary/media/Kroo.pdf [accessed 27 January 2013].

kWhOURS. 2013. *kWhOURS.* [Online]. Available at: http://www.kwhours.com [accessed 28 April 2013].

Lowe, M., Golini, R. and Gereffi, G. 2010. *U.S. Adoption of High-Efficiency Motors and Drives: Lessons Learned.* [Online]. Available at: http://www.cggc.duke.edu/pdfs/CGGC-Motor_and_Drives_Report_Feb_25_2010.pdf [accessed 29 May 2013].

McKinsey & Company. 2012. *Lighting the Way. Perspectives on the Global Lighting Market*. [Online]. Available at: http://www.mckinsey.com/~/media/McKinsey/dotcom/client_service/Automotive%20and%20Assembly/Lighting_the_way_Perspectives_on_global_lighting_market_2012.ashx [accessed 27 January 2013].

Moore, G. 1991. *Crossing the Chasm*. Chichester, HarperCollins.

Moram, M. 2011. *Energy-Efficient Lighting*. [Online]. Available at: http://www.breathingbuildings.com/media/4544/381878078_dr%20michelle%20moram-%20sustainable%20buildings%202030.pdf [accessed 27 January 2013].

The Motor Ship. 2010. 'Stena E-MAXair – Probably the Greenest Tanker in the World', *The Motor Ship*, 8 January 2010. [Online]. Available at: http://www.motorship.com/news101/ships-and-shipyards/stena-e-maxair-probably-the-greenest-tanker-in-the-world [accessed 28 April 2013].

Nanoco. 2013. *Nanoco Group PLC*. [Online]. Available at: http://www.nanocotechnologies.com [accessed 28 April 2013].

NASA. 2011. *Subsonic Ultra Green Aircraft Research: Phase I Final Report*. [Online]. Available at: http://newenergytimes.com/v2/news/2012/20120500NASA-CR-2012-217556-Subsonic-Ultra-Green.pdf [accessed 28 April 2013].

Neal, E., Molina, M. and Trombley, D. 2012. *A Defining Framework for Intelligent Efficiency*. [Online]. Available at: http://www.aceee.org/sites/default/files/publications/researchreports/e125.pdf [accessed 27 January 2013].

NGenTec. 2013. *About NGenTec*. [Online]. Available at: http://www.ngentec.com/about.asp [accessed 28 April 2013].

NRDC. 2012. *Is Cloud Computing Always Greener?* [Online]. Available at: http://www.nrdc.org/energy/files/cloud-computing-efficiency-IB.pdf [accessed 27 January 2013].

Nujira. 2013. *Nujira*. [Online]. Available at: http://www.nujira.com [accessed 28 April 2013].

OECD and Eurostat. 2005. *Oslo Manual. Guidelines for Collecting and Interpreting Innovation Data*. Third edition. [Online]. Available at: http://epp.eurostat.ec.europa.eu/cache/ITY_PUBLIC/OSLO/EN/OSLO-EN.PDF [accessed 27 April 2013].

O-Flexx. 2013. *About O-Flexx*. [Online]. Available at: http://www.o-flexx.com/en/company/about-o-flexx/about-o-flexx/ [accessed 28 April 2013].

Onzo. 2013. *Onzo*. [Online]. Available at: http://www.onzo.com [accessed 28 April 2013].

Patrão, C., Rivet, L., Fong, J. and Almeida, A. 2009. *Energy Efficient Elevators and Escalators*. [Online]. Available at: http://www.eceee.org/conference_proceedings/eceee/2009/Panel_4/4.037/paper [accessed 27 January 2013].

Patrão, C., Almeida, A., Fong, J. and Ferreira, F. 2010. *Elevators and Escalators Energy Performance Analysis*. [Online]. Available at: http://www.aceee.org/files/proceedings/2010/data/papers/1981.pdf [accessed 27 January 2013].

PAX Scientific. 2013. *PAX Scientific*. [Online]. Available at: http://www.paxscientific.com [accessed 28 April 2013].

Retroficiency. 2013. *Retroficiency*. [Online]. Available at: http://www.retroficiency.com [accessed 28 April 2013].

Rocky Mountain Institute, 2013. *U.S. Price vs. Rated Efficiency of 250-hp Motors*. [Online]. Available at: http://www.rmi.org/RFGraph-US_price_vs_rated_efficiency_250_hp_motors [accessed 29 May 2013].

Sefaira. 2013. *Sefaira*. [Online]. Available at: http://www.sefaira.com [accessed 28 April 2013].

Subrato, C., Widder, S. and Jackson, R. 2011. *50 Pilot Deep Energy Retrofits*. [Online]. Available at: http://apps1.eere.energy.gov/buildings/publications/pdfs/building_america/ns/eemtg082011_c7_50_pilot_deep.pdf [accessed 27 January 2013].

Sumitomo. 2013. *Sumitomo Electric Industries*. [Online]. Available at: http://global-sei.com/super/index.en.html [accessed 28 April 2013].

UK Department of Transport. 2009. *A Quick Guide to Truck Aerodynamics*. London, HMSO.

UKTI. 2012. *UK Advanced Engineering*. [Online]. Available at: http://www.ukti.gov.uk/investintheuk/uktipublications/item/289700.html [accessed 22 April 2013].

United States Department of Energy. 2011. *Best Practices Guide for Energy Efficient Data Center Design*. [Online]. Available at: http://www1.eere.energy.gov/femp/pdfs/eedatacenterbestpractices.pdf [accessed 27 January 2013].

United States Department of Energy. 2012. *Energy Savings Potential of Solid-State Lighting in General Illumination Applications*. [Online]. Available at: http://apps1.eere.energy.gov/buildings/publications/pdfs/ssl/ssl_energy-savings-report_jan-2012.pdf [accessed 27 January 2013].

University of Leicester. 2011. *When Size Matters: Nanotechnology for Energy Efficiency*. [Online]. Available at: http://www.alphagalileo.org/ViewItem.aspx?ItemId=105572&CultureCode=en [accessed 27 January 2013].

View Glass. 2013. *View Glass*. [Online]. Available at: http://www.viewglass.com [accessed 28 April 2013].

VPhase. 2013. *VPhase Voltage Optimisation*. [Online]. Available at: http://www.vphase.co.uk [accessed 28 April 2013].

Wasabi. 2013. *Wasabi Energy*. [Online]. Available at: http://www.wasabienergy.com [accessed 28 April 2013].

Weightman, D. and Field, J. 2012. *Office Plug Loads: Energy Use and Savings Opportunities*. [Online]. Available at: http://www.esource.com/esource/ getpub/members/webconference_slides/CEC-WC-1-12-PlugLoads.pdf [accessed 27 January 2013].

Wellington. 2013. *Wellington Energy Saving ECM Motors and Fans*. [Online]. Available at: http://www.wdtl.com [accessed 28 April 2013].

Woodley, A. 2012. *Composite Winglets Reduce Aircraft Emissions*. [Online]. Available at: https://connect.innovateuk.org/web/composites/articles/-/ blogs/composite-winglets-reduce-aircraft-emissions;jsessionid=498A060130 F05AA45203ADA730857E87.c6e65d2a570 [accessed 27 January 2013].

Wooley, J. 2011. *Fostering the Development and Commercialization of Climate Appropriate Cooling Technologies*. [Online]. Available at: http://aceee.org/files/ pdf/conferences/eer/2011/BS5E_Wooley.pdf [accessed 27 January 2013].

World Bank. 2012. *Air Transport and Energy Efficiency*. [Online]. Available at: http://siteresources.worldbank.org/INTAIRTRANSPORT/Resources/TP38. pdf [accessed 27 January 2013].

Zenex. 2013. *GasSaver*. [Online]. Available at: http://www.zenexenergy.co.uk/ Zenex1/index.php?option=com_content&view=article&id=9&Itemid=5 [accessed 11 May 2013].

Zhai, J., LeClaire, N. and Bendewald, M. 2011. 'Deep Energy Retrofit of Commercial Buildings: A Key Pathway Towards Low-Carbon Cities', *Carbon Management* 2(4): 425–30.

Zimmerann, M. and Andersson, J. (eds). 1998. *Low Energy Cooling. Case Study Buildings*. [Online]. Available at: http://www.ecbcs.org/docs/annex_28_case_ study_buildings.pdf [accessed 27 January 2013].

# 9

# Designing for Energy Efficiency

*All design can be seen as a process of resisting compromise.*
*Kevin McCloud, presenter of* Grand Designs

## Design Decisions Lock In Energy Use

The level of energy efficiency of any process, building, device – or indeed the whole economy – is largely a matter of choice; choice set at the design level. Of course, the management, operation and use of the process, building or device does deeply affect energy use and hence overall efficiency – in the case of buildings, it can vary by a factor of two or more for similar buildings. But the fundamental performance is constrained by decisions taken, usually very early on, in the design stage. We always have a choice in the process of design; we can design an efficient process, building or device, or we can design a standard one. Policy makers and concerned practitioners need to work to ensure that designers choose the more efficient option more often than is currently the norm. This is particularly important in buildings because the building stock is long lived and design decisions being made today will lock in energy use for decades and maybe even centuries but it also applies to all products and systems.

There are four issues that need to be addressed to ensure energy efficiency is incorporated into all designs. The first is that the further you get in any design and construction process the harder it is to incorporate energy efficiency measures. Initial decisions made early on in the process rapidly lock-in design features, and as time passes, and the amount of money spent on the design process increases, the potential to save energy through design choices is reduced. Clearly, in any design process there are other constraints, including time and money, as well as the overall objective, e.g. to move into a new building or implement a new industrial process. These objectives often have tight deadlines and take precedence over energy efficiency. Buildings are not built just to save energy but to meet other corporate or organizational objectives such as the need for more space or to relocate. The important thing is to explicitly consider energy efficiency at the right stage, and that stage is right at the beginning – the concept stage.

The second issue is that design has traditionally been organized in silos where, for example, an architect designs a building's orientation, layout and facades and then the design is handed to services engineers to design the services to meet required comfort levels. This lack of integration ignores the physical reality that factors such as orientation or layout interact with each other to determine energy use. Even within the design of services there are silos: HVAC engineers are separate from lighting engineers, but in reality heat gains from lighting energy use can affect HVAC design.

The third issue is conservatism within the design professions. Many designs are, in fact, simply copies of previous designs – 'this is what worked last time'. To a certain extent this is understandable as it is important to know that a design works, particularly if the designer's professional indemnity insurance is on the line. This encourages over-sizing of components such as boilers, fans and pumps which locks in significant energy and operations cost, as well as increased capital costs. Over-sizing can be encouraged by a fee structure which is based on capital expenditure rather than subsequent performance. There is little reward for innovation in the building services profession. A better balance between conservatism and innovation is needed.

The fourth issue is that natural conservatism on the part of engineers is also reinforced by design codes which are of course necessary, but do tend to lock in design approaches. Codes set a minimum standard needed and are usually component based rather than system based. In cable design, for instance, the standard typically sets the minimum cable size required for health and safety, i.e. the minimum required to prevent overheating and hence fire risk. The design process and codes do not encourage consideration of larger cables which will have a higher upfront cost but a lower operating cost, therefore producing a positive return on investment.

Ensuring energy efficiency is incorporated into any new building, vehicle or process design requires three conditions: an educated and determined client who is clear about the benefits of incorporating energy efficiency and what the potential to do so really is; an educated design team with the capability to produce and deliver an energy-efficient design (as well as match all the other client's requirements); and, finally, a different process to conventional design.

At the start of any design process it is important that a clear objective for energy use is established, along with all the other functional requirements in the brief. If it is not explicitly included, the energy use will be a matter of chance. The energy objective should have the full support of the client's senior management and a strong client advocate can help to keep the objective front and centre in the minds of the design team. In the energy field the design objective can be expressed compared to a benchmark such as energy per metre squared or as achieving a certain design standard such as Leadership in Energy and Environmental Design (LEED) Platinum (US Green Building Council 2012) or Passivhaus (Passivhaus UK 2012). Ambitious goals challenge designers more, but seem to work. An example is the United States General Services Administration's Net Zero Renovation Challenge (Carmichael 2011) which covers 30–35 buildings across the US and challenges ESCOs to achieve net-zero energy use, defined as 'a building that produces (and exports) at least as much renewable energy as it uses in a year'.

The design team must have the capability to deliver an energy efficient design. Capability is a combination of attitude, process, technical skills and available design tools.

A design approach that breaks away from the traditional silo approach is integrative or holistic design. This approach, practised by the Rocky Mountain Institute and others, is a collaborative process focused on whole-building design. The use of integrative design techniques has been proven to deliver significant energy savings at little or no extra capital cost – and often lower capital cost – in the design of both buildings, new builds and retrofits, industrial processes and transport. For further evidence of the effectiveness of integrative design see Lovins (2007a–d) and Rocky Mountain Institute (2012a, 2012b). The Sustainable Energy Authority of Ireland (SEAI) has done some very good work in promoting Energy Efficient Design (EED) which uses an integrative design approach and has been proven to result in lower energy costs, lower operational costs and capital costs (SEAI 2011), and can be integrated into existing design processes. The EED process has three phases:

- Undertake a facility energy balance. This should be done at the concept design stage and the purpose is to identify high-level energy-saving opportunities.

- Analyse and challenge. A list of measures is proposed, developed and prioritized. The interaction between measures is explicitly considered and a short list of projects for implementation drawn up.

- Implementation.

The EED process includes an EED specialist who is responsible for managing the process. EED has been proven to be highly productive. In the case of Lakeland Dairies, analysis of heat and cooling processes led to avoiding capital investment for additional cooling plant, reduced cooling and heating loads, reduced peak electrical loads, and to the development of a heat recovery project with an estimated payback period of six months (SEAI 2009). Energy savings achieved by applying EED have reached 50 per cent.

## Design Standards

A number of building design standards have been developed to assist building owners and designers to achieve higher levels of efficiency and environmental performance. Well known standards include LEED and Passivhaus. LEED was developed in the US but has been used in 135 countries (US Green Building Council 2012) in more than 7,000 projects covering 1.5 billion square feet. The LEED system uses a scorecard approach in which different features of a building attract points and different levels of performance are awarded Certified, Silver, Gold or Platinum LEED certification. Various rating schemes are used for different building types covering new build and retrofit, offices, health care and schools.

In the residential sector, Passivhaus is a voluntary standard that focuses on reducing energy losses from the building fabric and results in very low levels of energy use, so much so that conventional heating systems are not required. More than 30,000 Passivhaus buildings have been built worldwide and energy costs are reduced by a factor of five to ten compared to similar buildings built to conventional standards. Although overall Passivhaus achieves very high levels of efficiency compared to conventionally designed buildings, the use of mechanical ventilation could, in some cases, be replaced by passive ventilation.

Standards such as LEED and Passivhaus are extremely useful tools for promoting energy-efficient and environmentally sound building design. They make it easier for clients to specify high performance simply by saying 'I want a LEED Gold building'. But like all single measures of performance they do need to be fully understood and used with care. In LEED, for example, it is possible to score points for features such as bicycle racks. Although the encouragement of cycling can create a positive environmental impact it does not produce a direct economic benefit to the investor, and these kinds of softer feature can be offset to a certain degree against energy performance.

## Building Performance Compared to Design

Another important point when using any design standard is to remember that the 'as built' performance is not the same 'as designed' performance. The difference comes about from several factors including the inaccuracies of performance modelling, components not being built to the design, construction quality and poor commissioning of services. The poor performance of modelling tools is likely to become a major issue, particularly in financed schemes such as the UK's Green Deal in which savings are expected to exceed loan repayments. Incorrect calculation of savings levels in such schemes could lead to major hardships for consumers and possible legal action. New modelling tools which use the computing power available 'in the cloud', such as those from Sefaira (Sefaira 2013), allow more accurate, faster modelling that enables the rapid assessment of different design options.

## Conclusions

We now have the design techniques to achieve significant improvements in energy efficiency in new and existing buildings, industrial processes, energy systems and vehicles of all sorts. The challenge now is to build capacity in these techniques, both on the supply side and the demand side, and to accelerate their deployment such that they become the normal approach rather than the exception. Building capacity on the supply side is a challenge to the education system and the engineering and architecture professions, which often are inherently conservative. Building capacity on the demand side will require work within each sector to build knowledge of the power of these techniques and hence customer demand.

## References and Bibliography

Carmichael, C. 2011. *GSA Net Zero Renovation Challenge Charette*. [Online]. Available at: http://www.rmi.org/Knowledge-Center/Library/2011-18_GSANetZero [accessed 28 January 2013].

Kats, G. 2009. *Greening Our Built World: Costs, Benefits and Strategies*. Washington, DC, Island Press.

Lovins, A. 2007a. *Public Lectures in Advanced Energy Efficiency. 1. Buildings*. [Online]. Available at: http://www.rmi.org/Content/Files/E07-02_Stanford_1Buildings.pdf [accessed 27 January 2013].

Lovins, A. 2007b. *Public Lectures in Advanced Energy Efficiency. 2. Industry*. [Online]: Available at: http://www.rmi.org/Content/Files/E07-03_Stanford_2Industry.pdf [accessed 27 January 2013].

Lovins, A. 2007c. *Public Lectures in Advanced Energy Efficiency. 3. Transportation*. [Online]. Available at: http://www.rmi.org/Content/Files/E07-04_Stanford_3Transport.pdf [accessed 27 January 2013].

Lovins, A. 2007d. *Public Lectures in Advanced Energy Efficiency. 4. Implementation*. [Online]. Available at: http://www.rmi.org/Content/Files/E07-05_Stanford_4Implement.pdf [accessed 27 January 2013].

Lovins, A. 2007e. *Public Lectures in Advanced Energy Efficiency. 5. Implications*. [Online]. Available at: http://www.rmi.org/Content/Files/E07-06_Stanford_5Implications.pdf [accessed 27 January 2013].

New Buildings Institute. 2011. *NEEA Examples of Deep Energy Savings in Existing Buildings*. [Online]. Available at: http://www.betterbricks.com/sites/default/files/nbi_neea_deep_savings_search_phase_1_final.pdf [accessed 27 January 2013].

New Buildings Institute. 2012. *Buildings Database*. [Online]. Available at: http://buildings.newbuildings.org [accessed 27 January 2013].

Passivhaus UK. 2012. *Passivhaus. The World's First Fabric Approach to Low Energy Buildings*. [Online]. Available at: http://www.passivhaus.org.uk/standard.jsp?id=122 [accessed 27 January 2013].

Reed, B. and Fedrizzi, S.R. 2009. *The Integrative Design Guide to Green Building: Redefining the Practice of Sustainability*. Hoboken NJ, John Wiley & Sons.

Rocky Mountain Institute. 2012a. *Built Environment: Impact and Project Experience*. [Online]. Available at: http://www.rmi.org/rmi/retrofit_consulting_project_experience [accessed 27 January 2013].

Rocky Mountain Institute. 2012b. *True Stories*. [Online]. Available at: http://www.rmi.org/retrofit_depot_get_connected_true_retrofit_stories [accessed 27 January 2013].

SEAI. 2009. *Case Study: Lakeland Dairies*. Sustainable Energy Authority of Ireland. [Online]. Available at: http://www.seai.ie/Your_Business/Energy_ Agreements/Special_Working_Groups/EED_SWG_2008/EED_Lakeland_ Dairies.pdf [accessed 28 April 2013].

SEAI. 2011. *Energy Efficient Design Methodology*. [Online]. Available at: http:// www.seai.ie/Your_Business/Energy_Agreements/Special_Working_ Groups/EED_SWG_2008/EED_Methodology.pdf [accessed 27 January 2013].

Sefaira. 2013. *Sefaira*. [Online]. Available at: http://www.sefaira.com [accessed 28 April 2013].

US Green Building Council. 2012. *LEED*. [Online]. Available at: http://new. usgbc.org/leed [accessed 27 January 2013].

# 10

# Financing Energy Efficiency Investment

*There was some local resistance in Cornwall, where the new engines were certain to save costs in pumping out water from the tin mines, … the 'no cure, no pay' terms offered by Boulton and Watt – based on one third of the savings in fuel over a period of twenty-five years – saved the day.*

*Thomas Crump,*
The Age of Steam, London, Constable and Robinson, *2007, p. 58.*

## Introduction

For many years there has been great interest in the problems of financing investment in energy efficiency – particularly in how to bring in external, or third-party, finance to invest in cost-effective energy efficiency measures. This is because finance, or the lack of it, is held to be a major barrier to increasing the uptake of profitable energy efficiency projects. Although many energy efficiency projects have short payback periods, even shorter than the normal investment criteria of the host, often they are not actioned or implemented because organizations have limited funds available for investment and choose to invest elsewhere, for example in projects that increase sales (*offensive* spending as opposed to *defensive* cost-cutting spending). Many projects may have payback periods longer than the investment criteria but could still be considered profitable by external investors. Other projects are profitable from the point of view of society when compared to energy generation infrastructure and when all externalities are properly valued. We need to look at financing as many of these projects as possible.

The differences between what is invested in energy efficiency and what the potential is at different levels of economic viability are the energy efficiency gaps referred to in Chapter 3. Creating mechanisms by which third-party investors can invest in these projects is a way of improving energy efficiency and overall economic effectiveness. In recent years, with the advent of Property Assessed Clean Energy (PACE) schemes in the USA and on-bill financing schemes such as the Green Deal in the United Kingdom, there has been a surge of interest in third-party finance for energy efficiency investments, a surge of interest that is not yet matched by actual transaction volume.

Although the lack of finance is often cited as a major barrier to investing in energy efficiency, the real problem is not lack of finance per se, but rather a lack of structures that address investor concerns and therefore would enable funds with the optimum cost of capital to flow into energy efficiency projects. Despite the global financial crisis there is no shortage of investors in the world looking for stable low-risk returns, and the risk–return profile of energy efficiency projects should be attractive to many investors. The truth is that we are only at the beginning of the evolution of the energy efficiency financing market.

## How Much Investment Do We Need?

So how much investment would be needed to implement all cost-effective energy efficiency measures? In Chapter 3 we reviewed various studies of the potential for energy efficiency, some of which address the scale of investment needed. The 2008 McKinsey study, *How the World Should Invest in Energy Efficiency* (Farrell and Remes 2008), estimated that an annual investment of $170 billion per annum globally could halve the projected growth in energy demand and deliver half the carbon abatement required to keep atmospheric carbon levels to 450 ppm. This investment would, McKinsey estimated, provide an IRR of 17 per cent at an average oil price of $50 per barrel (with a minimum IRR for any particular category of investment of 10 per cent). Given that the average oil price is significantly above $50 per barrel, the projected IRRs would be far above 17 per cent, probably nearer 30 per cent, which is attractive to many equity investors.

The global investment number of $170 billion per annum should be compared with total investments in renewable energy. UNEP and Bloomberg New Energy Finance (2012) report that in 2011 global investment in renewable energy – covering all types of investment – reached $257 billion, an increase of 17 per cent from 2010 and six times the level in 2004. This number is still expected to grow despite cutbacks in subsidies for renewable energy in Europe, the USA and elsewhere. For comparison, the total global investment in the energy system is estimated to be $1,300 billion (GEA 2012), of which about $1,000 billion is in the supply side.

Increasing investment in energy efficiency to circa $170 billion per annum would appear to be achievable, at least in terms of available capital when compared to the investment in renewables and the energy sector generally. A major problem, however, is that unlike renewables it is difficult to assess how much is being invested in efficiency now, partly because of definition problems – do we count capital expenditure on a new process that is more efficient as energy efficiency capital expenditure? Probably not. There are major data collection problems because there are many small investments by many players rather than a few high-visibility investments such as in wind or solar power.

## Sources of Funds

The provision of finance for energy efficiency can come from four sources:

- Internal funds – capital spending budgets within companies or public sector organizations;

- State funding – usually as some form of subsidy but potentially as a profitable investment;

- Utility funding – which can effectively be state funded but is more likely to come indirectly from customers;

- Private finance directly from banks (debt) or investors (debt or equity).

There can, of course, be hybrid schemes that bring together state funding and private sector finance.

Here we are more concerned with the last three, which are external sources of funds to the project host. Increasing allocation of internal funds to energy efficiency within organizations is a matter for senior managers, assisted by energy managers and other agents of change, including government, who can implement policies to encourage this additional allocation of capital to energy efficiency. As such this is more of a matter of energy management and energy policy.

## STATE FUNDING MODELS

State funding, whether it comes from national, local or city governments, or, indeed, supra-national bodies such as the European Union, is essentially a subsidy in one form or another. It can take the form of rebates for energy efficiency equipment; tax breaks for investment in energy efficiency equipment; subsidies for technical assistance for energy surveys or other parts of the project development and implementation process; subsidized loans for energy efficiency investments or revolving funds.

## UTILITY FINANCED SCHEMES

Utility funding can either be mandatory or voluntary. Mandatory spending by utilities is driven by utility regulation and it represents a forced allocation of capital spending away from energy supply in favour of energy demand. It has the potential to be an important tool for policy makers now and in the future. The ultimate source of finance is the customer because the cost of any programme is added to consumers' bills in one form or another. As we discuss in Chapter 11, the justification for such mandatory schemes is generally to address market failures and to seek least-cost electricity systems, but there can also be other motivations for policy makers such as addressing fuel poverty.

Voluntary spending by utilities comes about because utility managements see energy efficiency as a business opportunity, either directly, as a standalone profit centre or, for example, as a tool to enhance returns from energy supply through increasing customer retention. Many of the examples of utility schemes come from the USA, which has seen much innovation in this area, but there are other examples from Europe, Asia and Africa. We address some of the issues involved in energy suppliers offering energy efficiency services in Chapter 12.

## PRIVATE FINANCE OPTIONS

The provision or arrangement of third-party private finance is usually associated with Energy Service Companies (ESCOs) and some form of 'shared savings' agreement, usually working under an Energy Performance Contract (EPC) or Energy Savings Performance Contract (ESPC). Third-party private finance can either be equity or debt, and can come from a wide variety of sources including individuals, either through some form of 'crowd' or community funding or tax-based scheme, family offices, funds, banks and institutional investors such as insurance companies and pension funds.

## Just What Is an Energy Services Company?

There is much confusion about the term ESCO and the business models employed by ESCOs. The basic idea behind the ESCO model is that capital expenditure for projects is funded by a party other than the host, and that energy costs after the projects have been implemented should be reduced by a sufficient amount to cover repayment of the capital expenditure and other costs such as ongoing monitoring. The ESCO provides some form of guarantee that energy cost savings will exceed the repayments of capital, thus providing net savings to the project host from the beginning of the contract, usually through an Energy Performance Contract (EPC) or Energy Savings Performance Contract (ESPC). The basic concept is not new, having been used by Boulton and Watt in the eighteenth century to finance installation of their more efficient pumping engines in Cornish tin mines. Because of the confusion in the market about the term ESCO, I would argue that we now ditch the term and instead simply talk about 'developers of energy efficiency projects', which could be consultants, end users, vendors or even a community group. For the moment, however, ESCO is still in common use and so we will use it here.

In order to clear up confusion about the ESCO term it is important to distinguish between the *concept*, the *entity* and the *contract form*.

### THE CONCEPT – SHARED SAVINGS

The concept of shared savings is straightforward: financial savings resulting from some form of energy efficiency improvement are shared over a period of time between the host, the provider of capital and the ESCO. The energy efficiency improvement itself could be an investment in technology such as high-efficiency lighting or a behavioural programme with no investment, for example. However, the implementation of this simple concept is fraught with difficulties in practice, some of which we will review below, and can be effected by a range of different business models, contract forms and financial arrangements. This has led to the confusion around the ESCO and EPC/ESPC concept amongst energy efficiency professionals, policy makers, suppliers and customers.

## THE ENTITY

The entity developing the projects is a developer and could be an ESCO, a Facilities Management (FM) company, a construction company, a consultant or a community group.

## THE CONTRACT FORM

The contract form can be one of several variants such as EPC, ESPC, Efficiency Services Agreement (ESA), Managed Energy Services Agreement (MESA) or some other variant.

Another reason for confusion is that there are many types of contract which are effectively energy services, such as the form traditionally used in France and other parts of Europe, called 'chauffage'. These involve the sale of heat at an all-in price which covers the capital costs of the boiler and distribution system, operations and maintenance costs, and fuel costs. Chauffage contracts, in their original form at least, do not produce end-use energy savings and, in fact, during the length of the contract the supplier is actually incentivized to sell the customer more heat, not less. It is true, of course, that the upfront installation of new heat plant, possibly Combined Heat and Power, can result in an energy saving when it replaces an old inefficient boiler plant and distribution system. In this case the contracts can be said to be shared savings (in some cases) because the total outgoings, including repayment of the capital costs during the contract, were less than the total outgoings on energy and maintenance prior to the investment. In some cases, however, total costs go up in order to pay for the capital upgrade, but there may be a re-allocation of costs between energy, maintenance and finance.

Large providers of chauffage contracts in their home markets, such as EDF and GDF-Suez in France, traditionally used their large cash flows and balance sheets to finance projects, as well as start or acquire operations in new markets, although this is becoming more difficult for them. In the UK, these operators entered the energy service market in the 1980s and dominated the market for many years, predominantly selling outsourced operations and maintenance of boiler houses, and making savings through automation and demanning. In the 1980s in the UK uniquely, this became known as Contract Energy Management (CEM).

As well as chauffage, selling heat, some energy service companies also expanded into the provision of multiple utilities including cooling, compressed air, treated water, effluent treatment and industrial gases. A leading example of this contract form is the series of Utility Alliance Agreements (UAAs) signed between Diageo and RWE Solutions UK (latterly RWE npower) which were 15-year multi-utility agreements. Like some chauffage contracts, these multi-utility contracts produced large upfront energy and maintenance savings, which were split between the client and the contractor, with the contractor recovering all costs, including capital expenditure, over the lifetime of the contract. These UAAs are another contractual form of the shared savings concept.

## General Risks of Energy Efficiency Projects and Financing

### HOW DO YOU MEASURE SAVINGS?

Before we look at the different forms of shared savings, let's look at a number of generic problems around the shared savings concept which occur irrespective of the contract form. Foremost among these, of course, is the issue of how you measure savings. Energy savings are always compared to a counterfactual, which in practice is a scenario for what would have happened if no action to improve energy efficiency had been taken. In that sense energy savings, which we commonly describe and quantify, are inherently an abstract concept. You cannot, in the case of an investment in energy efficiency in a building or a factory, have a control experiment. There may be some cases where it is possible to have a control experiment, for instance if the client owns two very similar buildings with similar use in the same geographical area, or when undertaking large-scale behavioural changes, but these are highly unusual. The problems of measurement of savings are made worse because energy use in any building or facility is not static but is affected by a host of variables, including production output, ambient temperatures and other weather factors such as wind levels and direction, patterns of occupation (hours of use, numbers of people) and the ways in which occupants behave in regard to their energy use.

This measurement problem needs to be addressed by the Measurement and Verification (M&V) techniques which are discussed in Chapter 6, and an M&V strategy needs to be agreed between all parties as part of negotiating a shared savings contract of any form, preferably using independent M&V consultants.

## CHANGE OF USE OR BUILDING CLOSURE

Another problem with shared savings is the fact that buildings and facilities close or change use altogether. What happens to the energy savings if the building is changed from an office to a hotel, or if a school expands its pupil roll by 25 per cent? Another, much discussed, problem in relation to commercial offices is the split incentive. Building owners own buildings for their investment value, both yield over time and capital growth. When they invest to upgrade their building's energy the direct benefit does not flow to the landlord unless they are paying the energy bill, which typically they do in the common parts but not the tenants' part. As we discussed in Chapter 3, the indirect benefits such as the ability to charge more rent, or have fewer voids, have been reported, and although interest in these benefits is growing in some jurisdictions they have not yet been fully recognized.

## CREDITWORTHINESS

The creditworthiness of the counterparty is a big issue in shared savings contracts. If an ESCO puts in place some form of shared savings contract which runs over a number of years, funded by a third party, the investor needs confidence that the customer will continue to pay their share of the savings to the investor. Traditionally, public sector clients are lower risk than many private sector companies, although the global financial crisis has brought even that assumption into question. In the UK we have recently seen National Health Service hospitals effectively go into administration, although it has to be said that, unlike private organizations, they have been kept in operation and effectively been guaranteed by the government.

## ENERGY PRICE FLUCTUATIONS

Energy prices go down as well as up, and this can cause problems in shared savings contracts. Cost savings from any energy efficiency measure are, of course, units of energy saved (e.g. kWh) times the price of energy (e.g. £/kWh). When the energy efficiency measure is implemented the price of energy at that time is known but the future price of energy is unknown, unless there is a fixed-price energy supply contract for the length of the EPC contract. Any increase in energy price leads to a proportionate increase in cost savings, and any reduction in energy price reduces energy cost savings. For both the client and the investor this variability of energy price affects actual financial returns compared to projected returns. Most descriptions, and particularly sales literature describing the shared savings concept, naturally enough assumes or implies that energy prices are on an unstoppable upwards trend. History shows the folly of making this assumption. Following the oil crises of 1973 and 1979 oil prices reached a peak of $35 per barrel in 1980 ($95 in today's prices) and many analysts predicted ever-increasing energy prices. Then in 1986 the oil price fell from $27 per barrel to below $10 due to a 'glut' of oil, or perhaps more accurately a 'temporary surplus'. One of the factors behind the surplus was sharp reductions in demand for oil in OECD countries in response to the oil crises. This history lesson, as well as the impact of shale gas in the USA which has produced a fall in gas prices from around $7 per 1,000 cubic feet (with a short-term spike to $12 after Hurricane Katrina in 2005) to about $2.50 per 1,000 cubic feet in 2012, should always be remembered when considering future energy price scenarios.

A number of strategies can be employed to mitigate the risks (downside and upside) of variable energy prices on shared savings contracts. First, the savings can be calculated throughout the lifetime of the contract at a constant energy price, usually the starting energy price. This ensures that all the price risk, downside and upside, is transferred to the host. In the event of an energy price fall, the host's gross savings are reduced but the amount paid out on the shared savings concept is constant. In the event of any increase in energy price the client gains all the upside.

Energy price risk can be shared equally by simply using the average price of energy paid by the client in any one period. This exposes both parties to the upside and downside risks equally. This approach may not be attractive to a third-party investor. However, the downside risk to the investor can be capped by setting a minimum energy price used to calculate the savings. This would typically be set at a level sufficient to guarantee a minimum required return on capital. It would also be typically balanced by setting an upside limit (collar), above which no further gain is passed back to the investor.

## POST-CONTRACT CHANGES THAT LEAD TO SAVINGS

Another big problem with shared savings, which is related to M&V, is the situation where the host implements something, perhaps a change of process, or its own behavioural programme aimed at reducing waste, and savings are produced and are shown by M&V, but direct causation is difficult to prove. In this case the host can rightly claim that the energy service company should not benefit from this action and this can lead to contractual disputes. Several shared savings contracts have foundered on this type of issue.

This problem reflects a fundamental fact about energy use: it is intimately tied into the mainstream activity of the user, whether it be an individual's lifestyle at home, the usage patterns of a building by a tenant or owner, or the production of beer, widgets or iron and steel. Generally in industry, the more energy intensive the process the harder it is to implement a shared savings type contract, as energy use is so determined by the process factors. The exceptions to this are investments that can be easily ring-fenced, for instance a Combined Heat and Power plant, a Waste Heat to Power plant or a waste-fuelled boiler. Even in buildings, the same principle applies: where energy use is intimately tied to a host's core activity, e.g. lighting in retailing, where colour rendition and perceived warmth of lighting can directly drive sales of vegetables for instance, shared savings contracts of any kind become more difficult to develop and implement.

## TOO GOOD TO BE TRUE

Shared savings contracts also suffer from issues which arise due to cultural factors. They can sometimes appear to be 'too good to be true'. This perception can inhibit their uptake, and is probably more of a factor in the UK than, for instance, in the USA. Another important barrier to ESCO activity is job protection on the part of incumbent energy managers or energy engineers, who naturally enough feel that they have done as much as they can and feel threatened by the arrival of an ESCO trumpeting the high level of savings it can achieve. Diplomatic engagement with the incumbent energy staff is an important skill for all ESCO sales and technical development teams.

## LONG CONTRACT DURATION

Fundamentally, shared savings contracts are usually long-lived in order to recover the investments made. Contracts typically vary between 7 and 15 years, but with some extending to 25 years or beyond. Many organizations are reluctant to sign long-term commitments of any kind and even when they do the contracts have to be able to survive many changes of management and circumstances.

## PROJECT UNDER-PERFORMANCE

Another risk is that energy efficiency projects may not perform as expected. They can be late, which affects returns, not work at all, or at least not produce the level of savings intended. These technical performance risks can be mitigated by using appropriate, proven technologies, appropriately experienced contractors and contract forms where the performance risk is passed to the contractor.

## CHANGES IN INTERNATIONAL ACCOUNTING STANDARDS

Finally, changes in international accounting standards – and harmonization of accounting standards between International Financial Reporting Standards (IFRS) and US Generally Accepted Accounting Principles (GAAP) – are making off-balance-sheet solutions and leasing types of solution more difficult to achieve. These changes have flowed from the Enron bankruptcy and other accounting scandals, and are now having an effect on the energy efficiency financing market. For many years some companies have offered leases for energy efficiency equipment, but leases will probably have to be recognized on the clients' balance sheets in future. In the public sector, accounting issues are further complicated by different standards and accounting practices in the health sector, local authorities, universities and central government departments.

## Contract Forms

### THE ENERGY PERFORMANCE CONTRACT

The most common and successfully implemented of the shared savings concepts has been the ESCO/EPC model which first developed in the USA in the 1980s and has been widely used in the US public sector at state and federal levels.

This model is described by the US Department of Energy as 'the use of guaranteed savings from the maintenance and operations budget (utilities) as capital to make needed upgrades and modernizations to your building environmental systems, financed over a specified period of time'. In this model the contractor or ESCO guarantees that the savings (avoided costs), including both utility and operations expenses, will meet or exceed the annual payments to cover all project costs over an agreed debt service period, or the ESCO pays the difference. This is the performance guarantee that gives EPCs their name.

Most often this model has relied on the client taking debt onto its balance sheet i.e. borrowing money. In the USA, 75–80 per cent of the EPC market is in the Municipalities, Universities, Schools and Hospitals (MUSH) market, i.e. the public sector. This market in the USA is characterized by its ability to raise cheap debt by issuing 'muni bonds', a form of tax-efficient debt in which the lender does not pay federal or state tax on the interest received which does not have an equivalent in many other countries. The muni-bond market is worth approximately $2.8 trillion (i.e. there is circa $2.8 trillion in outstanding bonds at any time) and, despite widely reported concerns about the financial health of some cities and districts, the sector as a whole appears to have been resilient, with defaults actually falling in the recession.

The ESCO/EPC model has been discussed at length over many years, but has never really achieved its full potential. Part of the problem can be traced back to the extensive and effective promotion of the EPC concept around the world, financed in part by the US government through agencies such as USAID throughout the 1990s. In the early 1990s there was a big promotion of the ESCO/EPC concept through trade missions to Eastern Europe, the former Soviet Union, Asia and Latin America, in which large US ESCOs visited the countries, trained people in the concept, and identified (and in some cases implemented) pilot projects. International Finance Institutions (IFIs) such as the World Bank, the Asian Development Bank (ADB) and the European Bank of Reconstruction and Development (EBRD) also promoted ESCOs/EPCs with varying degrees of success. The IFIs have been better at addressing the whole problem by arranging for debt facilities and capacity-building measures in financial institutions, but in most cases the original promotion of the concept by the USA only focused on ESCOs and the contract form – effectively only providing two parts of the three basic ingredients and neglecting the all-important source of funds. An ESCO sector and the EPC contract are only two thirds of the required equation; without access to appropriate levels of the right kind of funding, the market cannot develop its potential.

It is possible, of course, that the ESCO offering an EPC finances the project from its own balance sheet, either through debt or equity. Even for the largest ESCOs, however, there are only limited possibilities for doing this due to balance sheet constraints, and in recent years many of the large ESCOs have been trying to raise external finance to get existing and new EPC contracts off their balance sheet. For growing ESCOs, as projects are won the investment requirements increase and hence there is a constant need to raise capital. Some ESCOs will finance projects up until practical completion and acceptance by the client and then seek to refinance them. There is much reference to boosting ESCO balance sheets in developing markets but this often seems to be based on the assumption that ESCOs will finance projects themselves. As developers of projects ESCOs do not inherently need big balance sheets, although if they move into project construction, or provide performance guarantees they do require more capital unless these risks can be passed onto others such as insurance companies. The problem of financing projects should be separated from the problem of financing the ESCOs.

## ENERGY SAVINGS PERFORMANCE CONTRACT

The ESPC is essentially the same as an EPC. The term is often used in connection with US federal and state government contracts, particularly under the 'Super-ESPC' contracts. These umbrella contracts, put into place and supported by the US Department of Energy Federal Energy Management Program (FEMP) come in two varieties:

- A regional Super-ESPC covers a wide variety of energy efficiency equipment;

- A technology-specific Super-ESPC only covers one of three particular technologies: biomass and alternative biomethane fuels (BAMF), geothermal heat pumps (GHP) or solar photovoltaics (PV).

The use of the super-ESPC contract form allows federal agencies to bypass the normally cumbersome procurement processes and contract directly with an ESCO. FEMP has already taken a number of ESCOs through the necessary federal government procurement processes and awarded framework contracts to them. This reduces the time needed and cost of developing a project, and the use of Super-ESPCs has largely replaced standalone ESPCs in the federal government estate.

A recent step in the evolution of ESPCs in the US federal government market is the introduction of the Net Zero Renovation Challenge by the General Services Administration (GSA). The Net Zero Renovation Challenge sets qualifying ESCOs the target of renovating projects to achieve net-zero energy use.

A European equivalent to Super-ESPCs would be procurement frameworks such as RE:FIT in London (RE:FIT 2013). RE:FIT was established by the Greater London Authority (GLA) using EU money from the European Local Energy Assistance (ELENA) programme and was initially designed to facilitate the uptake of EPC contracts in London public sector organizations. It built upon a pilot scheme in which 42 public sector buildings covering Transport for London, the Metropolitan Police Service and the London Fire and Emergency Planning

Authority, with a total floor area of 146,000 m², achieved average energy savings of 28 per cent. Total investment was £7 million with a seven-year payback period. After the pilot, RE:FIT developed a standardized EPC contract and a framework in which a number of ESCOs were included. The framework and ESCOs went through the legally required and bureaucratic public procurement process. RE:FIT provides front-end technical assistance to help public sector organizations through the process of developing and contracting EPC projects using the ELENA funds. To date, RE:FIT has completed more than 100 projects with a capital expenditure of £13 million and energy savings of £2.1 million, and it has a pipeline of more than 400 projects. In December 2012, RE:FIT announced a new framework contract with some contract changes and more flexibility over funding sources.

### Evaluation of ESPC programmes

Given the size of the ESPC market in the USA it is perhaps not surprising that most independent assessment of such contracts has been in the USA, although there has been work elsewhere. In the USA, the most authoritative assessments are probably the General Accountability Office's report (GAO 2005), with the excellent headline title *Energy Savings Performance Contracts Offer Benefits, but Vigilance Is Needed to Protect Government Interests*, and the Oak Ridge National Laboratory's report *Evaluation of the Super ESPC Program—Reported Energy and Cost Savings* (ORNL 2007a).

The GAO report, although generally positive about ESPCs, pointed out that in some cases between 1999 and 2003 it was not possible to ascertain if savings produced exceeded costs. This presumably reflects a failure to use proper M&V processes. The ORNL study reported that in 100 projects with sufficient information, guaranteed savings totalled $42.9 million and actual savings were $46.4 million, 108 per cent of the guaranteed level. In 91 projects estimated savings were $45.3 million, reported savings were $44.8 million and guaranteed savings were $41.4 million. A later random sample of 27 of these projects were re-evaluated using actual energy prices instead of contract prices and savings were found to be 111 per cent of projected savings. These numbers should give confidence in the ability of ESCOs to achieve their estimated savings and (naturally enough) exceed their guaranteed savings. Failure to exceed guaranteed savings would lead to a short business life for the ESCO, and of course ESCOs are incentivized to 'bid low' on guaranteed savings.

## STRUCTURAL PROBLEMS WITH THE EPC/ESPC MODEL AND EMERGING MODELS

The EPC/ESPC model has a number of problems, particularly in markets other than the MUSH market. The first issue with EPCs and ESPCs is that although they are promoted and understood to be 'shared savings' (and they do share savings), the real incentives acting on the ESCO are to maximize capital expenditure, as the ESCO makes a margin on capital. This often leads to a capital-expenditure-driven approach in which the net savings to the client are quite small, as opposed to a savings-driven approach where techniques such as retro-commissioning and even training and motivation programmes produce savings with little or no capital expenditure. Some ESCOs operating in the North American public sector have been making very good margins on capital expenditure, and when they have tried to transition to the private sector, particularly in the commercial office market, customers have demanded greater transparency and been unwilling to pay for those margins.

The traditional EPC approach also has a problem with the classic split incentive in commercial tenanted offices. The split-incentive problem is most often expressed as if the landlord is making the capital expenditure while the tenants get the benefit of reduced energy expenditure, but the same problem applies to EPCs. If the EPC produces savings for the tenants then somehow the repayments to the EPC investor need to be recovered from the tenant. Arranging this contractually, particularly in multi-tenanted buildings, is especially difficult and remains a barrier to applying the EPC contract form in this market. In the commercial building market many buildings are funded by mortgages, and covenants in these mortgages prevent building owners taking on more debt to finance energy efficiency projects. Furthermore, the guarantee from an ESCO does not actually enhance the credit rating of the building or owner. Other issues include the fact that existing long-term facilities management (FM) contracts are often in place, and layering an EPC contract on top of these adds to the already high transaction costs.

In recent years in the USA a number of providers have created variants of the Managed Energy Services Agreement (MESA or sometimes just ESA) which has a number of advantages over the EPC/ESPC, including enabling off-balance-sheet treatment for the client; creating a contract form that can be externally financed; ensuring that the risks are held by appropriate parties; the structure targets high cash yields over an eight to ten year period; the structure offers multiple methods of recourse and the investor retains ownership of assets.

Providers of ESA/MESA structures in the USA include Metrus, SCI energy, Green City Finance and Abundant Power Group, amongst others. A small number of UK providers are known to be working on the MESA contract form for the UK public sector and commercial office markets, and the contract form is gaining interest globally.

## Problems with Energy Efficiency from the Investor Perspective

Energy efficiency represents an interesting opportunity to some investors, notably those with an interest in sustainability or impact investing, and some property and infrastructure investors, but it also presents a number of problems. These include a lack of understanding of the processes, benefits and risks, and high transaction costs. In addition, small investment size compared to renewable energy, property or infrastructure projects can be an issue. To illustrate this, in the well-reported retrofit project in the Empire State Building, which was part of a $500 million refurbishment project, the incremental cost resulting from the energy efficiency projects was only $13 million, a level below that required by many institutional investors (Empire State Building n.d.). Even in the USA, where there have been some individual programmes at the level of tens of millions of dollars, they are still below the critical mass required to attract the large international banks into the market.

For investors, energy efficiency does not fit naturally into any particular asset allocation, e.g. property. Major institutional investors operate on agreed asset allocations and if something does not fit that allocation it is difficult to invest in. Also, the contract life presents problems for many investors. Banks are increasingly restricted by regulation, notably the Third Basel Accord (Basel III), from making long-term loans coincident with the tenors (durations) required by many energy efficiency projects (7 to 15 years).

Lack of standardization can also pose problems. To date, there has not been any standardization of M&V, assessment of projects or contract terms. Large-scale investment will only come with standardization, and this will be helped by developments such as the Environmental Defense Fund's Investor Confidence Project (ICP 2013).

Another problem for investors with energy efficiency projects is that there is as yet no secondary market and therefore any investment in energy efficiency is illiquid, i.e. the investor/lender cannot easily recover his or her money. Analysts are talking about developing a secondary market, possibly based on the bond market, but to date even in the USA the volume of transactions is too small for the bond market which operates at large scale. Bond markets also seek a high degree of standardization and will require some form of rating from the rating agencies. This will take time and much capacity building to acquire. In March 2013, a significant development for the secondary market occurred when the state of Pennsylvania Treasury sold 4,700 loans made through its Keystone Home Energy Loan Program (CDFA 2013).

In the USA in particular, but also in other markets, the major challenge now for energy efficiency financing programmes is to transition from publicly funded energy efficiency programmes (many of which were funded by the stimulus packages such as the American Recovery and Reinvestment Act of 2009) to privately funded schemes. In order for this to happen the problems listed above will need to be solved. Projects such as the Environmental Defense Fund's Investor Confidence Project are underway to agree standardized processes and build investor understanding and confidence in energy efficiency projects.

## Implementation of EPC Contracts and Other Outsourced Solutions

There is extensive literature on the process and problems of implementing contracts with ESCOs, particularly from the USA. In my previous book *Outsourcing of Energy Management* (Fawkes 2007) I stressed that any form of outsourcing, and any shared savings contract, whether it be an EPC, ESPC, ESA, MESA or any other contract form is effectively outsourcing, is a strategic decision that needs to be taken and supported at the most senior levels of the organization, and that successful outsourcing requires good planning as well as a clear process for dealing with the inevitable conflicts that will happen before, during and after contract signature.

## Barriers to Growth of Third-Party Finance Models

The barriers to the growth of the third party energy efficiency finance market are a combination of demand, i.e. lack of demand for financing energy efficiency, and supply, i.e. availability of finance. The lack of demand barrier, however, is decreasing in importance as end users increasingly recognize the need for energy efficiency investment to counter high prices and meet environmental objectives.

Evidence from talking to vendors of equipment and associated financial services, as well as numerous end users in the public and private sectors, suggest that there is growing interest in third-party-financed solutions, but in most sectors the number of completed transactions remains small compared to the potential market. There is a need to improve end-user understanding of the concept, as well as for ESCOs to sell cash flow to CFOs and CEOs rather than technology solutions to engineers, and there is undoubtedly still potential to develop new business models and new contract forms that appeal to new groups of customers and investors.

## Actual Risks and Returns from Efficiency Investments

Despite the risks described above, a body of evidence supports the view that energy efficiency is a relatively high return/low risk investment. Work by Aspen Systems Corp. and the US Environmental Protection Agency (Rickard et al. 1998) in 1998 demonstrated that energy efficiency projects exhibited a similar risk profile to US municipal and long-term bonds while showing higher returns. Of course, US municipal bonds are traditionally regarded as very low risk, but since the date of the study the risk profile of US municipal bonds has changed considerably due to the deterioration of state, county and city finances.

The Lawrence Berkeley National Laboratory in the US compiled a 15-year database of more than 3,500 energy efficiency projects – see, for example, Larsen et al. (2012) – and found that more than 85 per cent achieved better energy savings than the project developer originally predicted. A study of the performance of 102 'Super ESPC' projects in the Federal government estate by the Oak Ridge National Laboratory (referred to above) showed that the value of the actual cost savings was 108 per cent of projected savings (ORNL 2007b).

## Other Financing Models

### ON-BILL FINANCING

On-bill financing, the repayment of capital cost over an extended period through an addition on consumers' energy bills, started in the USA in the early 1980s with programmes introduced by Pacific Gas and Electric (PGE) and the Tennessee Valley Authority (TVA). PGE installed wall and attic insulation while the TVA programme installed insulation and wood stoves. The use of on-bill financing has grown both in terms of the number of programmes and the range of measures implemented. California and New York have now enacted legislation that mandates investor-owned utilities (IOUs – as opposed to community-owned utilities) to introduce on-bill financing schemes. This has the potential to increase the market by a factor of 10.

In the UK the Green Deal is on-bill financing with capital costs paid directly to the Green Deal Provider installing approved measures, with capital provided by financial institutions and collections carried out by the electricity suppliers. The debt incurred is tied to the electricity meter rather than the individual householder. (The Green Deal is described in more detail below.)

## PACE

Property Assessed Clean Energy financing (PACE) is a modification of an old approach to funding public goods. Benjamin Franklin invented the original concept in the 1700s to finance investment in public infrastructure such as sewers and the system is still commonly used to finance sewers and projects to put utility wires underground. PACE is a senior obligation which is on an equal footing with other local taxes on the house and therefore has precedence over any mortgage. It is tied to the house and not the owner or tenant.

It was first used for energy efficiency in California and the first schemes were operated in two very different Californian markets, Berkeley – which has a mild, wet climate and liberal politics – and Palm City – which has a hot, dry climate and conservative politics – and it was a success in both markets.

Despite its subsequent adoption in 28 states and Washington, DC, PACE in the residential market has been stopped by a controversial decision by the Federal Housing Finance Agency (FHFA) to limit its use in the residential sector. This decision is still being challenged. Several states are now starting to implement PACE schemes in the commercial sector and these hold great promise. The potential for commercial PACE is estimated at $2.5–7.5 billion annually in 2015, with a total opportunity of $88–180 billion in large commercial buildings alone.

## Publicly Funded Finance Schemes

In some circles the term 'energy efficiency financing' still implies public funding of efficiency projects and programmes – an assumption that we need to move away from. Over the years there have been examples of publicly funded schemes in many countries to promote efficiency and invest in efficiency projects, including funds to finance ESCO-developed Energy Performance Contracts. As well as government funded schemes there have been a number of schemes supported by international financial institutions (IFIs). The problem with any publicly funded scheme, of course, is that it is limited in budget, particularly in the current economic climate where government budgets everywhere are under pressure, and it is subject to changes of policy and/or government. We cannot massively scale up investment in energy efficiency by relying on public funds, we have to access the capital markets.

Experience of financing schemes around the world supported by organizations such as the EBRD suggests that there are some basic ingredients that are required but not always present:

- First, of course, is availability of long-term debt finance. This is best provided by local banks and therefore some capacity building within the banks is needed. They may also require some form of credit enhancement.

- There is a need for some form of technical assistance to help project hosts develop projects and move them through the process from concept to implementation.

- Some form of relatively easy procurement process, particularly in the public sector. This may be in the form of a framework contract with pre-approved ESCOs.

- Finally, there needs to be sufficient technical capacity within ESCOs or similar organizations to provide suitable technical assistance to project hosts.

The ideal design of scheme seems to be to use public funding or some sort of 'soft financing' to provide technical assistance, programme management, and private long-term debt finance to fund projects. The United Nations Development Programme (UNDP) Global Environment Facility (GEF) project in Romania is a good example of what can be achieved. The project achieved a multiplier effect of more than 25: $2m of UNDP GEF funds catalysed more than $50m of investing from local banks into energy efficiency projects (Velody 2006).

Given the pressure on government spending everywhere, the challenge to anybody concerned with designing finance schemes is to devise programmes that utilize private finance and are not dependent on public funding. In the US, we are now seeing a transition away from publicly funded schemes, many of which were supported by American Recovery and Reinvestment Act (ARRA) stimulus funding which is now drying up. We need to see that trend elsewhere as well.

## The United Kingdom's Green Deal

The UK Green Deal is probably the most ambitious energy efficiency financing scheme to date and has attracted global interest. It is aimed at the residential and small and medium enterprise (SME) market, and began operation in January 2013.

The Green Deal is an on-bill finance mechanism introduced as a centrepiece of the UK Coalition government's programmes on energy efficiency. It is aimed at the residential sector and was intended to be fully privately financed, with householders borrowing to pay for energy efficiency measures. The Green Deal operates under a 'Golden Rule' which is that the expected savings from carrying out the energy saving measures must exceed the repayments. Assessments of houses have to be carried out by accredited advisers and work has to be installed by accredited installers operating as Green Deal Providers. The scheme has an ambitious target of catalysing £14 billion of private finance over 10 years and, after a long process of design and legislation, it kicked off with some pilot programmes in late 2012. As well as the private finance, the scheme allows the use of ECO funds (Energy Company Obligation – the money that energy suppliers have to spend on energy efficiency as part of their licence condition), to be added to the private capital in cases where the returns do not satisfy the Golden Rule. It is planned that an additional £13 billion of ECO money will go towards the Green Deal. It is also envisaged that the scheme will create 65,000 new jobs.

The Green Deal was enabled by the Energy Act 2011, and a not-for-profit Green Deal Finance Company (GDFC) has been established with a wide range of members including energy suppliers such as British Gas and E.On, banks such as HSBC and Goldman Sachs, contractors such as Carillion and local authorities such as Newcastle City Council. It is envisaged that other Green Deal Providers will be able to join the GDFC and that membership should be open to both large and small suppliers.

Some local authorities, notably Birmingham City Council, are taking an innovative approach to the Green Deal. Birmingham is aiming to finance projects from public funding, warehouse them and then re-finance them.

At the time of writing it is not clear how successful the Green Deal will be as it faces issues including customer uptake; customer trust; technical viability; performance of technical measures; erosion of savings by increased comfort as well as by technical degradation or failures over the lifetime of the repayments.

Customer uptake, as in all residential energy efficiency programmes, may be a major problem. In the UK, some free-at-the-point-of-use schemes funded by utilities under their mandatory programmes, such as Carbon Emissions Reduction Target (CERT) and Community Energy Saving Programme (CESP) (now replaced by the Energy Company Obligation, ECO), have reported that even when free it is hard to get people to take up the offer. In some cases you literally cannot give improved energy efficiency away. Why this should be, particularly when there are problems of fuel poverty, and at a time when energy bills are generally rising and perceived to continue to rise in future, is a problem for behavioural scientists and marketing experts. Part of the problem is undoubtedly the hassle factor – having builders come into your house is generally regarded as a traumatic experience in many parts of the world. At the very least it can be a major disruption to everyday life and one which requires a significant upside to justify. The fact that improved energy efficiency is invisible, unlike a new extension, a new conservatory or a new kitchen, is also undoubtedly a major factor. It should always be remembered that the availability of financing solutions don't make consumers decide to buy a product, they only enable the purchase once a buying decision has been made.

Customer trust is also a major issue. In the UK, energy suppliers are amongst the least trusted brands. Energy suppliers are, perhaps rightly, regarded as having problems such as inaccurate billing, over-complex tariffs, and putting up prices when international fuel prices rise but not reducing them when the opposite occurs. They have a real issue building customer trust, particularly for complex projects that cross the meter and enter the customers' homes, and if energy suppliers are involved in schemes this can be a turn-off. Some people believe that the involvement of local authorities is essential as they are trusted more than commercial companies, but even public bodies may have trust issues.

Technical viability is still a big issue. Energy efficiency enthusiasts, the author included, tend to say that all the technology we need exists, and this is true in a general sense. However, once we start looking at large-scale retrofits, either in the residential or the commercial market, there are still areas where we need technological development. This is particularly true in insulation, which has been a traditional industry. In situations such as older buildings with solid walls, buildings which are protected in some way for cultural reasons, or in areas where a particular aesthetic is an essential part of the built environment, e.g. the Cotswolds, or cities such as Edinburgh or Cambridge, we don't yet have suitable technologies; materials like aerogels hold promise, although they are too expensive for general building applications.

Another aspect of technical viability concerns the modelling tools used to assess and evaluate technical measures. We need to ensure that these models are accurate if they are going to be used as the basis of financial deals or consumer lending. There have been reports that the models used in California for assessing residential energy saving have turned out to have a 20 per cent error.

One common effect when measures such as insulation and draught proofing are installed is that some of the projected savings are taken in the form of improved comfort. This is most pronounced in cases where the existing comfort conditions are poor, which is typical of households in fuel poverty, but even in 'normal' households there is often a noticeable improvement in comfort. Taking some benefits in the form of increased comfort can reduce energy savings below the estimate produced by building models.

The perceptions and expectations about savings are also likely to be critical in the Green Deal and similar schemes. This is particularly relevant to the Green Deal where the Golden Rule promises that *estimated* savings will be more than the repayments. Even if this is achieved, i.e. the measures perform exactly as predicted, increases in energy prices will lead to a situation where the total bill being paid by the consumer plus the repayment could exceed the old energy bill. Even though sophisticated consumers will recognize this, these schemes almost by definition include large numbers of consumers spanning all ranges of sophistication who will only see increased energy bills.

Another technical issue that has not been widely addressed is the degradation of savings over time as equipment performance degrades and ultimately fails. Over a financing term of 20 or 25 years it is likely that some technical measures will need to be replaced or repaired. This obviously eats into savings and reduces the benefits to the consumer.

## LESSONS FROM THE US MARKET

There are some very interesting lessons to be learnt from the US experience, even though any application of that experience needs to take into account local legislation, practices and culture. A major lesson is that there is no one-size-fits-all policy or programme. Different market segments buy energy efficiency in different ways and face different problems. These segments need a different approach to selling energy efficiency and accompanying finance. Small businesses buy differently than large businesses, and schools buy differently than food retailers or science laboratories. We definitely need to imbue the energy efficiency industry with better marketing skills.

A growing number of banks in the USA are now viewing energy efficiency loans as a low-risk product. They are certainly less risky than home equity release loans (second mortgages), as with these loans the bank has no control over what the money is used for. Consumers can take equity out of their homes and buy a new car, a new boat or fly to Las Vegas and bet the whole lot on black. With energy efficiency loans the money is not released until the energy efficiency measures have been installed and their proper installation and commissioning is independently verified. The consumer should then be better off, as savings exceed the repayments on the loan. Data on actual loan performance, i.e. the level of defaults, is hard to collect but there is a growing pool of data that shows the low-risk nature of these loans.

As mentioned above, the total size of energy efficiency funding is still relatively small, and most schemes are in the $20–50m range, but this suits small local banks and Community Development Finance Institutions in the US.

To further develop the finance market in the USA, and everywhere else, now requires standardization: standardization of contracts, standardization of M&V protocols, and standardization of project evaluation methods. Only when a high degree of standardization is achieved can low-cost finance such as bonds be put in place and a mass finance market developed. This process is being helped by projects such as the Environmental Defense Fund's Investor Confidence project.

## Conclusions

The potential for third-party energy efficiency project financing has been talked about for many years, but the market is still only at the early stages of an evolutionary process. Many schemes to date have relied on public funding, which is essentially unsustainable and will not be able to fill the need. Only by making investment into energy efficiency projects understandable, standardized and reliable can we unlock the required amounts of capital needed to achieve the large potentials for efficiency improvement we know to be there. There are very encouraging signs that the finance community is finally paying attention to the problem and this will help pull the market forward. The finance community and energy efficiency project developers need not only to speak to each other, but to evolve a common language – something that can be inherently difficult but which has happened in other related areas such as renewable energy financing over the last two decades. Over the next 5 to 10 years I expect to see a big growth in energy efficiency financing as more and more investors wake up to the opportunity and solutions to the various problems are identified and implemented. As the primary market grows in size we will also eventually see a secondary market – most likely in the form of bonds of some description. There is also considerable scope for growth of community, or peer-to-peer type financing enabled through on-line platforms.

## References and Bibliography

Adler, M. 2012. *Revolving Fund for Housing in Estonia*. [Online]. Available at: http://www.e3g.org/images/uploads/E3G_EEFinance_061112_M-Adler_(Estonia).pdf [accessed 28 January 2013].

Angell, C. 2009. *Addressing the Energy Efficiency Financing Challenge: The Role and Limitations of a Green Bank*. [Online]. Available at: http://web.law.columbia.edu/sites/default/files/microsites/climate-change/files/Publications/Students/Angell_AddressingtheEnergyEfficiencyFinanceChallenge.pdf [accessed 28 January 2013].

BASE and UNEP. 2006. *Public Finance Mechanisms to Increase Investment in Energy Efficiency*. [Online]. Available at: http://www.sefalliance.org/fileadmin/media/base/downloads/pfm_EE.pdf [accessed 28 January 2013].

Berger, S. 2011. *Energy Saving Partnership Berlin. Supporting ESCO Markets on a Regional Basis*. [Online]. Available at: http://www.seai.ie/News_Events/Previous_SEAI_events/Susanne%20Berger.pdf [accessed 28 January 2013].

Bleyl-Androschin, J.W. 2009. *Integrated Energy Contracting (IEC). A New ESCo Model to Combine Energy Efficiency and (Renewable) Supply in Large Buildings and Industry.* [Online]. Available at: http://www.ieadsm.org/Files/Tasks/Task%2016%20-%20Competitive%20Energy%20Services%20(Energy%20Contracting,%20ESCo%20Services)/Publications/091026_T16_Integrated%20Energy%20Contracting_GEA_Bleyl.pdf [accessed 28 April 2013].

Bloomberg. 2012. *Brazil May Invest $3 Billion in Energy Efficency as Loans Rise.* [Online]. Available at: http://www.bloomberg.com/news/2012-03-23/brazil-may-invest-3-billion-in-energy-efficiency-as-loans-rise.html [accessed 28 January 2013].

Bocskay, S. 2012. *Financing Your Retrofit.* [Online]. Available at: http://www.sustainablemelbournefund.com.au/sites/default/files/Financing_your_retrofit_25_July_2012.pdf [accessed 28 January 2013].

Borgeson, M., Zimring, M. and Goldman, C. 2012. *The Limits for Financing Energy Efficiency.* [Online]. Available at: http://eetd.lbl.gov/ea/emp/reports/limits-financing-ee-2012.pdf [accessed 28 January 2013].

Brown, M. 2008. *State Energy Efficiency Policies. Options and Lessons Learned. Brief #1. Funding Mechanisms for Energy Efficiency.* [Online]. Available at: http://ase.org/sites/default/files/file_Brief_1v3.pdf [accessed 28 January 2013].

Brown, M.H. and Braithwaite, H. 2011. *Energy Efficiency Finance: Options and Roles for Utilities.* [Online]. Available at: http://www.swenergy.org/publications/documents/Energy_Efficiency_Finance_Options_for_Utilities_Oct_2011.pdf [accessed 28 January 2013].

Bulgaria Housing Association. 2012. *Energy Saving Measures in Residential Buildings in Bulgaria.* [Online]. Available at: http://www.e3g.org/images/uploads/E3G_EEFinance_061112_E-Gaydarova_(Bulgaria).pdf [accessed 28 January 2013].

Buonicore, A.J., O'Neil, K.E. and Bailey, J. 2013. *Underwriting Energy Efficiency Financing in The Innovative Connecticut PACE Program.* [Online]. Available at: http://www.srmnetwork.com/wp-content/uploads/Whitepaper_CT_PACE_Final_01-15-13.pdf [accessed 28 January 2013].

California First. 2013. *Save Energy. Increase Cash Flow. Low-Cost, Long-Term Financing.* [Online]. Available at: https://californiafirst.org/overview [accessed 27 January 2013].

California Statewide Communities Development Authority. 2012. *Sustainable Energy Bond Program.* [Online]. Available at: http://www.cacommunities.org/fileadmin/hb/cscda/energy_finance_programs/CSCDA_FREE_Webinar__9-13-12.pdf [accessed 28 January 2013].

CDFA (2013). *The Pennsylvania Treasury Department Executes a Secondary Market Sale of Consumer Energy Loans.* [Online]. Available at: http://www.cdfa.net/cdfa/cdfaweb.nsf/ordredirect.html?open&id=bostonia-paHELP-casestudy.html [accessed 29 May 2013].

Clarkson, D. 2012. *Using Public and ARRA Funds to Leverage Private Capital to Finance Energy Efficiency Projects.* [Online]. Available at: http://www.eefinance.net/docs/EEFC%20Presentation--ACEEE--5-20-10.pdf [accessed 28 January 2013].

Clinton Climate Initiative. 2009. *Contracting Financing Options EPC Toolkit for Higher Education.* [Online]. Available at: http://www2.presidentsclimatecommitment.org/documents/ccitoolkit/Energy_Performance_Contracting_Financing_Options.pdf [accessed 28 January 2013].

Clinton Climate Initiative. 2011. *Policy Brief. Property Assessed Clean Energy (PACE) Financing: Update on Commercial Programs.* [Online]. Available at: http://eetd.lbl.gov/ea/ems/reports/pace-pb-032311.pdf [accessed 28 January 2013].

Copithorne, B. and Fine, J. 2011. *On-Bill Repayment: Unlocking the Energy Efficiency Puzzle in California.* [Online]. Available at: http://www.edf.org/sites/default/files/On-Bill%20Repayment-Unlocking-the-Energy-Efficiency-Puzzle-in-California.pdf [accessed 29 January 2013].

Cruceru, M., Voronca, M.M. and Palita, V. 2009. *Projects Financing in the Field of Rational Use of Energy.* [Online]. Available at: http://synenergy.teipir.gr/papers/I_2.pdf [accessed 28 January 2013].

Duenas, M. 2012. *Securing Finance for Energy Efficiency: EIB Experience and Strategic View.* [Online]. Available at: http://www.e3g.org/images/uploads/E3G_EEFinance_061112_M-Duenas_(EIB).pdf [accessed 28 January 2013].

Empire State Building. n.d. *The Empire State Building: Creating a Replicable Model for Energy Efficiency Reinvestment.* [Online]. Available at: http://www.esbnyc.com/documents/sustainability/presentations/ESB_London_converted_revised.pdf [accessed 27 April 2013].

Energy Policy Institute. 2010. *Energy Efficiency Financing Mechanisms.* [Online]. Available at: http://stuff.mit.edu/afs/athena/dept/cron/project/urban-sustainability/Energy%20Efficiency_Brendan%20McEwen/Financing%20Energy%20Efficiency/Energy%20Policy%20Institute-%202010-%20energy%20efficiency%20financing%20mechanisms%20may%202010.pdf [accessed 28 January 2013].

Energy Star. 2007. *Financing Guidebook for Energy Efficiency Program Sponsors.* [Online]. Available at: http://www.energystar.gov/ia/home_improvement/downloads/FinancingGuidebook.pdf [accessed 28 January 2013].

Farrell, D. and Remes, J. 2008. 'How the World Should Invest in Energy Efficiency', *The McKinsey Quarterly*, July 2008. [Online]. Available at: http://besustainable.pbworks.com/f/McKinsey+Quarterly_How+the+world+should+invest+in+energy+efficiency.pdf [accessed 28 April 2013].

Fawkes, S. 2007. *Outsourcing Energy Management*. Aldershot, Gower Publishing.

Freehling, J. 2011. *Energy Efficiency Finance 101: Understanding the Marketplace*. [Online]. Available at: http://aceee.org/files/pdf/white-paper/Energy%20Efficiency%20Finance%20Overview.pdf [accessed 28 January 2013].

GAO. 2005. *Energy Savings: Performance Contracts Offer Benefits, But Vigilance Is Needed to Protect Government Interests*. [Online]. Available at: http://www.gao.gov/assets/250/246803.pdf [accessed 27 January 2013].

GEA. 2012. *Global Energy Assessment – Toward a Sustainable Future*. Cambridge UK and New York NY, Cambridge University Press,and the International Institute for Applied Systems Analysis, Laxenburg, Austria.

Gerdes, J. 2012. 'San Francisco Announces Biggest Commercial Clean Energy PACE Retrofit'. *Forbes*. [Online]. Available at: http://www.forbes.com/sites/justingerdes/2012/11/19/san-francisco-announces-biggest-commercial-clean-energy-pace-retrofit/ [accessed 27 January 2013].

Ghekier, L. 2012. *ERDF as a Lever to Mobilise Co-Financing*. [Online]. Available at: http://www.e3g.org/images/uploads/E3G_EEFinance_061112_L-Ghekiere_(France).pdf [accessed 28 January 2013].

Hayes, S., Nadel, S., Granda, C. and Hottel, K. 2011. *What Have We Learned From Energy Efficiency Financing Programs?* [Online]. Available at: http://aceee.org/research-report/u115 [accessed 28 January 2013].

ICP. 2013. *Investor Confidence Project*. [Online]. Available at: www.eeperformance.org [accessed 28 April 2013].

IFC. 2011. *IFC Energy Service Company Market Analysis*. [Online]. Available at: http://www1.ifc.org/wps/wcm/connect/dbaaf8804aabab1c978dd79e0dc67fc6/IFC+EE+ESCOS+Market+Analysis.pdf?MOD=AJPERES [accessed 29 January 2013].

International Energy Agency. 2011. *Joint Public–Private Approaches for Energy Efficiency Finance*. [Online]. Available at: http://www.iea.org/publications/freepublications/publication/finance-1.pdf [accessed 28 January 2013].

International Energy Agency. 2012a. *Plugging the Energy Efficiency Gap with Climate Finance*. [Online]. Available at: http://www.iea.org/publications/freepublications/publication/PluggingEnergyEfficiencyGapwithClimateFinance_WEB.pdf [accessed 28 January 2013].

International Energy Agency. 2012b. *The Future of Energy Efficiency Finance*. [Online]. Available at: http://www.iea.org/media/workshops/2012/energyefficiencyfinance/workshop_report.pdf [accessed 28 January 2013].

Jollands, N. 2012. *Sustainable Energy Finance Facilities in the Residential Sector*. [Online]. Available at: http://www.e3g.org/images/uploads/E3G_EEFinance_061112_N-Jollands_(EBRD).pdf [accessed 28 January 2013].

Kapur, N., Hiller, J., Abramson, A. and Langdon, R. 2011. *Show Me the Money. Energy Efficiency Financing Barriers and Opportunities*. [Online]. Available at: http://nicholasinstitute.duke.edu/climate/other/show-me-the-money-energy-efficiency-financing-barriers-and-opportunities [accessed 28 January 2013].

Kim, C., O'Connor, R., Bodden, K., Hochman, S., Liang, W., Pauker, S. and Zimmermann, S. 2012. *Innovations and Opportunities in Energy Efficiency Finance*. [Online]. Available at: http://www.wsgr.com/publications/PDFSearch/WSGR-EE-Finance-White-Paper.pdf [accessed 28 January 2013].

Kirkpatrick, A.J. 2012. *Closing the 'Energy-Efficiency Gap': An Empirical Analysis of Property Assessed Clean Energy*. [Online]. Available at: http://pacenow.org/wp-content/uploads/2012/08/Kirkpatrick_PACE_MP.pdf [accessed 28 January 2013].

Kuma, S. 2010. *Promoting Innovative Energy Efficiency Financing Mechanisms*. [Online]. Available at: http://asiaesco.org/pdf/presentation/6-2.pdf [accessed 29 January 2013].

Larsen, P., Goldman, C. and Satchwell, A. 2012. *Evolution of the U.S. Energy Service Company Industry: Market Size and Project Performance from 1990–2008*. LBNL-5447-E, July. [Online]. Available at: http://emp.lbl.gov/sites/all/files/lbnl-5447e.pdf [accessed 27 April 2013].

MacLean, J. 2008. *Mainstreaming Environmental Finance Markets (I) – Small-Scale Energy Efficiency and Renewable Energy Finance*. [Online]. Available at: http://www.eefinance.net/images/MacLean%20KfW%20Paper%20on%20EE-RE%20Finance%20Final%20Nov%2021.pdf [accessed 28 April 2013].

McCaffree, M. 2010. *Alternative Financing Mechanisms for Energy Efficiency*. [Online]. Available at: http://www.edisonfoundation.net/IEE/Documents/IEE_AltFinancingMech_McCaffree.pdf [accessed 28 January 2013].

Miliken Institute. 2009. *PACE Finance: Innovative Funding to Accelerate the Retrofitting of America's Buildings for Energy Independence*. [Online]. Available at: http://www.milkeninstitute.org/presentations/slides/GC09_PACE.pdf [accessed 28 January 2013].

Miliken Institute. 2010. *Financing the Residential Retrofit Revolution*. [Online]. Available at: http://www.milkeninstitute.org/pdf/FILab_Res_Retrofit_April_20.pdf [accessed 28 January 2013].

Nakagami, H. 2010. *Recent Activity of the ESCO Industry in Japan and Asian Countries*. [Online]. Available at: http://www.asiaesco.org/pdf/presentation/3-1.pdf [accessed 28 January 2013].

National Governors Association. 2011. *State Clean Energy Financing Guidebook.* [Online]. Available at: http://www.nga.org/files/live/sites/NGA/files/pdf/1101CLEANENERGYFINANCING.PDF [accessed 28 January 2013].

Neme, C., Gottstein, M. and Hamilton, B. 2011. *Residential Efficiency Retrofits: A Roadmap for the Future.* [Online]. Available at: http://www.raponline.org/search/document-library/?keyword=918&submit=Submit&publish_date_preset=&publish_date_start=&publish_date_end=&document_type_id=&sort=publish_date&order=desc&CommunityId=15636 [accessed 28 January 2013].

ORNL. 2007a. *Evaluation of the Super ESPC Program – Reported Energy and Cost Savings.* [Online]. Available at: http://www.ornl.gov/sci/femp/pdfs/200705_interim_report.pdf [accessed 27 April 2013].

ORNL. 2007b. *Evaluation of the Super ESPC Program – Level 2 – Recalculated Cost Savings.* [Online]. Available at: http://info.ornl.gov/sites/publications/files/Pub6386.pdf [accessed 27 January 2013].

PACENow. 2013. *What is PACE?* [Online]. Available at: http://pacenow.org/about-pace/what-is-pace/ [accessed 27 January 2013].

Palmer, K., Wells, M. and Gerarden, E. 2012. *An Assessment of Energy-Efficiency Financing Programs.* [Online]. Available at: http://www.rff.org/RFF/Documents/RFF-Rpt-Palmeretal%20EEFinancing.pdf [accessed 28 January 2013].

Peretz, N. 2009. *Growing the Energy Efficiency Market Through Third-Party Financing.* [Online]. Available at: http://www.felj.org/docs/elj302/15growing-the-energy-efficiency-market091020.pdf [accessed 28 January 2013].

Planning Commission, Government of India. 2008. *Eleventh Five Year Plan (2007–2012).* [Online]. Available at: http://planningcommission.nic.in/plans/planrel/fiveyr/11th/11_v1/11th_vol1.pdf [accessed 29 January 2013].

Planning Commission, Government of India. 2011. *Faster, Sustainable and More Inclusive Growth. An Approach to the Twelfth Five Year Plan.* [Online]. Available at: http://planningcommission.nic.in/plans/planrel/12appdrft/approach_12plan.pdf [accessed 29 January 2013].

PWC. 2011. *Financing Mechanism for Energy Efficiency Projects and Programmes.* [Online]. Available at: http://www.iea.org/media/workshops/2011/ipeecweact/Kumar.pdf [accessed 28 January 2013].

RE:FIT. 2013. *RE:FIT.* [Online]. Available at: http://www.refit.org.uk [accessed 28 April 2013].

Rezessy, S. and Beroldi, P. 2010. *Financing Energy Efficiency: Forging the Link Between Financing and Project Implementation.* [Online]. Available at: http://ec.europa.eu/energy/efficiency/doc/financing_energy_efficiency.pdf [accessed 28 January 2013].

Rickard, S., Hardy, B., Von Neida, B. and Mihlmester, P. 1998. *The Investment Risk in Whole Building Energy-Efficiency Upgrade Projects.* [Online]. Available at: http://gaia.lbl.gov/federal-espc/working-groups/SavingsVerification/The-Investment-Risk-in-Whole-Building-Energy-Efficiency-Upgrades.pdf [accessed 27 January 2013].

Savage, M. and Blyth, W. 2011. *Financing Energy Efficiency: A Strategy for Reducing Lending Risk.* [Online]. Available at: http://www.chathamhouse.org/sites/default/files/19462_0511pp_blythsavage.pdf [accessed 28 January 2013].

Schlein, B. 2009. *Citi Energy Efficiency Finance Initiative: An Integrated Approach.* [Online]. Available at: http://www.c2es.org/docUploads/July14_Schlein_Citi.pdf [accessed 28 January 2013].

Taylor, P.T., Govindrarajalu, C., Levin, J., Meyer, A.S. and Ward, W.A. 2008. *Financing Energy Efficiency. Lessons from Brazil, China, India and Beyond.* [Online]. Available at: http://3countryee.org/FinancingEnergyEfficiency_Lessons.pdf [accessed 28 January 2013].

UNEP and Bloomberg New Energy Finance. 2012. *Global Trends in Renewable Energy Investment 2012.* [Online]. Available at: http://fs-unep-centre.org/sites/default/files/publications/globaltrendsreport2012final.pdf [accessed 27 January 2013].

United Nations Environment Programme. 2009. *Energy Efficiency and the Finance Sector.* [Online]. Available at: http://www.unepfi.org/fileadmin/documents/Energy_Efficiency.pdf [accessed 28 January 2013].

United States Department of Energy. 2012. *Commercial Property Assessed Clean Energy (PACE) Primer.* [Online]. Available at: http://www1.eere.energy.gov/wip/pdfs/commercial_pace_primer_revised.pdf [accessed 28 January 2013].

USAID. 2009. *Innovative Approaches to Financing Energy Efficiency in Asia.* [Online]. Available at: http://pdf.usaid.gov/pdf_docs/PNADR150.pdf [accessed 28 January 2013].

Velody, M. 2006. *Energy Efficiency – Releasing the Investment Potential.* [Online]. Available at: http://www.ecologic-events.de/climate2012/sofia/documents/8_mark_velody.pdf [accessed 28 January 2013].

White, P. 2010. *An Awakening in Energy Efficiency: Financing Private Sector Building Retrofits.* [Online]. Available at: http://www.johnsoncontrols.com/content/dam/WWW/jci/be/solutions_for_your/private_sector/Financing_PrivateSector_whitepaper_FINAL.pdf [accessed 28 January 2013].

Wilson, K., Spoonhour, B. and Alvarez, M.C. 2011. *Property Assessed Clean Energy (PACE) and the New Normal.* [Online]. Available at: http://growthandinfrastructure.org/proceedings/2011_proceedings/wilson_pace.pdf [accessed 28 January 2013].

World Bank Independent Evaluation Group. 2010. *Assessing the Impact of IFC's China Utility-Based Energy Efficiency Finance Program.* [Online]. Available at: http://ieg.worldbankgroup.org/content/dam/ieg/pubs/CHUEEWebBook.pdf [accessed 29 January 2013].

World Economic Forum. 2011. *A Profitable and Resource Efficient Future: Catalysing Retrofit Finance and Investing in Commercial Real Estate.* [Online]. Available at: http://www3.weforum.org/docs/WEF_IU_CatalysingRetrofitFinanceInvestingCommercialRealEstate_Report_2011.pdf [accessed 28 January 2013].

Xin, L. 2010. *China's Experience of Financing in Energy Efficiency.* [Online]. Available at: http://www.unece.org/fileadmin/DAM/energy/se/pp/eneff/Astana_EEForum_Sep2010/d1s2_2_LiuXin.pdf [accessed 28 January 2013].

# 11

# Energy Efficiency Policies

*Policy making is the process by which governments translate their political vision into programmes and actions to deliver 'outcomes', desired changes in the real world.*

Modernising Government,
UK Government White Paper 1999

## Introduction

The extent to which energy efficiency policy exists, the level of commitment to that policy, and the emphasis and balance of the policy, naturally varies widely between countries, dependent on their specific energy situation, state of development, geopolitical issues and the government's view of the future scenarios and risks it is facing.

My view, of course, is that energy efficiency policy should be given a higher priority than it generally has at present at national, regional and local levels in all countries. However, within energy efficiency policy there will always be differing degrees of emphasis. For instance, in an emerging economy such as India, where 70 per cent of the buildings needed in 2050 have not yet been built, an emphasis on ensuring that new buildings are highly efficient will have a greater effect on long-term energy use than measures to improve efficiency of existing buildings. In a developed economy such as the UK, more emphasis on improving existing buildings is needed as most of the buildings which will be in use in 2050 already exist.

In this chapter we will explore:

- what the objectives of energy efficiency policy should be;

- the range of policy levers that governments can control;

- how the effectiveness of energy policy should be measured;

- the two elephants in the room of fossil fuel subsidies and how to bring energy efficiency into the electricity market;

- specific policy examples from different countries, regions and communities;

- a holistic model of energy efficiency policy.

## Why Have an Energy Efficiency Policy?

The justifications for an energy efficiency policy flow from the stresses and strains on the global energy system we discussed in Chapter 2, as well as country- and region-specific energy problems. To recap, these problems are the threat of resource depletion; energy security; ageing energy infrastructure (in developed economies); the need to rapidly expand energy supply infrastructure (in emerging economies); the economic costs of importing energy; the threat of climate change; the pollution and resulting health effects related to energy use; fuel poverty in developed economies and the associated health effects; fuel poverty in developing countries (i.e. the 1.3 billion people without access to electricity); and the safety and public acceptance of nuclear power.

An energy efficiency policy is a response to the various energy risks facing governments (national, regional or local). These include the risk that energy supplies are disrupted, which will cause economic disruption and possibly social unrest; the risk that some of the population is unable to pay its energy bills, which leads to social problems; the risk of climate change; the risk of energy-intensive companies moving out of the country if energy prices are too high; and, in developing countries, the risk of wasted brainpower and talent that occurs due to an absence of commercial energy. As well as the direct opportunity costs from the educational impact there is the risk of poorly educated youth being engaged by extremists.

As we saw in Chapter 3, accelerating the adoption of energy efficiency, although it cannot remove them entirely, can help to mitigate all these risks.

Policy is essentially about choosing a preferred future from various scenarios. In the energy arena we can continue to ignore or neglect energy efficiency and end up in a high-energy-using future with increased stress on energy infrastructure, energy supplies, energy security and the environment – or we can choose a more efficient future where these stresses are lower than they would otherwise have been.

## The Difficulties of Energy Efficiency for Policy Makers

Advocates of improving energy efficiency policy have to first acknowledge the many difficulties that energy efficiency presents for policy makers. First, there is the fact that capacity, i.e. human capacity of understanding and know-how around energy efficiency amongst politicians and civil servants is limited compared to the capacity around the energy supply sector. Energy supply is more familiar and inherently easier to understand. Secondly, energy efficiency still has an association with conservation or getting by on less, which is not a popular political message, even if it is not entirely without merit. Next, energy efficiency is invisible, the result is less of something, and energy efficiency hardware is not photogenic and rarely (if ever) suitable as a backdrop for a political photo opportunity. This can be demonstrated by searching for 'energy efficiency' in one of the online photo libraries. The results either show a low-energy light bulb, a box of some description, or some abstract symbol. Wind turbines, solar panels or even nuclear power stations are far more photogenic. This illustrates what I refer to as 'the ribbon problem': energy efficiency projects rarely present photogenic ribbon-cutting opportunities for politicians.

The next problem is the small size, and hence budget, of traditional energy efficiency projects and programmes. Politicians are, even more so these days after the global financial crisis and trillion-dollar stimulus packages and deficits, used to dealing with large budgets, and energy efficiency usually isn't a 'big ticket' item. This does not mean that the potential benefits are not huge, it is just that traditionally energy efficiency is about many small projects. An additional dimension to the problem is that the energy efficiency industry, which in itself is hard to define, is fragmented, with many different types of company and many small to medium firms that lack the lobbying power of large energy suppliers. They also often lack a common voice, with each firm pushing their own technology or preferred solution rather than a holistic approach. Trade associations and groups of stakeholders can play a part to improve this situation.

Another problem is that the benefits have been hard to measure. There is no excuse for poor measurement and verification of energy use these days, with a combination of protocols such as IPMVP and low-cost smart meters and software. The other aspect of this problem, as we saw in Chapter 4, is that the many and varied benefits of energy efficiency fall outside the immediate system boundary of the decision maker, making them hard to measure and even harder to capture value. The benefits from improved energy efficiency cut across system and organizational boundaries. Agreeing on interdepartmental issues is difficult for most (all?) governments, and a minister for energy is unlikely to get much credit for intervening in the area of responsibility of another department of state.

Another issue is the lack of disaggregated data on important questions, such as what is the real energy consumption of different types of housing (as opposed to theoretical consumption)? What is the real make-up of the housing stock? What do people spend on energy? And so on. A final issue is that the level of understanding on energy efficiency behavioural change is low.

These are the problems that policy makers, and influencers, who want to improve energy efficiency policies face in all countries.

## The Foundations of Energy Efficiency Policy and Engaging Policy Makers

When looking at energy efficiency policy we need to think through how to improve the quality of policy thinking and practice. The evidence from several examples, notably Singapore, over many years, is that a long-term and systematic approach to energy policy is necessary – this seems natural considering that energy infrastructure is by its very nature long term and systematic. This is essentially the technocratic approach which has worked so well in many policy areas in Singapore for many years but may not, however, sit comfortably with short-term political requirements, the 24-hour news cycle and public demand for engagement. A long-term view is the first essential starting point at all levels, from local through to national and supra-national levels.

The second essential building block of energy efficiency policy, and perhaps of policy in all areas nowadays, is a solid understanding of consumer (including industrial and commercial consumer) behaviour and the ability to apply the latest ideas in behavioural change along with the often missing ingredient of emotional connection. Agents of change inside government must understand consumers' beliefs and the habits that guide their actions, as well as work with outside partners who know how to change behaviour by creating a collective spirit and changing the social norm. This understanding is only now beginning to emerge through a combination of academic research and practical projects.

In many parts of the world these two essential elements currently sit in a miasma of distrust and disengagement which manifests itself in different ways. In India we see protests by fishermen against the commissioning of a new nuclear power station that has delayed its start up. In Europe, following the financial crisis, there is deep distrust of companies in the banking and energy sectors, as well as distrust of government and general voter apathy. Any energy policy, and the policy formation process itself, should seek to engage with the public and address this distrust and disengagement.

An important question is, if you do not have this level of high-quality policy making in a country or region, how do you achieve it? Often, policy makers only act when there is a crisis, but energy is a subject where avoiding crises is very important. Even a few hours without electricity carries huge economic and social costs, and longer disruptions will cause a major crisis in all countries.

In a similar way to the discussion in Chapter 6 on management, there is the issue of how to change policy makers' actions in ways other than relying on a crisis. One approach that seems to work well is to reframe the debate to focus on the economy and job creation potential instead of energy and the environment, which remains abstract for most people. One example of this is given by an energy strategy study on a US city which owned its own utility and relied on an old coal fired plant, close to the end of its life, which needed to be replaced at an estimated cost of several hundred million dollars. Rather than just procuring a new plant, the city council was enlightened enough to commission a far-reaching energy study that identified the baseline energy situation and financial flows across the city and then looked forward over a 25-year period under a number of scenarios: business as usual, varying levels of energy efficiency investment, energy efficiency plus renewables, and developing a multi-utility-services model. The partners in the study framed the results in a way that would engage the policy makers and the widest range of stakeholders – thereby addressing their concerns about the amount of value kept in the community. Explicitly stating the amount of money that was going up the chimneys of the power station (tens of millions of dollars per year) and how much money was leaving the community to pay for coal, much of which was imported from out of the country, was the key to getting engagement to make a policy decision and implement it. This approach provided a common cause for all stakeholders whereas other issues such as climate change would have divided people and made effective action more difficult.

## The Two Large Elephants in the Room

When addressing energy efficiency policy there are two very large elephants in the room that are often ignored and which very few countries have even begun to get to grips with: fossil-fuel subsidies and bringing energy efficiency into the electricity system.

### ELEPHANT NUMBER ONE – FOSSIL-FUEL SUBSIDIES

Any country or region that really wants to address energy efficiency policy fully needs to address the big issue of fuel and electricity subsidies. In many, or even all, countries the fuel and electricity industries benefit from subsidies of different kinds to varying degrees, whether it be direct payments to suppliers or tax breaks or price-support mechanisms for consumers. This reflects the close links between energy use and social and economic objectives. The fossil fuel industry in particular has benefited from subsidies for many decades and throughout its history nuclear power has always received direct and indirect subsidies.

The Global Subsidies Initiative of the International Institute for Sustainable Development (IISD 2012) estimate that fossil-fuel subsidies are about $600 billion a year, with $100 billion going straight to suppliers. In 2009 the G20 countries, followed by more than 50 other countries, signed up to eliminate fossil-fuel subsidies. Since then, however, subsidies have risen to an estimated $775 billion in 2012, of which $630 billion are consumption subsidies in developing countries (Worldwatch Institute 2012). In comparison, renewable subsidies are estimated at $66 billion, although it is undoubtedly true that the energy gain per dollar of renewable subsidies is a lot less than for fossil-fuel subsidies.

There is no question that subsidizing fossil fuels encourages demand growth. However, in emerging economies fuel subsidies are very difficult to remove because for large parts of society, particularly low-income segments, they have become part of the economic background, have driven demand patterns and technology choice, and reduce the cost of living. An example is India, where diesel is subsidized and part of the rationale is that diesel-fuel usage is linked to food production. Sudden removal could lead to mass social unrest, as happened in November 2012 in Jordan, a country that imports 96 per cent of its energy and is dependent on imported Egyptian gas. The Jordanian government's aim in making changes was to reduce the overall government deficit by increasing fuel prices (diesel by 33 per cent, cooking gas by 50 per cent and transport fuel by 15 per cent) and there was some redirection of subsidies so that the lower-income groups would receive cash payments. The moves were met by several days of riots and previously unheard-of calls to bring down King Abdullah. This is an example of the problems for all governments making energy decisions that are painful in the short term but make sense in the medium and long term.

## ELEPHANT NUMBER TWO – BRINGING ENERGY EFFICIENCY INTO THE ELECTRICITY SYSTEM

Another important intersection of policy areas is the very clear link between energy efficiency policy and electricity supplier (utility) regulation. Electricity markets are highly regulated everywhere, and the traditional underlying world view behind electricity supply has been, and generally continues to be, that demand is an external uncontrollable factor and that it is necessary to build sufficient supply to meet increasing demand. This view leads to excess generation capacity being built, particularly to meet peak demands, which then operates at sub-optimal efficiency for long periods.

A growing body of evidence from around the world suggests that when the electricity market is incentivized to exploit energy efficiency, a large, fast and cost-effective resource is made available to the system and total costs are reduced. The hard question is how to actually introduce energy efficiency into the electricity market. PJM, the Independent System Operator in the north-east USA, has introduced a Forward Capacity Market which allows demand-side projects to bid into it and then be implemented (PJM 2009). Other possible mechanisms include some form of premium payment or Efficiency Feed-in Tariff (E-FiT) which would operate in a similar way to renewable FiTs. As well as designing the mechanics of any scheme, the other issue is overcoming the natural resistance of the electricity industry, which often wants to block these kinds of initiative and denigrates the demand-side resource.

Separating policies for electricity supply from those for energy demand perpetuates a long-term problem in policy making – that there is insufficient attention to investment in our energy infrastructure that takes into account the trade-offs between supply-side and demand-side investment.

## The Need for an Investment-Grade Energy Efficiency Policy

Groups representing very significant investors, including the European-based Institutional Investors Group on Climate Change (IIGCC), the North-American-based Investor Network on Climate Risk (INCR), and the Investor Group on Climate Change Australia/New Zealand (IGCC), along with the United Nations Environment Programme Finance Initiative (UNEP FI), reported in September 2011 on the need for, and essential design elements of, an investment grade climate policy (IIGCC-INCR-IGCC-UNEP 2011).

Energy efficiency has to be a key component of any efforts to mitigate climate change. Even where there is scepticism on climate change – or if the climate models turn out to be wrong – increased energy efficiency brings many benefits in terms of increased productivity and profitability; insulation from energy price volatility; job creation; increased comfort and reduced pollution. Therefore, adopting more aggressive energy efficiency policies should be an obvious choice, a 'no brainer' everywhere.

To meet the challenge and scale up energy efficiency we need to scale up three things: demand for energy efficiency, supply of energy efficiency goods and services, and the flow of finance into energy efficiency. Therefore, the fundamental aim of policy makers should be to create an investment-grade energy efficiency policy that works to increase the flow of investment at all levels.

One of the first principles of investment-grade policies has to be that there is a long-term target with short- and medium-term intermediary targets, and that the target stays in place over the long term.

The overall objective of energy efficiency policy should be to increase the historic rate of improvement of energy intensity. If we can increase the rate of reduction in energy intensity above the rate of economic growth, overall energy use will decline. As we have seen, energy intensity also depends on the structure of industry and this effect needs to be disentangled when considering progress on improving energy intensity. This fits with the view of the International Energy Agency (IEA) in its *2012 World Energy Outlook* (IEA 2012), which discusses a scenario of accelerated uptake of energy efficiency, the Efficient World Scenario, which can boost 'cumulative economic output through 2035 by $18 trillion – equivalent to the current size of the economies of the United States, Canada, Mexico and Chile combined'. This scenario also halves global growth in primary energy demand by 2035 relative to the IEA's New Policies Scenario, improves energy intensity at 2.6 times the rate of the last 25 years, and significantly reduces $CO_2$ emissions after 2020.

The objective of increasing the rate of improvement of energy intensity will be achieved by maximizing the uptake of economic energy efficiency opportunities and maximizing the rate of developing new opportunities through new technologies or techniques. In addition, the uptake of socially economic energy efficiency investments – which are sub-economic at the level of the individual decision maker – need to be encouraged.

## Measuring the Effects of Energy Efficiency Policy

As well as implementing appropriate energy efficiency policies, policy makers need to put in place appropriate and transparent measures of success for different levels of the economy. If it is not measured it can't and won't be managed.

At the highest level the measure will be energy intensity. Under the macro target of energy intensity we need to develop a whole range of indicators covering different sectors, sub-sectors and individual plants. The appropriate indicators would include:

- Country level: energy intensity (energy/GDP);

- Sector and sub-sectors: sectoral energy intensity (energy/GDP) and sectoral energy productivity (energy/unit of production);

- Individual plant productivity (energy/unit of production).

Government, working with the industrial sectors to get their engagement, needs to develop these indicators, based on combining economic and energy data that already exists, and report on them on a regular basis.

An additional indicator of overall progress on energy efficiency is the total investment in energy efficiency which, given the diversity of investment type and investor, raises the question of how to measure and collect this data. Different approaches are possible and, as with other long-term measurements, it is important to maintain consistency. Within each sector they can be used to gauge the success of sector-specific programmes.

Individual sectoral measures and programmes have to have specific measures of success that support the higher-level objectives. Suitable measures for programmes such as PACE in the USA or the Green Deal in the UK, in addition to energy saved, will include the number of houses insulated or energy-saving devices installed, market penetration and amount of capital deployed, and the number of jobs created. For programmes such as the Non-Domestic Energy Efficiency work of the UK Green Investment Bank, for instance, the amount of private capital invested in energy efficiency compared to the public capital used is an important measure of success. As previously discussed, any energy efficiency programme has to utilize robust measurement of energy savings based on protocols such as IPMVP. This should be a requirement for any projects utilizing public expenditure.

## A Note on Diverging Energy Policies Between the USA and Europe

When we compare and contrast the energy policies of the USA and Europe at the moment we see a very pronounced and crucial difference. Europe is set on a high-energy-price policy, with a heavy emphasis on expensive renewable technologies, driven by concerns over resource depletion and climate change, whereas the USA seems to be on a path of low energy prices based on an idea of energy abundance, mainly in the form of shale gas and unconventional oil, coupled with aggressive improvement in energy efficiency (at least in some states). Given the interactions between energy and the economy, which are probably much more important than most economists recognize, the next few years and decades will demonstrate which of these approaches is right. Of course both could be right as Europe and the USA face different circumstances but, if a low-energy-price economy drives innovation and economic growth more than a high-energy-price economy, we may see an increasing divergence of the two economies and increased internal strains within Europe.

## The Danger of Just Encouraging Low-Hanging Fruit

One of the most often-heard expressions around energy efficiency is 'low-hanging fruit', meaning easy, fast-return measures or projects. Stephen Chu, US Energy Secretary, once said energy efficiency was more about 'fruit lying on the floor' (EERE 2009). Although simple quick return measures, particularly those that are of an operational or 'good housekeeping' nature, should never be discouraged, there is a danger of energy efficiency policies focusing too much on the 'low-hanging fruit' if these measures are carried out in a piecemeal way without considering a wider systems view. The risk is threefold: first, that once these measures are implemented the host organizations stop looking at efficiency because they do not have an ongoing energy management programme; secondly, the danger that small individual measures are sub-optimal compared to a proper integrative design project; and thirdly that the opportunity for radical improvements is missed and that it may be many years (or decades) before a suitable renovation opportunity presents itself again.

## A Holistic View of Energy Efficiency Policy

The triple aims of scaling up demand for energy efficiency, supply of energy efficiency products and services, and flow of finance, require a focus on what innovation theory calls 'enabling conditions'. The enabling conditions have to be thought through and understood for each sector of the economy and for each segment of each sector. This requires a deep understanding of the segments, almost from a marketing perspective. Unlike all successful sales organizations (whether selling to consumers or business), energy efficiency actors in business and policy, as well as energy efficiency policy analysts and energy supply companies, generally do not truly understand market segmentation. We tend to stay at sector level, e.g. housing, non-domestic buildings, industry, transport.

For any segment, the enabling conditions will be a combination of things that are best addressed by government, regulations for example, and things that are best addressed by industry but which can be encouraged, catalysed or supported by the government.

If we take commercial property, a sub-sector of the building sector, as an example, we can start to think through what the enabling conditions are likely to be. The actual enabling conditions need to be worked out by government and industry working together, sector by sector and segment by segment. The following is a first pass at a set of possible enabling conditions for the commercial property market:

- Operating Energy Performance Certificates to provide transparency.

- Valuation mechanisms that recognize additional value from energy efficiency, assuming the data shows that is in fact true. (In the USA, it does seem that this proposition has been accepted by the valuation professionals and hence the property industry, whereas in the UK it remains controversial and unproven. If the industry says it is unproven then there needs to be a work programme for proving or disproving it, possibly supported by public money as well as private sector support.)

- Standardization of Measurement and Verification through adoption of the International Performance Measurement and Verification Protocol as a norm or requirement.

- All companies to adopt the ISO 50001 energy management standard or to ensure that their FM suppliers have it.

- Better, independently verified, data on the performance of relevant energy saving investments.

- Regulations that cover a) new build, b) retrofit, and c) renovation, the distinction between retrofit and renovation being that a retrofit is undertaken primarily for energy reasons; a renovation is primarily done for other reasons. A renovation represents a major opportunity to incorporate energy efficiency features very cost effectively, an opportunity that is still all too often being missed. The enforcement of such regulations needs to be improved; many buildings in many countries which purport to meet regulations or codes do not, as enforcement is poor.

- The split incentive between landlords and tenants. The well-known barrier in commercial property energy efficiency has to be addressed through different mechanisms such as Green Leases, but until a standard answer is developed and widely adopted by the industry, scale-up of energy efficiency retrofits will be inhibited.

- The standard clause in many, if not all, commercial leases that requires tenants to reinstate the building to how it was when they took on the lease also needs to be addressed. If a retrofit is to take place, the clause needs to be modified.

- Designers of buildings, architects and engineers, need to understand and apply holistic or integrative design techniques which have been proven to produce large and very cost-effective energy savings compared to conventional design techniques.

- Owners and specifiers of buildings need to understand and insist upon their design teams using integrative design techniques.

Energy efficiency policy needs to take a holistic approach designed to build capacity in demand for energy efficiency services and products, to build capacity for supply of energy efficiency services and products, and to build capacity for energy efficiency financing.

## A Framework for Policy – The Policy Levers

Many frameworks for thinking about the policy levers open to governments on energy efficiency have been published over the years.

Janssen (2008) identifies six policy options. These are:

1. Economic instruments;

2. Information programmes;

3. Financial incentives;

4. Regulations and standards;

5. Voluntary agreements;

6. Research, demonstration and development.

According to Jansen:

> *the choice of instrument depends on a variety of factors, including cost and ease of delivery; 'strength' and 'durability' of effectiveness in overcoming barriers and providing energy efficiency improvements in the short term and long term; public, political and administrative acceptability; and effectiveness in improving energy efficiency.*

## ECONOMIC INSTRUMENTS

Economic instruments cover pricing of energy, and taxes such as carbon taxes. Politicians often talk about using taxation to encourage or discourage socially desirable actions. Examples include using tax on cigarettes to reduce smoking. So-called 'green taxes' such as the UK Air Passenger Duty became popular during the period of booming interest in environmental matters from the mid 2000s. Whether such taxes are really effective or really motivated by green ambitions is highly debatable, but there is no doubt that the taxation system can be used to influence behaviour.

## INFORMATION PROGRAMMES

Information programmes cover the dissemination of information. In the 1970s and 1980s, following the oil crises, many governments initiated information programmes aimed at consumers and businesses. In the UK we had the 'Save It' advertising campaign. The effectiveness of simply providing information is now rightly questioned. We are bombarded with information about what we should and shouldn't do in relation to health and many other matters, but information by itself is not enough. In order to take effective action you need to know what to do – know-how – and have the motivation to do it. Building know-how means training in some form. Building motivation requires incentives and feedback and can also be added to by effective training. Work in Australia and elsewhere points to the importance of emotional connection to create motivation, and the results of making this emotional connection effectively are graphically illustrated by the success of water-saving campaigns in Victoria, Australia (Liubinas and Harrison 2012). Due to the threat of reservoir water running out, caused by many years of below average rainfall, Victoria implemented a highly successful programme based on a campaign that sought to make an emotional connection. In a programme that has a lot to teach energy efficiency professionals, water use per capita was reduced by 20 per cent.

A new aspect of information, enabled by information technology and 'big data' techniques is to make energy data available on an open data basis, as has been done in Chicago and New York (NYC Open Data 2013). Chicago recently held a 'hackathon' where developers competed to use the city's energy usage data, which has been released on a Census block basis, as well as 100 sustainability data sets, to come up with new solutions to the city's energy and sustainability challenges (Center for Neighborhood Technology 2013). This open and big data approach to improving energy efficiency has great promise although of course issues such as privacy do need to be addressed.

## FINANCIAL INCENTIVES

Financial incentives can provide 'market pull'. Examples of incentives include the various rebate programmes in the USA by which utilities pay a rebate to consumers investing in energy efficiency measures as part of demand-side management programmes.

## REGULATIONS AND STANDARDS

Regulations cover efficiency standards for buildings, vehicles and appliances. Regulations provide 'market push'. Examples include the tightening of vehicle fuel efficiency standards in Europe and the USA which has sparked off a range of innovations from automobile manufacturers including stop/start technologies, more efficient engines and weight reduction, all of which have increased average fuel efficiency significantly in the last few years. Regulations, of course, do require enforcement, and in many countries building regulations are not as well enforced as they could be. Most regulations are static in that they are set and then remain in place for a period before renegotiation. Renegotiation, particularly of building regulations, can be a long and painful process subject to lobbying and pressure from vested interests.

In 1998, Japan introduced dynamic regulations in the form of the Top Runner programme which was designed to stimulate continuous improvement in the energy efficiency of appliances and vehicles (Kodaka 2008; Kimura 2010). In the Top Runner programme the future efficiency standard was set at the level of performance of the most efficient appliance or vehicle within the category, whereas previously it had been set at the average level. The regulations required every manufacturer to reach the current highest standard, the top runner, by a fixed date. A weighted average according to units shipped is used to assess performance. By 2010, 23 different products were covered by the Top Runner programme, and the overall results have been impressive. Air conditioners achieved an energy efficiency improvement between FY1997 and FY2004 of 67.8 per cent compared to an initial expectation of 66.1 per cent. Refrigerators achieved an improvement of 55.2 per cent between FY1998 and FY2004 compared to an expectation of 30.5 per cent. Gasoline-powered passenger vehicles achieved a 22.8 per cent improvement between FY1995 and FY2005, in line with expectations.

## VOLUNTARY AGREEMENT

Voluntary agreements cover industries or market segments coming together to voluntarily adopt a standard, an example being Energy Star in the USA. Energy Star celebrated its twentieth anniversary in 2012 and the programme reports that it has saved end users $230 billion in utility bills since inception (Energy Star 2012).

## RESEARCH, DEMONSTRATION AND DEVELOPMENT

Research, development and demonstration remains an important part of energy efficiency policy as we need to continue to develop new technologies and demonstrate their effectiveness. Energy efficiency has traditionally, as in all areas, been the Cinderella of publicly funded energy research and development budgets, with large sums being spent on research and development in energy supply technologies, particularly nuclear, and very little spent on efficiency research.

## ALTERNATIVE CLASSIFICATION

The Australian government's classification of energy efficiency policy options is also helpful. It covers:

- *Standards* – standards for performance of buildings, vehicles or appliances push suppliers to reach higher levels of energy efficiency.

- *Disclosure* – disclosure through measures such as energy labelling (Energy Performance Certificates) for buildings and appliances makes energy performance visible and comparisons can create 'competition' to achieve better results and customer pull.

- *Training and accreditation* – helps to build capacity and underpins long-term cultural change.

- *Awareness and information* – the provision of information addresses information barriers and raises awareness of the potential for energy efficiency and what steps can be taken to improve efficiency.

- *Demonstration* – demonstration of technologies helps to make technical possibilities visible and reduce their risk profile.

- *Technology and innovation* – encouraging innovation creates the possibility of more stringent standards and helps to define future best practices.

- *Incentives* – financial incentives, which can be negative or positive, can be used to support activities in all of these areas.

## Energy Efficiency Policies Can Be Local As Well As National

We most often think about policy as being about national government direction, but we should not forget the power of regional and local governments. In the United States, even during the time that George W. Bush was President and there was little national policy support for measures on energy efficiency or greenhouse gas abatement, many states, counties and cities had very active and innovative policies. Since then the number of states, counties and cities with explicit energy policies and plans has increased and we are now seeing a great deal of innovation in state policy making. In the UK and Europe we are seeing innovative city and local energy planning with an emphasis on investing in smart and sustainable energy infrastructure, often based on some form of community participation.

Whatever the overarching national policy framework, regional and local governments can devise and implement their own policies and action plans, although clearly their powers are constrained compared with national governments – for example in their ability to set technical standards or levy taxes.

## Conclusions

Relative to the size of the opportunity, in both energy and financial terms, and the significant benefits, efficiency policy has been and is still neglected – it is usually a poor cousin to energy supply policy. This is understandable given the history of the energy sector, its social and economic impact and the strength of the supply-side lobby. However, the combination of energy problems that all countries and regions are facing now requires a new approach, one that is balanced between the supply and demand sides and recognizes efficiency as a resource just like any other energy resource. We now need to develop and implement advanced investment-grade energy policies and energy efficiency policies that enable the efficiency resource to be utilized.

Countries, cities and localities around the world are introducing a range of innovative efficiency policies and these are starting to have a demonstrable effect on energy use. The challenge for policy makers now is fourfold:

- To break away from the old supply-side-dominated view of the world;

- To truly balance the supply and demand side of energy policy by ensuring demand is viewed as an energy resource and is always represented properly in energy policy;

- To implement policies that scale up demand for energy efficiency, the supply of energy efficiency goods and services, and the flow of finance into energy efficiency finance;

- To design mechanisms that capture and truly value the various benefits of energy efficiency projects and programmes.

## References and Bibliography

Becker, D. and Motta, J. 2011. *Broader and Deeper. A Comprehensive Approach.* [Online]. Available at: http://aceee.org/files/pdf/conferences/eer/2011/BS1A_Becker.Motta.pdf [accessed 28 January 2013].

Boardman, B. 2012. *Achieving Zero. Delivering Future-Friendly Buildings.* [Online]. Available at: http://www.eci.ox.ac.uk/research/energy/achievingzero/achieving-zero-text.pdf [accessed 28 January 2013].

Burr, A.C. 2012. *Energy Disclosure and The New Frontier for American Jobs.* [Online]. Available at: http://www.imt.org/uploads/resources/files/Energy_Disclosure_New_Frontier.pdf [accessed 29 January 2013].

Burr, A.C., Keicher, C. and Leipziger, D. 2011. *Building Energy Transparency: A Framework for Implementing U.S. Commercial Energy Rating and Disclosure Policy.* [Online]. Available at: http://www.buildingrating.org/sites/default/files/documents/IMT-Building_Energy_Transparency_Report.pdf [accessed 29 January 2013].

Burr, A.C., Majersik, C. and Stellberg, S. 2012. *Analysis of Job Creation and Energy Cost Savings from Building Energy Rating and Disclosure Policy.* [Online]. Available at: http://www.imt.org/uploads/resources/files/Analysis_Job_Creation.pdf [accessed 29 January 2013].

Cabinet Office Behavioural Insights Team, Department of Energy and Climate Change and Department of Communities and Local Government. 2011. *Behaviour Change and Energy Use.* [Online]. Available at: http://www.cabinetoffice.gov.uk/sites/default/files/resources/behaviour-change-and-energy-use.pdf [accessed 28 January 2013].

Calwell, C. 2010. *Is Efficiency Sufficient? The Case for Shifting our Emphasis in Energy Specifications to Progressive Efficiency and Sufficiency.* [Online]. Available at: http://www.eceee.org/sufficiency/eceee_Progressive_Efficiency.pdf [accessed 28 January 2013].

Center for Neighborhood Technology. 2013. *Urban Sustainability Hackathon.* [Online]. Available at: http://www.cnt.org/events/reinventing-chicago/hackathon [accessed 31 May 2013].

Centre for Analysis of Social Exclusion. 2012. *Getting the Measure of Fuel Poverty.* [Online]. Available at: http://sticerd.lse.ac.uk/dps/case/cr/CASEreport72_Executive_Summary.pdf [accessed 28 January 2013].

Constantinescu, T. 2009. *Energy Efficiency and Renewable Energy – Challenges and Opportunities in Romania.* [Online]. Available at: http://www.iene.gr/3rdSEEED/articlefiles/Session_IX/Constantinescu.pdf [accessed 28 January 2013].

Cooper, M. 2011. *Locating Energy Efficiency in a 21st Century Least Costs Planning Environment.* [Online]. Available at: http://aceee.org/files/pdf/conferences/eer/2011/BS1C_Cooper.pdf [accessed 28 January 2013].

ECEEE. 2010. *Workshop Summary: Is Efficient Sufficient?* [Online]. Available at: http://www.eceee.org/eceee_events/Is_Efficient_Sufficient_/Presentations/WorkshopSummary.pdf [accessed 28 January 2013].

EERE (Energy Efficiency and Renewable Energy). 2009. Obama Administration Launches New Energy Efficiency Efforts. US Department of Energy website, 29 June 2009. [Online]. Available at: http://apps1.eere.energy.gov/news/news_detail.cfm/news_id=12607 [accessed 27 April 2013].

Energy Star. 2012. *Energy Star Celebrating Twenty Years*. [Online]. Available at: http://www.energystar.gov/ia/about/20_years/ES_20th_Anniv_brochure_spreads.pdf?c719-f3d8 [accessed 31 May 2013].

Goldman, C., Reid, M., Levy, R. and Silverstein, A. 2010. *Coordination of Energy Efficiency and Demand Response*. [Online]. Available at: http://eetd.lbl.gov/ea/ems/reports/lbnl-3044e.pdf [accessed 28 January 2013].

Greene, D. and Pears, A. 2003. *Policy Options for Energy Efficiency in Australia*. [Online]. Available at: http://www.acre.ee.unsw.edu.au/downloads/AEPG%20Energy%20Efficiency%20report%20-%202003.pdf [accessed 28 January 2013].

Growitsch, C. and Höffler, F. 2011. 'Impact of Fukushima on the German Energy Policy Debate', *IAEE Energy Forum*, Fourth Quarter 2011. [Online]. Available at: http://www.iaee.org/documents/2011FallEnergyForum.pdf [accessed 28 January 2013].

Guertler, P. 2011. *Levelling the Playing Field Through Least-Cost Energy Planning: In Limbo, Too Late or Just Right?* [Online]. Available at: http://www.ukace.org/wp-content/uploads/2011/07/ACE-Research-2011-06-1-233-Guertler.pdf [accessed 28 January 2013].

Hayes, L., Service, O., Goldacre, B. and Torgerson, D. 2012. *Test, Learn, Adapt: Developing Public Policy with Randomised Controlled Trials*. [Online]. Available at: http://www.cabinetoffice.gov.uk/sites/default/files/resources/TLA-1906126.pdf [accessed 29 January 2013].

Hayes, S., Young, R. and Sciortino, M. 2012. *The ACEEE 2012 International Energy Efficiency Scorecard*. [Online]. Available at: http://www.aceee.org/research-report/e12a [available 29 January 2013].

Hirschey, M. and Britt, M. 2010. *Energy Performance Certification of Buildings*. [Online]. Available at: http://www.iea.org/publications/freepublications/publication/buildings_certification-1.pdf [accessed 28 January 2013].

IEA. 2012. *World Energy Outlook 2012 Fact Sheets*. [Online]. Available at: http://www.worldenergyoutlook.org/media/weowebsite/2012/factsheets.pdf [accessed 28 April 2013].

IIGCC-INCR-IGCC-UNEP. 2011. *Investment-Grade Climate Policy: Financing the Transition to the Low Carbon Economy*. [Online]. Available at: http://globalinvestorcoalition.org/wp-content/uploads/2012/11/2011-Investment-Grade-Policy-Report-1.pdf [accessed 27 April 2013].

IISD (2012). *Untold Billions: Fossil-Fuel Subsidies, Their Impacts and the Path to Reform*. [Online] Available at: http://www.iisd.org/gsi/untold-billions-fossil-fuel-subsidies-their-impacts-and-path-reform [accessed 31 January 2013].

International Energy Agency. 2007. *Mind the Gap. Quantifying Principal-Agent Problems in Energy Efficiency*. [Online]. Available at: http://www.iea.org/ publications/freepublications/publication/mind_the_gap.pdf [accessed 28 January 2013].

International Energy Agency. 2010. *Energy Efficiency Governance Handbook.* [Online]. Available at: http://www.iea.org/publications/freepublications/ publication/gov_handbook.pdf [accessed 28 January 2013].

International Energy Agency. 2011a. *Innovations in National Energy Efficiency Strategies and Action Plans.* [Online]. Available at: http://www.iea.org/ publications/freepublications/publication/Innovations.pdf [accessed 28 January 2013].

International Energy Agency. 2011b. *25 Energy Efficiency Policy Recommendations.* [Online]. Available at: http://www.iea.org/publications/freepublications/ publication/25recom_2011.pdf [accessed 28 January 2013].

International Energy Agency. 2012. *Progress Implementing the IEA 25 Energy Efficiency Policy Recommendations.* [Online]. Available at: http://www.iea.org/ publications/insights/progress_implementing_25_ee_recommendations.pdf [accessed 28 January 2013].

Janssen, R. 2008. *Energy Efficiency Policy Explained: An Introduction.* [Online]. Available at: http://www.helio-international.org/EEPolicyExplained.pdf [accessed 28 January 2013].

Janssen, R. and Staniaszek, D. 2012. *How Many Jobs? A Survey of the Employment Effects of Investment in Energy Efficiency of Buildings.* [Online]. Available at: http:// www.euroace.org/LinkClick.aspx?fileticket=3R8RB3xG_YU%3D&tabid=69 [accessed 28 January 2013].

Joshi, B. and the Regulatory Assistance Project. 2012. *Best Practices in Designing and Implementing Energy Efficiency Obligation Schemes.* [Online]. Available at: http://www.ieadsm.org/Files/AdminUpload/(1)RAP_IEADSM%20 Best%20Practices%20in%20Designing%20and%20Implementing%20 Energy%20Efficiency%20Obligation%20Schemes%202012%20June(6).pdf [accessed 28 January 2013].

Larson, D. 2011. *Energy Efficiency as a Resource.* [Online]. Available at: http://aceee. org/files/pdf/conferences/eer/2011/Opening_Larson.pdf [accessed 28 January 2013].

Liubinas, A. and Harrison, P. 2012. *Saving a Scarce Resource: A Case Study of Behavioural Change.* [Online]. Available at: http://marketing.conference-services.net/resources/327/2958/pdf/AM2012_0124_paper.pdf [accessed 28 April 2013].

Managan, K., Layke, J., Araya, M. and Nesler, C. 2012. *Driving Transformation to Energy Efficient Buildings. Policies and Actions: 2nd Edition*. [Online]. Available at: http://www.institutebe.com/InstituteBE/media/Library/Resources/Energy%20 and%20Climate%20Policy/Driving-Transformation-to-EE-Buildings.pdf [accessed 28 January 2013].

NYC Open Data. 2013. *Electric Consumption by Zip Code 2010*. [Online]. Available at: https://nycopendata.socrata.com/Environmental-Sustainability/Electric-Consumption-by-ZIP-Code-2010/74cu-ncm4 [accessed 31 May 2013].

PJM. 2009. *Reliability Pricing Model Demand Response and Energy Efficiency*. [Online]. Available at: http://www.pjm.com/~/media/markets-ops/ rpm/20090406-dr-ee-in-rpm-collateral.ashx [accessed 27 April 2013].

Rocky Mountain Institute and Institute for Building Efficiency. 2011. *Proposal for a New Deep Retrofit Program*. [Online]. Available at: http://aceee.org/files/ pdf/conferences/eer/2011/BS1A_Bell.pdf [accessed 28 January 2013].

Steenblik, R. 2012. *A Subsidy Primer*. [Online]. Available at: http://www.iisd. org/gsi/sites/default/files/primer.pdf [accessed 29 January 2013].

Sudarshan, A. and Sweeney, J. 2008. *Deconstructing the 'Rosenfeld Curve'*. [Online]. Available at: http://piee.stanford.edu/cgi-bin/docs/publications/ Deconstructing_the_Rosenfeld_Curve.pdf [accessed 28 January 2013].

Supple, D. and Sheikh, I. 2010. *Public Policies Driving Energy Efficiency Worldwide*. [Online]. Available at: http://www.institutebe.com/InstituteBE/media/ Library/Resources/Energy%20and%20Climate%20Policy/Public-Policies-Driving-Building-Efficiency.pdf [accessed 29 January 2013].

UNIDO. 2011. *Policy Options to Overcome Barriers to Industrial Energy Efficiency in Developing Countries*. [Online]. Available at: http://www.unido.org/ fileadmin/user_media/Services/Research_and_Statistics/WP132011_Ebook. pdf [accessed 29 January 2013].

Wade, J., Guertler, P., Croft, D. and Sunderland, L. 2011. *National Energy Efficiency and Energy Savings Targets*. [Online]. Available at: http://www.eceee.org/Policy/ Targets/TargetsFinalReport24May2011.pdf [accessed 29 January 2013].

Weeselink, B., Harmsen, R. and Eichhammer, W. 2010. *Energy Savings 2020. How to Triple the Impact of Energy Saving Policies in Europe*. [Online]. Available at: http://roadmap2050.eu/attachments/files/1EnergySavings2020-FullReport. pdf [accessed 28 January 2013].

World Energy Council. 2010. *Energy Efficiency: A Recipe for Success*. [Online]. Available at: http://www.worldenergy.org/documents/fdeneff_v2.pdf [accessed 28 January 2013].

World Energy Council. 2011. *World Energy Perspective: Nuclear Energy One Year After Fukushima*. [Online]. Available at: http://www.worldenergy.org/documents/world_energy_perspective__nuclear_energy_one_year_after_fukushima_world_energy_council_march_2012_1.pdf [accessed 28 January 2013].

Worldwatch Institute. 2012. *Fossil Fuel and Renewable Energy Subsidies on the Rise*. [Online]. Available at: http://www.worldwatch.org/fossil-fuel-and-renewable-energy-subsidies-rise-0 [accessed 31 January 2013].

York, D., Molina, M., Neubauer, M., Nowak, S., Nadel, S., Chittum, A., Elliott, N., Farley, K., Foster, B., Sachs, H. and Witte, P. 2013. *Frontiers of Energy Efficiency: Next Generation Programs for High Energy Savings*. [Online]. Available at: http://www.aceee.org/research-report/u131 [accessed 28 January 2013].

Zimrig, M., Borgeson, G., Hoffman, I., Goldman, C., Stuart, E., Todd, A. and Billingsley, M. 2011. *Delivering Energy Efficiency to Middle Income Single Family Households*. [Online]. Available at: http://eetd.lbl.gov/ea/emp/reports/lbnl-5244e.pdf [accessed 28 January 2013].

# 12

# Energy Efficiency Policy Examples

*Vitally we are putting energy efficiency where it should be at the heart of our energy policy.*

*David Cameron,*
*Prime Minister of the United Kingdom, February 2013*

As with the energy management examples, there are many different cases of energy efficiency policy available online and in books. Here we present summaries of only a few national and local energy polices from many excellent examples around the world. In all countries energy efficiency policies are evolving as the subject rises up the policy agenda. As well as national policies we now have sufficient variation in state and local policies, particularly in the USA, that we are close to being able to determine which policies have the most effects.

## Brazil

Brazil uses 1.2 toe per capita compared to a global average of 1.8 toe, and total energy usage grew rapidly between 1990 and 2008, in line with the rapid economic growth in the country. The global financial crisis led to a reduction in growth and growth in energy consumption in 2009 before picking up again. Energy intensity decreased by 0.5 per cent per annum from 2000 to 2009. The total installed electricity capacity in the country is about 109 GW, and total electrical consumption was 470 TWh in 2011. Oil provides 40 per cent of the country's primary energy, with non-commercial biomass supplying 32 per cent, hydro 14 per cent, gas seven per cent, coal five per cent and nuclear three per cent. Industry accounts for 40 per cent of consumption, with the residential sector only accounting for 22 per cent.

In 2008 the President signed into law the National Climate Change Plan (PNMC), and energy efficiency falls into the PNMC. The target was to reduce electrical consumption by 10 per cent by 2030 compared to a reference scenario. There are targets for improving energy efficiency in industry, transport and buildings, including replacing one million old refrigerators a year for 10 years.

The rationale for improving energy efficiency includes cost reduction and an increase in competitiveness for consumers and producers; an increase in economic efficiency; reducing diesel and LPG imports; delaying the need for new investments in generation, transmission and distribution infrastructure; and reducing social and environmental impacts.

Previous energy efficiency programmes in Brazil included CONSERVE, which encouraged substitution of oil by alternative fuels; PECO, which encouraged automobile fuel efficiency; and PRO-ALCOOL, the programme to encourage use of sugar-derived ethanol – this is not an energy efficiency programme, but rather is aimed at reducing fuel imports. In 2000, a one per cent wire charge on utilities revenue (PEE) was introduced to support energy efficiency and research and development (R&D), and in 2001 a National Energy Efficiency Law (MEPS) was introduced.

There has been extensive work, involving cooperation between the manufacturers and government, on introducing energy labelling for various appliances including refrigerators, freezers, showers, air conditioners, motors, compact fluorescent lamps and ovens. The labelling schemes began as voluntary but have since been made mandatory.

The National Electricity Conservation Programme, PROCEL, which ran from 1986 to 2005, invested a total of R$858 million in energy efficiency measures and produced cumulative savings of 21.8 TWh/year, reducing demand by 5.1GW and avoiding investment of R$14.9 billion in new supply, transmission and distribution equipment.

The National Programme for the Rationalization of the Use of Oil and Natural Gas Derivatives (CONPET) addressed passenger and cargo transportation, labelling and education and capacity building. It led to 348 stove models being labelled, 25 gas water heater models being labelled and 130,000 vehicles monitored. It led to savings of 320 million litres of diesel annually and a reduction in $CO_2$ emissions of 860,000 tonnes and a reduction of 19,000 tonnes of particulate matter emissions annually.

Between 1998/99 and 2004/05 the wire charge on utilities revenue led to a cumulative peak demand reduction of 1,395 MW and savings of 4,653 GWh per year.

The National Energy Efficiency Law has set maximum energy consumption or minimum efficiency standards for three-phase motors, refrigerators, air conditioners, gas ovens and gas water heaters.

In 2007 a decree was passed making energy efficiency a requirement in public procurement exercises and encouraging energy performance contracting in the public sector.

The national energy plan foresees 5 per cent 'autonomous conservation' resulting from the evolution of appliances and voluntary actions (around 55,700 GWh) and 5 per cent induced conservation resulting from public policy.

## Singapore

The island state of Singapore imports almost 100 per cent of its energy and due to its small land area it only has a relatively small potential for renewable energy sources such as wind or solar that have a low land-use density. Energy demand, however, is expected to increase by 2.5 to 3 per cent per annum over the next 10 years.

Energy efficiency is regarded as a key element of energy policy with the aims of improving energy security, economic competitiveness, environmental sustainability and innovation in energy efficiency technologies. The National Environment Agency (NEA) is the key agency for climate change and energy efficiency and is a statutory board under the MEWR (Ministry of the Environment and Water Resources). The Energy Efficiency Programme Office (E²PO) is a multi-agency committee which is led by the NEA and the Energy Market Authority (EMA). As well as the NEA (responsible for households) and the EMA (which is responsible for electricity markets in Singapore), the E²PO consists of the Land Transport Authority (LTA) for transport, the Building and Construction Authority (BCA) for buildings and the A*Star office for R&D. The overall mission is to achieve greater efficiency through supporting the adoption of energy efficiency measures, raising awareness to stimulate energy efficiency, developing capability to drive and sustain energy efficiency, and supporting energy efficiency research and development.

In April 2009, Singapore released a Sustainability Development Blueprint with specific targets for energy of:

- reducing energy intensity by 20 per cent from 2005 to 2020;

- reducing energy intensity by 35 per cent from 2005 to 2035.

A number of incentive schemes were introduced, including:

- Design for Efficiency Scheme (DfE). The DfE provides up to 80 per cent funding, or up to $600,000 whichever is lower, for large consumers of energy to conduct design workshops aimed at producing more efficient designs.

- Energy Efficiency Improvement Assistance Scheme (EASe). EASe provides financial support, up to 50 per cent of the costs, for companies without in-house expertise to engage consultants to carry out energy audits. The scheme reports that it delivers $5 to $10 of annual energy savings for every $ spent on an energy audit. The EASe budget is SGD 10 million.

- Grant for Energy Efficient Technologies (GREET). GREET provides 50 per cent funding, capped at SG$2m, to encourage owners and operators of industrial facilities to invest in energy efficient equipment.

- Accelerated tax depreciation allowance for energy efficiency equipment and technologies.

- Training grant for Singapore Certified Energy Manager (SCEM) programme.

- Green Mark scheme and the Green Market Incentive Scheme. The Green Mark scheme requires all new buildings and existing buildings undergoing major refurbishment work – above 2,000m² in gross floor area (GFA) – to meet the Green Mark certified standard. The Green Mark standard assesses energy efficiency as well as a range of environmentally friendly features and, in a similar way to the LEED scheme in the USA, it can certify buildings as Gold, Gold$^{PLUS}$ or Platinum (Building and Construction Authority of

Singapore 2013). The Green Mark Incentive scheme is designed to encourage developers to achieve higher Green Mark ratings. New and retrofitted buildings with GFA above 5,000m² that achieve the Gold Green Mark and above receive a cash incentive based on the GFA and the rating achieved.

- Building Control Regulations – sets an Envelope Thermal Transfer Value (ETTV) standard to regulate heat loss, minimum efficiency standards for commercial air conditioning units and a maximum for lighting power consumption.

- Mandatory energy labelling scheme – all household refrigerators, air conditioners and clothes driers sold in Singapore must have an energy performance label.

- One of the pilot projects launched in November 2009 was the Intelligent Energy System (IES) which was designed to test a range of smart grid technologies to enhance the capabilities of the power grid. This included tests in multiple sites of advanced metering and communications infrastructure, demand response management systems, and management systems for distributed energy sources.

Other energy efficiency initiatives include the Energy Efficiency National Partnership, which is a voluntary programme to assist companies to improve their own energy efficiency. The initiative includes an annual award to recognize best practice.

Singapore also operates an Energy Services Company (ESCO) accreditation scheme to help build the quality of services offered and improve confidence in the ESCO market. In addition, the Economic Development Board (EDB) administers an investment allowance scheme which gives a capital allowance for investment in qualifying equipment that results in, amongst other factors, improved energy efficiency.

In addition to the other agencies, the Energy Studies Institute has been established at the National University of Singapore to promote and develop policy-orientated research in energy.

In 2012, the EDB announced a programme to establish a financing mechanism for energy efficiency investment in the industrial sector.

## Korea

Korea is a rapidly growing economy with a heavy emphasis on high technology industries, automobiles and shipping, and its leading companies such as Samsung and Daewoo have global presence. Energy demand has been growing rapidly, at 4.9 per cent per annum between 1990 and 2009 (ABB 2011c), but the country has very limited supplies of indigenous natural resources, leading to a high reliance on imports. The cost of energy imports in 2011 was $172.5 billion (nearly one-third of total imports) which was made up of $100.8 billion on oil, $24 billion on LNG and $18.5 billion on coal. This level of expenditure on imports is greater than the $95.5 billion of exports from the semiconductor and automobile industry combined.

Oil accounted for 39.7 per cent of Korea's primary energy in 2010, with coal accounting for 28.9 per cent, nuclear 16.4 per cent, LNG 12.2 per cent and renewables 2.8 per cent. Industry is the largest consumer of energy, at 59.4 per cent compared to 19.2 per cent in buildings and 19.1 per cent in transport. Total $CO_2$ emissions were 607.6 Mt.

The Korean Energy Management Corporation (KEMCO) was created in 1980 through the Rational Energy Utilization Act, and implements energy efficiency and renewable energy programmes. KEMCO, according to their website, 'seeks to implement projects efficiently for the rationalization of energy use, thereby reducing carbon dioxide emission and contributing to the sound development of the national economy' (KEMCO 2013). The Rational Energy Utilization Act (1979) was amended in 2002, 2003 and 2008 to introduce new energy-saving measures. Three labelling programmes have been launched to promote high-efficiency appliances: the Energy Efficiency Standards and Labeling Program (1992), the High-efficiency Appliances Certification Program (1996) and the E-Standby Program (1999).

The government of Korea (in 2008) set an ambitious energy efficiency target of improving energy intensity to 0.185 toe/$1,000 between 2008 and 2030. Achieving this aim would reduce energy use in 2030 by 46 per cent compared to a business-as-usual scenario. The government has established sectoral measures for industry, transport, buildings and the public sector, as well as cross-sector programmes covering smart grid, ESCOs, R&D, energy prices and public awareness.

In the industrial sector, which is dominated by energy-intensive industries such as steelmaking, the government worked with industry to establish

Greenhouse Gas–Energy Reduction Commitments (GERC) for the largest energy users. In all, these cover 463 companies (in 2012) of which 366 are in industry, 47 in buildings and 50 in agriculture, livestock and waste. These commitments cover 67 per cent of GHG emissions and 64.9 per cent of energy consumption in Korea. In 2012, companies emitting over 25,000 tonnes $CO_2$ or using over 100TJ of energy were included in the scheme, and in 2014 this will be extended to companies emitting over 15,000 tonnes $CO_2$ or using 80 TJ.

To assist smaller companies a green credit scheme was introduced in which SMEs can receive technology and capital from large companies to improve their energy efficiency and the large companies can credit some of the results from the SME within their own commitment. The government agency KEMCO certifies energy management systems within companies and can provide financial assistance for energy-saving investments.

In the buildings sectors an energy labelling scheme has been introduced which applied to new buildings from 2010, existing houses and office buildings in 2012 and all buildings from 2013. A mandatory 'energy efficiency mark' is recorded for each building. The GERC referred to above applies to the building sector, the first 47 buildings in 2012. An energy-saving target has been imposed on energy suppliers and incentives for meeting the target have been introduced in 2012.

In the transport sector the fuel efficiency measurement system has been changed to better reflect real-world fuel economy, and all vehicles have to be labelled. Methods for measuring the fuel economy of Plug-in Hybrid Electric Vehicles (PHEVs) have been introduced. To encourage the use of high-efficiency tyres, a tyre labelling scheme for passenger cars has been introduced in 2012 and will be expanded to the light truck market in 2013.

A road map and strategy has been developed for promoting 'green cars', and a target of 1.2 million green cars in Korea and exports of 0.9 million green cars by 2015 has been set. A new fuel economy programme for heavy duty vehicles will be introduced in 2015.

In the equipment and appliance markets, energy efficiency labelling and certification programmes have been introduced, as well as a programme to improve the efficiency of items on standby. The labelling scheme covers 35 items including refrigerators, white goods, fans, boilers, air conditioners, lamps and automobiles. The certification programme covers 41 items, including LED lighting, while the e-standby programme covers 22 items such as set-top boxes. Labelling has improved the energy efficiency of refrigerators by 60 per cent between 1996 and 2010 and lowered energy per litre from 1.75kWh/litre to 0.719kWh/litre, while the performance of washing machines has improved 21 per cent between 2004 and 2010, improving from 15Wh/kg to 11Wh/kg.

## Netherlands Approach to Retrofitting Housing

There are almost no subsidies for energy efficiency in the Netherlands because it is believed that subsidies are unsustainable and don't lead to the correct long-term actions from investors. Policy instead has been focusing on creating a sense of urgency, enthusiasm and support around energy efficiency. The feeling in the Netherlands is that any mandatory energy targets will be counterproductive and instead an agreement (covenant) has been reached between the government, housing associations and other parties to set voluntary energy targets for housing refurbishments. Energy certificates have been incorporated into the rent-setting mechanism (which is defined in law), in order that a higher-performing building can be leased at a higher rent. The overall concept is to look at the Total Cost of Living, so that rent can be increased to fund retrofit measures as long as the increase is less than the reduction in energy spend – in a similar way to the UK Green Deal's 'golden rule'.

## Melbourne, Australia

The City of Melbourne is the state capital of Victoria, Australia. According to the city's web site the municipality covers 37.6 km² and has a residential population of around 98,860 (as of 2011). Metropolitan Melbourne has a population of 3.6 million. On an average day, around 805,000 people use the city, and Melbourne hosts more than a million international visitors each year. Melbourne enjoys a temperate climate with average maximum summer (December to February) temperatures of 25°C, (14°C minimum), average maximum autumn (March to May) temperatures of 20°C (11°C minimum), average maximum winter (June to August) temperatures of 14°C (7°C minimum) and average maximum winter (September to November) temperatures of 20°C (minimum 10°C).

The city established a leadership position by being active in greenhouse gas policy and mitigation programmes from the mid 1990s, and joined the International Cities for Climate Protection (ICCP)™ in 1998 and the Australian national Greenhouse Challenge in 2000. The city sees early action on greenhouse gas emissions as a driver of economic growth rather than as a cost. In 2003 the city adopted the 'Zero Net Emissions by 2020' strategy, and identified three main pathways to achieving the goal: improved building design (in both new builds and retrofits), use of renewable energy, and sequestration by tree planting.

The strategy also explicitly recognizes that energy efficiency is the most financially attractive route and should come before renewables and sequestration. The city council seeks to minimize its energy use in its own buildings, facilities (street lights) and other operations. The council has implemented a number of retrofit projects in buildings and installed energy-efficient street lighting. The latter is made more difficult by a split incentive caused by the distribution company owning the infrastructure, but with the council picking up the energy bill. However, the council has worked strategically with the distribution companies, Citipower and Alinta, to ensure the most efficient technologies are used, emphasizing the ability of energy efficiency to minimize total costs of supplying infrastructure to the city.

It is worth noting that Victoria – and Melbourne – implemented a very successful water-saving campaign in the late 2000s in response to a threat of severe water shortages caused by many years of rainfall being significantly below the long-term average. The programme used a marketing campaign based on emotional connection to initiate behavioural change, as well as incentives to encourage water recycling and grey water use. Water use was cut by 40 per cent per head of population, and the behavioural change aspects of this programme are worth studying by energy professionals seeking to build demand for energy efficiency services and products.

In the building sector, the City of Melbourne has implemented sub-sector-specific programmes as follows:

- Existing office buildings: a large-scale programme to retrofit about 70 per cent or 1,200 of the commercial office buildings within the City of Melbourne has been created: '1200 Buildings' (City of Melbourne 2013).

- New office buildings: tightening building codes (regulations) by requiring all new buildings to achieve Australian Building Greenhouse Rating (ABGR) 5 Stars or greater (an increase on the previous code).

- Education, health and community buildings: facilitating this sector to establish a programme to retrofit buildings.

- Retail and tourism sector: encouraging the accommodation and retail/wholesale sector to retrofit buildings and facilitate new standards for new buildings in these sectors.

- In the domestic sector, the focus is on implementing the least-cost measures which are space and water heating, lighting and common areas in high-rise developments. In this sector the Council is:
  - facilitating a house-to-house audit programme targeting space, water and insulation in approximately 12,000 households,
  - enabling retrofits on common areas in 75 per cent of all high rise developments and communal hot water and space heating where feasible,
  - launching a behaviour change programme to encourage resident demand for the audit programme and to provide broad energy efficiency advice and information.

The City has also implemented a mandatory disclosure programme whereby building owners have to disclose energy performance.

## THE MELBOURNE 1200 BUILDINGS PROGRAMME

The Melbourne 1200 Buildings programme 'aims to encourage and support building owners, managers and facility managers to improve the energy/ water efficiency and reduce waste to landfill of commercial buildings in the municipality of Melbourne' (City of Melbourne 2013). They also aim to retrofit about 1200 buildings in the City, about 70 per cent of the total. Owners and managers of commercial buildings can sign up to the programme, which gives them the ability to promote their buildings using the 1200 Buildings logo; access to environmental upgrade finance (see below); the latest news on industry approaches, technologies, initiatives and case studies; and training and engagement.

The programme also uses the state's Industry Capability Network, through which suppliers of relevant services and products can offer their services and access tenders; organizes events and training; and publishes information guides on the different aspects of retrofits from the high-level overall process down to individual technologies.

The financing scheme put in place by Melbourne, Environmental Upgrade Finance or EUF, is a world-leading scheme which allows the city council to levy a new form of statutory charge, called the environmental upgrade charge. The council can partner with private financial institutions to enter voluntary agreements with building owners to finance upgrades for non-residential buildings. The funds are collected by the council through the environmental upgrade charge and the charge remains in place until the financier is repaid in full. Property owners can pass on, with the occupier's consent, some of the upgrade charge to the occupiers. The scheme is administered through the Sustainable Melbourne Fund, a city-sponsored fund that invests in sustainable projects (separately from the environmental upgrade programme).

The Melbourne programme sits in a context of, and takes advantage of, Victoria Province-wide and national programmes. Victoria has a tradeable energy efficiency certificate scheme (VEET) and mandatory disclosure of energy performance on sale or leasing of buildings greater than 2,000 m$^2$ in area. The national rating scheme, the National Australian Building Energy Rating Scheme (NABERS), has been cleverly used by Melbourne to set aggressive, higher than normal, energy performance targets for buildings over 2,000 m$^2$.

The Melbourne programme is an excellent example of a local government providing vision as well as practical leadership through getting its own house in order and supporting the development of a holistic suite of policies, addressing the need to create demand through market disclosure, providing incentives through the VEET programme, and facilitating a financial mechanism whereby private investment can be brought into commercial building retrofits.

## Chicago

The city, which is famous for its architecture and whose official motto is 'Urbs in Horto' or 'city in a garden', has the aim of being more liveable, more competitive and more sustainable. It has had sustainability programmes for a number of years and has achieved the following:

- been voted 'most sustainable large community';

- number 1 in number of LEED certified buildings;

- has the largest urban solar capacity (10 MW on brown field site);

- number 1 in green roofs, with more than 5 million square feet;

- has the 3rd largest concentration of green jobs in the US;

- has recently shut down two urban coal fired plants, thus improving air quality.

The city's sustainability efforts have been accelerated under the leadership of Mayor Rahm Emmanuel and the city has 24 goals for 2015 in 7 key areas ('24/7') with 100 specific activities being monitored. Number 2 in the 7 key areas is 'Energy efficiency and clean energy'. Energy efficiency also clearly links in with number 1, creating jobs, and number 7, addressing climate change (Weigert 2013).

The city undertook a study of energy use split into census blocks and the numbers show that there is $3 billion a year spent on energy in 600,000 buildings and that 71% of Chicago's carbon dioxide emissions come from buildings. This realization led to the creation of the Retrofit Chicago programme which has three sub-programmes, one for public buildings, one for commercial buildings and one for the residential sector.

In the public sector the City set a target of reducing energy use by 20% in its 10 million square feet of facilities. Recognizing that finance could not come from public funds the City created the Chicago Infrastructure Trust which is designed to bring in multiple, private sector finance partners to invest in infrastructure upgrades. Although less than a year old, and still, as the Deputy Mayor described it at the recent ACEEE Financing Forum, an 'infant that has probably got too much attention', it is working on financing energy efficiency retrofits in buildings, large pumping stations and schools.

The Commercial Buildings Initiative (CBI) was launched as a voluntary, opt-in, programme. It initially had 14 million square feet of buildings owned by major real estate companies signed up but now has 32 buildings with 28 million square feet. It both "makes it easier" for building owners to have a retrofit and provides recognition. Interestingly enough finance is not considered a barrier in the CBI as these are major buildings owned by large real estate companies.

The Residential Partnership used the data on energy use at a census block level to identify twelve zones with a high potential for energy efficiency.

This information is available through the city's information portal and the city is encouraging people to come up with new ways of using the data. After less than a year 1,300 retrofits have now been undertaken with a total of 2,600 across the city (including areas outside the 12 zones). As in other residential retrofit schemes a critical issue is accelerating demand and the city uses an out-reach team using various techniques including house parties.

## Summary

Efficiency policies are evolving everywhere as the large potential of efficiency to meet energy objectives of increasing energy security, reducing energy costs and reducing environmental impact is increasingly recognized and given higher priority. We are seeing innovation in national and local policies and programmes, and the variety of policies will soon allow us to quantitatively determine the most effective set of policies.

## References and Bibliography

ABB. 2011a. *Brazil: Energy Efficiency Report*. [Online]. Available at: http://www05.abb.com/global/scot/scot316.nsf/veritydisplay/1b6ed2d18136aa5bc1257864004d09a6/$file/brazil.pdf [accessed 28 January 2013].

ABB. 2011b. *Saudi Arabia: Energy Efficiency Report*. [Online]. Available at: http://www05.abb.com/global/scot/scot316.nsf/veritydisplay/f90e53733342b472c125786400519e97/$file/saudi%20arabia.pdf [accessed 28 January 2013].

ABB. 2011c. *South Korea: Energy Efficiency Report*. [Online]. Available at: http://www05.abb.com/global/scot/scot316.nsf/veritydisplay/124041516f0075a1c12578640051c021/$file/south%20korea.pdf [accessed 28 January 2013].

AECOM. 2010. *City of San Bernardino: Energy Efficiency Conservation Strategy Summary*. [Online]. Available at: http://www.sustainablesanbernardino.org/documents/SB_EECS_strategy_final.pdf [accessed 28 January 2013].

Building and Construction Authority of Singapore. 2013. *About BCA Green Mark Scheme*. [Online]. Available at: http://www.bca.gov.sg/greenmark/green_mark_buildings.html [accessed 27 April 2013].

California Energy Commission. 2009. *California Energy Demand 2010–2020: Adopted Forecast*. [Online]. Available at: http://www.energy.ca.gov/2009publications/CEC-200-2009-012/CEC-200-2009-012-CMF.PDF [accessed 28 January 2013].

California Energy Commission. 2010. *Incremental Impacts of Energy Efficiency Policy Initiatives Relative to the '2009 Integrated Energy Policy Report' Adopted Demand Forecast.* [Online]. Available at: http://www.energy.ca.gov/2010publications/CEC-200-2010-001/CEC-200-2010-001-CTF.PDF [accessed 28 January 2013].

City of Melbourne. 2013. *About 1200 Buildings.* [Online]. Available at: http://www.melbourne.vic.gov.au/1200buildings/Pages/About1200Buildings.aspx [accessed 28 April 2013].

Community Energy Cooperative. 2007. *Re-energizing Illinois. Building Real Demand for Energy Efficiency.* [Online]. Available at: http://www.cntenergy.org/download/25/FullReport-2007.03.08FINAL.pdf [accessed 25 April 2013].

Energy Conservation Center of Ho Chi Minh City. 2011. *Energy Efficiency Policies in Ho Chi Minh City.* [Online]. Available at: http://www.iges.or.jp/en/kuc/pdf/activity20110314/4_WS-S1A-2-ECC-HCMC_E.pdf [accessed 28 January 2013].

Energy Market Authority. 2010. *Update on Energy Efficiency Policies and Programmes in Singapore.* [Online]. Available at: http://www.egeec.apec.org/www/UploadFile/5-%20Singapore%27s%20EE%20update.pdf [accessed 29 January 2013].

European Commission. 2011. *Energy Efficiency Plan 2011.* [Online]. Available at: http://eur-lex.europa.eu/LexUriServ/LexUriServ.do?uri=COM:2011:0109:FIN:EN:PDF [accessed 28 January 2013].

Fawkes, S. 2013. 'Foundations Laid for UK Energy Efficiency Policy', *Energy World* 412 (February 2013).

Garforth International LLC. 2011. *Community Energy Efficiency and Conservation Strategy Plan (CEP).* [Online]. Available at: http://hollandsenergyfuture.files.wordpress.com/2011/10/sept19.pdf [accessed 28 January 2013].

Garforth International LLC and City of Holland Board of Public Works. 2011. *Holland Community Energy Efficiency and Conservation Strategy.* [Online]. Available at: http://cleanwater.org/files/publications/mi/final_cep_for_suscom_sept_9_2011_for_website.pdf [accessed 28 January 2013].

Heffner, G. 2010. *Positioning to Deliver on Australia's Energy Efficiency Potential.* [Online]. Available at: http://aie.org.au/StaticContent/Images/SYD110823_Presentation_Grayson.pdf [accessed 29 January 2013].

IEE Japan. 2012. *Japan Energy Brief* 18 (March 2012). [Online]. Available at: http://eneken.ieej.or.jp/en/jeb/1203.pdf [accessed 29 January 2013].

International Energy Agency. 2008. *Energy Policy Review in Indonesia.* [Online]. Available at: http://www.iea.org/publications/freepublications/publication/Indonesia2008.pdf [accessed 28 January 2013].

Jupesta, J. and Suwa, A. 2011. 'Sustainable Energy Policy in Japan, Post Fukushima', *IAEE Energy Forum* (Fourth Quarter 2011). [Online]. Available at: http://www.iaee.org/documents/2011FallEnergyForum.pdf [accessed 28 January 2013].

KEMCO. 2013. *Objective of Establishment and History*. [Online]. Available at: http://www.kemco.or.kr/new_eng/pg01/pg01030000.asp [accessed 28 April 2013].

Ki-hyun, L. 2007. *Korea's Promotion Policies for Energy-Efficient Products*. [Online]. Available at: http://www.asiapacificpartnership.org/pdf/BATF/energy_efficiency_workshop/Promotion%20Policies%20for%20EE%20Products-Lee.pdf [accessed 28 January 2013].

Kimura, O. 2010. *Japanese Top Runner Approach for Energy Efficiency Standards*. [Online]. Available at: http://www.climatepolicy.jp/thesis/pdf/09035dp.pdf [accessed 29 January 2013].

Kodaka, A. 2008. *Japan's Top Runner Program: The Race for the Top*. [Online]. Available at: http://www.eceee.org/eceee_events/product_efficiency_08/programme_presentations/Kodaka_TopRunnerProgram.pdf [accessed 29 January 2013].

Korea Energy Management Corporation. 2010. *Energy Efficiency Policies in Korea*. [Online]. Available at: http://siteresources.worldbank.org/EXTENERGY2/Resources/4114199-1276110591210/Korea.pdf [accessed 28 January 2013].

Levine, D. 2010. *Energy Efficiency in China: Glorious History, Uncertain Future*. [Online]. Available at: http://www.aps.org/units/maspg/meetings/upload/levine.pdf [accessed 28 January 2013].

Massachusetts Secretary of Energy and Environmental Affairs. 2010. *Massachusetts Clean Energy and Climate Plan for 2020*. [Online]. Available at: http://www.mass.gov/eea/docs/eea/energy/2020-clean-energy-plan.pdf [accessed 28 January 2013].

McCormick, K. and Neij, L. 2009. *Experience of Policy Instruments for Energy Efficiency in Buildings in the Nordic Countries*. [Online]. Available at: http://www.lowcarbonoptions.net/Downloads/files/Norway_EE_policyIns.pdf [accessed 29 January 2013].

Mihlmste, P., Anderson, D., Dube, S., Hathaway, D., Medeiros, L. and Sankovski, A. 2010. *BRIC'd Up Energy Efficiency: Energy and Climate Policies in Brazil, Russia, India, and China*. [Online]. Available at: http://www.aceee.org/files/proceedings/2010/data/papers/2027.pdf [accessed 28 January 2013].

Nair, N.T. 2010. *Energy Conservation Act: Indian Example*. [Online]. Available at: http://www.sari-energy.org/PageFiles/What_We_Do/activities/SAWIE/wiser/cap_dev_program_for_afghan_women_march_22-30_2010/PRESENTATIONS/24032010/ENGLISH/Energy_Conservation_Act_2001_NT_Nair.pdf [accessed 28 January 2013].

Neubauer, M., Watson, S., Laitner, J.A., Talbot, J., Trombley, D., Chittum, A. and Black, S. 2009. *South Carolina's Energy Future: Minding its Efficiency Resources*. [Online]. Available at: http://aceee.org/research-report/e099 [accessed 28 January 2013].

New Zealand Ministry of Business, Innovation and Employment. 2013. *Energy Efficiency and the Environment*. [Online]. Available at: http://www.med.govt. nz/sectors-industries/energy/energy-environment [accessed 28 January 2013].

North East Energy Efficiency Partnerships. 2012. *A Regional Roundup of Energy Efficiency Policy in the Northeast and Mid-Atlantic States*. [Online]. Available at: http://neep.org/uploads/policy/2012%20Regional%20Roundup_FINAL_ 1-2-13.pdf [accessed 28 January 2013].

Schlegel, J. 2011. *Profiles in (EE) Courage: EE Leadership in New England*. [Online]. Available at: http://aceee.org/files/pdf/conferences/eer/2011/Schlegel_ Closing.pdf [accessed 29 January 2013].

Sciotino, M., Nowak, S., Witte, P., York, D. and Kushler, M. 2011. *Energy Efficiency Resource Standards: A Progress Report on State Experience*. [Online]. Available at: http://aceee.org/research-report/u112 [accessed 28 January 2013].

Sciotino, M. and Watson, S. 2011. *State Energy Efficiency Resource Standard (EERS) Activity*. [Online]. Available at: http://aceee.org/files/pdf/policy-brief/ State%20EERS%20Summary%20October%202011.pdf [accessed 28 January 2013].

Singapore National Environment Agency. 2013. *Energy Efficient Singapore*. [Online]. Available at: http://app.e2singapore.gov.sg [accessed 28 January 2013].

Weigert, K. 2013. *Sustainable Chicago*. Presented at the American Council for an Energy Efficient Economy's 7th Annual Financing Forum, Chicago, 13–14 May 2013. [Online]. Available at: http://www.aceee.org/files/pdf/ conferences/eeff/2013/Weigert_1A.pdf [accessed 31 May 2013].

World Energy Council. 2011. *Policies for the Future. 2011 Assessment of Country Energy and Climate Policies*. [Online]. Available at: http://www.worldenergy. org/documents/wec_2011_assessment_of_energy_and_climate_policies.pdf [accessed 28 January 2013].

# 13

# Energy Suppliers and Energy Efficiency

*Our role is the optimization of the use of electricity. That is our future.*
*Jim Rogers, CEO Duke Energy*

## Introduction

Energy supply businesses are companies which generate, transmit or distribute electricity, producers or distributers of gas, coal and oil, and fuel distribution companies. They sell electrons, cubic feet (metres) of natural gas, tonnes of coal, or gallons (litres) of fuel, and their revenues and profits are, with a few exceptions, directly linked to the volume of energy they sell. Therefore, at first glance at least, they should be against improving energy efficiency – and in fact they often are. In almost all jurisdictions, however, we find energy suppliers – particularly electricity suppliers – active in some form of energy efficiency activities, running demand-side management programmes, buying energy efficiency companies, running on-bill financing programmes or various types of efficiency programmes. In some cases, and cynics would probably argue in all cases, this energy efficiency activity is only window dressing or is a legal requirement resulting from local electricity market regulations. In other cases energy suppliers seem to be genuinely attempting to develop and implement new business models that incorporate energy efficiency, driven by the profit motive and a belief that it is the right thing to do. The truth is that some energy suppliers are only in energy efficiency because they are required to be by law, and will do the minimum necessary. Others are actively considering, and trying to develop, futures in which they can profitably sell energy efficiency as well as electrons or cubic meters of gas because they see the economic and social benefits.

For policy makers, energy companies – and especially the electricity suppliers – represent a potentially very powerful resource for improving energy efficiency, a resource that cannot and should not be ignored. The evidence from places like California and New England, where aggressive utility energy efficiency programmes have started to push down demand, is that utilities can be a powerful tool to promote a more efficient economy. Activating and deploying that resource, however, requires a systematic approach to energy policy, and particularly electricity markets, which has been lacking in most jurisdictions to date and is just beginning to emerge in some countries. Fundamentally, it does require decoupling of utility profits from energy volumes, something that is now being achieved in some US markets.

## The Rationale for Mandating Energy Efficiency in the Electricity Supply System

The main rationale for engaging energy suppliers in energy efficiency is that doing so has been proven to lower the cost of providing energy services. The effective 'delivered cost of energy' derived from energy efficiency measures has been proven to be less than the cost of building new plants. So where there are energy efficiency programmes, average electricity costs are cheaper because less new generation, transmission, distribution and supply capacity is needed. As we saw earlier, investment in energy efficiency can defer or eliminate the need for capital expenditure on enlarging networks.

Energy suppliers have a number of advantages as a tool for implementing large-scale energy efficiency. They are large organizations with considerable financial, organizational, marketing and technical skills, although in recent years many of them have suffered financially and no longer have the strong balance sheets they once did. Their other big advantage is that they touch all energy consumers on a regular basis and, in principle, they have sophisticated billing systems – although in some cases these are legacy systems and not fit for purpose in the modern world, even without adding the requirements and potential complexities of energy efficiency services.

## Beware the Law of Unintended Consequences

Like most laws and regulations, decoupling of utility revenues from energy sales can have unintended consequences. In Washington, DC, which was subject to extreme hot weather and storms in July 2012 leading to blackouts, lasting up to six or seven days for some customers, it subsequently came to light that the utilities PEPCO and BGE were being paid for the undelivered energy as if it had resulted from energy efficiency measures. This was approved by the Maryland Public Service Commission (in a restricted way) but the Commission did question whether they had 'inadvertently eliminated the incentive for the companies to quickly restore lost service to customers' (WUSA 2012). Clearly, we should design regulations and incentive schemes such that they don't promote failures of supply as if they were useful energy efficiency measures being implemented.

## Methods of Mandating Utilities

Any discussion of using policies to force electricity companies to provide energy efficiency sources has, of course, to be rooted in a discussion of the regulatory framework in which utilities operate, which itself can be a moving target. Generally, around the world there are two types of regulatory environment: nationalized and deregulated. Even in the so-called deregulated markets, electricity companies are, of course, subject to considerable regulation and input into the price-setting process.

Utilities can be forced to invest in energy efficiency or provide energy efficiency services through a number of regulatory mechanisms, including energy efficiency portfolio standards (equivalent to renewable energy portfolio standards) in which utilities are mandated to purchase a set quantity of efficiency; and also requirements to spend a certain amount on energy efficiency programmes, usually linked to volumes of energy supplied such as the UK Energy Company Obligation (ECO) scheme.

## Energy Suppliers and Energy Efficiency Activities

The various types of energy efficiency activities that energy suppliers could engage in are many and varied and cover the whole energy value chain. They can provide everything from energy efficiency consulting, conducting energy audits, energy monitoring and targeting, right through to project implantation and financing programmes.

The main categories of programme include:

- education and awareness aimed at different markets – residential, customer, industry;

- provision of technical assistance programmes such as energy audits and consultancy;

- provision of financial incentives such as grants or rebates for buying efficient equipment such as high-efficiency motors or lighting;

- provision of performance contracts;

- provision of finance.

## The Importance of Monitoring Utility Efficiency Programmes

It is also important that utility programmes are properly monitored and evaluated to show that the claimed benefits are in fact being achieved. Some early Demand-Side Management (DSM) schemes in the USA did not do this and subsequently became discredited.

We also need to consider how energy efficiency ties in with other programmes that utilities are either forced to implement by regulations or are considering for commercial reasons. There are clear interactions with Demand Response (DR) programmes, programmes designed to reduce peak loads for short periods to alleviate potential supply problems. DR is only concerned with short-term peak lopping or load-shape shifting rather than long-term destruction of demand. The 'smart grid' is a much used term that incorporates many technologies and practices such as smart metering, active demand response and demand management. The smart grid is held up as a model in which the power grid operates in a two-way mode with increased data flows and control systems enabling active load management and storage using electric vehicles. Smart grid programmes will help to improve efficiency and DR programmes. In many countries, for instance the UK, parts of the grid – notably the high-voltage transmission system – is already pretty smart. It is the lower-voltage distribution network that is not smart. As we have seen, the majority of infrastructure was installed long before the age of communications and the internet, and although its fundamental structure may still be sound its operation can often be economically improved by the addition of sensing and communication technology.

## Turning Energy Companies into Energy Service Companies

In all energy supply companies, energy efficiency, whether it is undertaken for mandatory, corporate social responsibility, or profit reasons, is a 'bolt-on' activity rather than fully integrated into the company's product and service offerings. The ultimate model held out by energy efficiency enthusiasts is the true energy service company, a company that only provides services such as set standards of illumination or thermal comfort and is not selling energy in the form of electricity, gas or oil. Such a company would be motivated to invest in the most efficient methods of delivering energy services. To date there have been no real examples of true energy services companies and it represents a massive leap from where most energy suppliers are and a real departure from their core skills. However, it does represent a more radical alternative than just bolting-on energy efficiency services to an existing energy supply model, but reaching this ideal raises a number of problems.

The fundamental problem, over and above regulation, which usually sets the method of reward and links it to energy sales, is centred on the age-old problem of changing the direction and culture of large organizations. Since the advent of the large-scale electricity industry (starting in the 1930s) the organization of utilities, their systems and their skills sets have been based on building large centralized generating plants coupled with retail organizations with customer service and billing functions.

Electricity companies are either generators or retailers – or both in vertically integrated markets. The generation side of the business always has a very high level of technical skills and the ability to manage large projects based around the particular type or types of generating assets in the portfolio, be it coal, nuclear, gas turbine or renewables. The staff on the generating side are used to the problems of designing, building, commissioning, operating and maintaining large-scale generating plants, which are very different skills to those required in energy efficiency work. On the retail side, energy suppliers have a mix of skills including marketing, advertising, billing, customer service and meter reading – where this falls within their remit. For most if not all energy suppliers the missing skill sets are those which are required to go beyond the meter and into the consumers' premises to identify, implement and, where appropriate, finance energy efficiency projects. These are skills that either need to be built in-house, brought in through corporate acquisition, acquired through appropriate partnering or outsourced to third parties.

When considering requiring increased levels of energy efficiency activity from energy suppliers, their leaders and our policy makers need to bear in mind the issues of human capacity and put in place programmes to build capacity in the areas needed to design and implement effective energy efficiency programmes.

Senior management in utilities has grown up in the old world of utilities that maximize supply. They are not so familiar with the technologies, techniques, contracts and risks concerning demand-side projects. They almost certainly won't have come from an energy services background. Senior managers of utilities that are publicly quoted also have to consider the opinions of their major investors and the impact of any change of strategy on shareholder value. Utility investors are interested in relatively low but safe returns and, whatever the facts, they may not consider a switch into different services with different issues and risk profiles as something they want to see. Any proposed change has to carry major shareholders with it.

## HOW DO THEY GET THERE?

Even if the goal of becoming an energy service company is accepted there is the hard question of strategy – how to get there from here? How should a supplier actually make the transition to being an energy services company? What research does it undertake to show what its existing customers, and others, actually want from energy efficiency suppliers? Has it fully surveyed the market to understand what new and emerging technologies, techniques and contract forms are out there? Should it start new businesses, or acquire existing businesses? If it acquires existing businesses, in which sub-sectors of energy efficiency markets and activities should these be? Should they be in sectors that are related to the core competencies of the utilities, such as medium-scale Combined Heat and Power, or should they be in areas outside the core competencies? How should these different businesses be integrated into a holistic customer offering? Or do they need to be?

These are all questions that are hard to answer and, in addition, there are the normal business acquisition problems such as how do you integrate dynamic, entrepreneurial small to medium sized companies with the typical, safe, slow, bureaucratic structures and systems found in utilities? We have seen examples of utilities going on spending sprees to acquire companies in different areas of energy efficiency such as Building Management Systems and home automation, without any coherent plan for how these can be knitted together. Initiatives such as community energy projects and companies can raise even more difficulties for utility managers, as they require a transition from a mindset of 'we have the answers' to facilitating other groups to find an answer.

The minimum requirements to build a true energy services company would seem to be:

- Real-time monitoring of customers' energy demands;

- Integration of real-time monitoring with energy purchasing;

- Excellent communication between client and energy service company such that changes in operating patterns, demands, etc. are communicated in good time and the effects calculated in a transparent way;

- Long-term but flexible contracts;

- Pre-agreed allocation of all the risks inherent in energy services contracts;

- Recognition in the customer that energy is not a core business skill;

- Trust in the energy service company to run mission-critical functions such as HVAC, refrigeration or industrial processes.

Despite the risks, I believe we will see more utilities moving towards becoming energy services companies. The risk of not doing it, under growing legislative and public pressure to improve efficiency, will outweigh the risks of doing it. This will require strong leadership from the top of the utility industry.

## Utility Programme Examples

### ESKOM

ESKOM, the South African monopoly electricity supplier, launched an energy efficiency and demand-side management programme in 2003 in response to severe power shortages. The power shortage was highlighted again in May

2013 when on the 23rd May ESKOM's reserve margin reached a frighteningly low figure of 0.4 per cent (Moneyweb 2013). Since 2004 ESKOM's programme have reduced peak demand between the critical hours of 1800 and 2000 by 2,372 MW. In 2010, ESKOM combined its various efficiency programmes into a new group, the Integrated Demand Management (IDM) division (ESKOM 2011). IDM run several large-scale demand-side management programmes, including:

- Energy Efficiency Demand Side Management (EEDSM) – identifies and promotes more efficient electricity use through improvements to technology and behavioural change;

- Energy Management Programme (EMP) – assists corporate customers to improve energy efficiency;

- Solar Water Heating (SWH) – provides financial incentives for consumers to switch to solar water heating;

- Power awareness and communications campaigns;

- Energy Conservation Scheme (ECS) – aims to achieve a 10 per cent reduction amongst consumers using more than 25 GWh per annum;

- Demand Response (DR) – a scheme where the system operator pays customers to reduce load on instruction;

- ESCO project funding – ESKOM provides funding up to a set benchmark level for approved and Monitored and Verified energy efficiency and demand response projects carried out by ESCOs. The scheme is based on a standard contract.

Since the inception of the IDM programme it has saved a verified 19,158 GWh. One of the most successful programmes has been the roll-out of compact fluorescent lamps (CFLs). Since its inception in December 2003, ESKOM has distributed more than 47 million CFLs in the residential sector, which achieved a demand reduction of 1,958 MW.

In addition, ESKOM runs its own internal energy efficiency programme which aims to achieve a 15 per cent reduction in non-essential consumption in buildings and substations by 2015. The target represents over 1.2 GWh.

## PJM

PJM is the Regional Transmission Operator (RTO) in a large part of the north-eastern and mid-western USA, with an electricity system covering all or part of 13 states and the District of Columbia. It is the largest competitive wholesale electricity market in the world and serves 60 million customers. PJM has 185 GW of generating capacity (more than Canada and Mexico combined), and more than 65,000 miles of transmission lines. In 2011, PJM delivered more than 778 TWh of electricity, more than twice the total power delivered in the United Kingdom (PJM 2012).

In 2007, PJM introduced its Reliability Pricing Model (RPM) which is designed to 'obtain sufficient resources' through a capacity auction. The capacity auction allows demand-response and energy efficiency resources to be bid into the system. In the first auction, for delivery year 2011/12, the energy efficiency that cleared the auction amounted to 78 MW; in the most recent auction for delivery year 2015/16 this reached 923 MW.

Although the PJM RPM capacity market is not without its critics, it, along with some other similar initiatives in the USA, has demonstrated that energy efficiency can provide a reliable, low-cost resource for the electricity system. The challenge is to design market mechanisms that allow the resource to be exploited.

## OPOWER

Although not itself an energy supplier, Opower represents one of the newer options for suppliers considering energy efficiency services in the residential sector. Opower is a software as a service (SAAS) company established in 2007 that works with utilities to encourage energy efficiency amongst residential consumers. It has a range of products including individualized energy reports using billing data to compare consumers' energy use with that of their neighbours and suggest energy-saving measures with the aim of changing consumer behaviour. The average consumer receiving Opower's reports has saved 2.5 per cent of their energy usage, compared to a non-participating control group as measured in statistically significant randomized trials. Extended programmes, such as that in SMUD (Sacramento Municipality Utility District) in California, show that these savings can be maintained over an extended period. These savings have been delivered at an average cost of $0.03/kWh compared to the average of $0.05/kWh for utility energy efficiency programmes in the USA. As well as reducing energy consumption the Opower programmes have been proven to reduce peak load and, importantly, increase customer engagement and satisfaction for the host utility. Opower is now working with 75 utilities and is reaching 15 million customers.

## Conclusions

Policy makers need to recognize the importance of the energy suppliers in accelerating energy efficiency and reform electricity markets to encourage energy efficiency investments. In some jurisdictions this is beginning to happen, but the overwhelming scale of the energy industry and its lobbying power tends to impede progress. Even without these reforms energy supply industry leaders need to consider how they can profit from the massive business opportunity that energy efficiency represents. Developing these new markets will need new organizations, new business models and new financing systems and, above all else, high-quality leadership.

## References and Bibliography

ACEEE. 2012a. *Energy Efficiency Programs for Utility Customers*. [Online]. Available at: http://aceee.org/topics/energy-efficiency-programs [accessed 29 January 2013].

ACEEE. 2012b. *Lost Margin Recovery*. [Online]. Available at: http://aceee.org/sector/state-policy/toolkit/utility-programs/lost-margin-recovery [accessed 29 January 2013].

Center for Climate and Energy Solutions. 2012a. *Revenue Decoupling – An Overview*. [Online]. Available at: http://www.c2es.org/us-states-regions/policy-maps/decoupling/detail [accessed 29 January 2013].

Center for Climate and Energy Solutions. 2012b. *Decoupling Policies*. [Online]. Available at: http://www.c2es.org/sites/default/modules/usmap/pdf.php?file=7016 [accessed 29 January 2013].

Dadakis, J. 2009. *Energy Efficiency and Utility Decoupling*. [Online]. Available at: http://web.mit.edu/colab/pdf/papers/Energy_Efficiency_and_Utility_Decoupling.pdf [accessed 29 January 2013].

Emery, A. 2012. *An Overview of Energy Efficiency and Demand Side Management in South Africa*. [Online]. Available at: http://www.coaltech.co.za/Annual_Colloquium/2012/An%20overview%20of%20energy%20efficiency%20and%20demand%20side%20management%20in%20South%20Africa.pdf [accessed 31 May 2013].

Energy Efficiency Resource Central. 2012. *Starting an Energy Efficiency Program for Your Utility and Community.* [Online]. Available at: http://www. publicpower.org/files/PDFs/StartinganEfficiencyprogramBrochure.pdf [accessed 29 January 2013].

Energy Innovation Business Council. 2012. *Economic Impact of Residential/ Commercial Energy Efficient Products in Michigan.* [Online]. Available at: http://assets.fiercemarkets.com/public/sites/energy/reports/eibc.pdf [accessed 29 January 2013].

ESKOM. 2011. *ESKOM Integrated Report 2011.* [Online]. Available at: http:// financialresults.co.za/2011/eskom_ar2011/downloads/eskom-ar2011.pdf [accessed 28 April 2013].

Etzinger, A. 2011. *Eskom's Approach to Integrated Demand Management.* [Online]. Available at: http://www.sanea.org.za/CalendarOfEvents/2011/ SANEALecturesJHB/Jul19/AndrewEtzinger-Eskom.pdf [accessed 29 January 2013].

Geller, H. 2012. *The $20 Billion Bonanza. Best Practice Electric Utility Energy Efficiency Programs and Their Benefits for the Southwest.* [Online]. Available at: http://swenergy.org/publications/20BBonanza/20B_Bonanza-COMPLETE_ REPORT-Web.pdf [accessed 29 January 2013].

Jannuzzi, G.M. 2008. *Incentives and Disincentives for Utility-Driven DSM in Brazil.* [Online]. Available at: https://cdm.unfccc.int/UserManagement/FileStorage/ Z1GDMJ3C4N8H6G3ANP7TWRD9106ORT [accessed 25 April 2013].

Moneyweb. 2013. *Power Reserve for Thursday Less than 0.4% of Capacity.* [Online]. Available at: http://www.moneyweb.co.za/moneyweb-south-africa/power-reserve-for-thursday-less-than-04-pct-of-cap [accessed 31 May 2013].

National Association of Regulatory Utility Commissioners. 2007. *Decoupling for Electric and Gas Utilities; Frequently Asked Questions (FAQ).* [Online]. Available at: http://www.epa.gov/statelocalclimate/documents/pdf/supp_ mat_decoupling_elec_gas_utilities.pdf [accessed 29 January 2013].

National Renewable Energy Laboratory. 2009. *Decoupling Policies: Options to Encourage Energy Efficiency Policies for Utilities.* [Online]. Available at: http:// www.nrel.gov/docs/fy10osti/46606.pdf [accessed 29 January 2013].

Natural Resources Defense Council. 2012. *Gas and Electric Decoupling.* [Online]. Available at: http://www.nrdc.org/energy/decoupling/ [accessed 29 January 2013].

PG&E. 2012. *How PG&E Makes Money.* [Online]. Available at: http://www.pge. com/myhome/myaccount/rateinfo/howwemakemoney/ [accessed 29 January 2013].

PJM. 2012. *2015/2016 RPM Base Residual Auction Results.* [Online]. Available at: http://www.pjm.com/~/media/markets-ops/rpm/rpm-auction-info/20120518 -2015-16-base-residual-auction-report.ashx [accessed 27 April 2013].

Quackenbush, J.D., Isiogu, O.N. and White, G.R. 2011. *2011 Report on the Implementation of P.A. 295 Utility Energy Optimization Programs*. [Online]. Available at: http://www.michigan.gov/documents/mpsc/eo_legislature_report2011_369985_7.pdf [accessed 29 January 2013].

Rocky Mountain Institute. 2011. *Turbocharging Energy Efficiency Programs*. [Online]. Available at: http://www.oilendgame.com/Content/Files/RMI_TEE_hi.pdf [access 29 January 2013].

Science Daily. 2013. 'Doubling Down on Energy Efficiency'. *Science Daily*, 17 January 2013. [Online]. Available at: http://www.sciencedaily.com/releases/2013/01/130117142552.htm [accessed 29 January 2013].

Smith, R. 2009. 'Less Demand, Same Great Revenue'. *The Wall Street Journal*, 8 February 2009. [Online]. Available at: http://online.wsj.com/article/SB123378473766549301.html [accessed 29 January 2013].

The Brattle Group. 2011. *An Empirical Study of Impact Decoupling on Cost of Capital*. [Online]. Available at: http://www.brattle.com/_documents/UploadLibrary/Upload952.pdf [accessed 29 January 2013].

WUSA. 2012. 'Pepco, BGE Outage Bills OK'd Under Energy Conservation Order', *WUSA 9*, 13 July 2012. [Online]. Available at: http://www.wusa9.com/news/article/212651/158/Pepco-BGE-Outage-Bills-OKd-Under-Energy-Conservation-Order [accessed 27 April 2013].

# Summary and Conclusions

*Despite all our centuries of technological progress we've reached the
stunning global energy efficiency of about 11 per cent.*
Dr Steven Fawkes, ECO Summit Berlin, July 2012

This book has tried to summarize the major aspects of energy efficiency,
including the potential in different dimensions; the barriers to achieving that
potential; the process of energy management; energy efficiency technologies;
policies to encourage greater energy efficiency; designing for energy efficiency;
financing energy efficiency; the actual and potential roles of energy suppliers;
and new and emerging opportunities.

Improving energy efficiency, and specifically the rate of improving
efficiency, has so many advantages for individuals, organizations and nations,
that it is sometimes hard to see why it is not given greater attention and
resources than it currently receives. In most countries it remains the Cinderella
of energy policy, working hard but never quite making it to the ball at the
centre of energy policy. It remains a massive potential cost-effective resource
that seems doomed to be always underexploited. There are encouraging
signs that in many markets, particularly the USA, this may be changing and
that energy efficiency could become the mass market that it has for so long
promised, bringing with it great economic and environmental benefits.

The positive signs include:

- increasing attention from policy makers;

- increasing attention from financiers;

- increased recognition of the massive value potential for business;

- increased recognition of the massive potential for economic growth and job creation;

- increased recognition of energy security risks;

- the arrival of new holistic design techniques that increase savings;

- the arrival of new structures for financing, such as ESAs;

- increased austerity leading to greater pressure on renewable energy subsidies.

The negative factors include:

- reduced focus on global warming;

- energy efficiency is still seen as all too difficult;

- the risk of energy prices coming down because of shale gas or other supply innovations.

I think the next 5 to 10 years will be the acid test for energy efficiency around the world. On balance I am optimistic (as Winston Churchill said, 'For myself I am an optimist – it does not seem to be much use being anything else'), and I believe that we will see strong growth in the rate of energy efficiency implementation and financing. If that happens we will be living in a slightly better world.

In the words of the late, great science fiction and science writer Arthur C. Clarke, when thinking about the future, 'people tend to overestimate what can be accomplished in the short run but to underestimate what can be accomplished in the long run'. This will also apply in the energy efficiency arena, and in the longer-term future we will achieve far higher levels of energy efficiency than we believe are possible today. Much of that, of course, will be through new technologies, but also through better design techniques. If that happens we will be living in a far better world.

I hope that one of the main messages from this book is that we actually have a choice over how energy efficient our technologies, our organizations and our societies are – it is not out of our control. With any luck this book will help more people make the right choices over their behaviour, their designs, their purchases and the policies they enact.

What I have tried to show in this book is the need, and benefits, of taking a systems view of energy efficiency. This applies at all levels, from designing an energy management system that can produce cost savings consistently, to the technical design of energy-consuming systems and equipment, to the design and implementation of financing systems and the design and implementation of policies to encourage the uptake of energy efficiency opportunities. At all those levels, many, many individual decisions determine both the short-term and longer-term energy efficiency of the household, the building, the firm, the government department, and ultimately the whole economy.

Improving energy efficiency is an ongoing, and sometimes tedious, task which requires dedicated professionalism from a wide range of people across many disciplines, often focused on relatively small and incremental projects that don't necessarily capture headlines. This effort, however, is really part of a higher purpose of improving human existence through the application of scientific, engineering and management expertise – a purpose shared by many energy efficiency practitioners, past, present and future.

Steven Fawkes

# Appendix 1:
# The Energy Efficiency Ecosystem

There are many different types of company and organization active in energy efficiency and it is important for everyone involved in energy efficiency, particularly those involved in policy setting, to properly understand these types and organizations and their different activities and roles.

While many organizations and businesses play obvious roles, there is often confusion in the market place about the meaning of terms; in particular, the term Energy Service Company (ESCO) is often used to describe companies with different types of contractual models, some of which were discussed in Chapter 10. This appendix sets out a typology of organizations operating in the energy efficiency ecosystem. Like all ecosystems the energy efficiency ecosystem is evolving; recent arrivals include Measurement and Verification service providers. The companies mentioned are predominantly based in the US or the UK, but similar companies exist in all markets, to a greater or lesser extent.

## Evolution of the Ecosystem

The energy efficiency industry is rapidly evolving as new entrants arrive and new models are developed. The process of developing energy efficiency projects is not dissimilar to that in energy supply, with different steps, including origination, development, financing, underwriting, implementation and Operations and Maintenance. We will probably see an evolution towards companies specializing in one or more of these stages.

## Architects and Engineers (A&E)

Providers of design and supervision services for new buildings, building services and processes. Usually operate on a fee-for-service model using A&E standard contracts and fee structures, which traditionally have been based on capital spend.

## Behavioural Change Companies

Companies that design and run programmes designed to effect behavioural change. As well as several specialized consultancies there are a few larger players, notably Opower.

## Building Analytics Companies

Building analytics is an emerging field that covers several types of software-based service. Analytics companies provide software tools to collect and analyse energy use in buildings. Examples include kWHOURS, Sefaira and Energy Deck.

## Building Management System (BMS) Bureaus

Monitor and control BMS operation in buildings. Ensure the BMS operates the buildings in an optimal fashion, identifies areas of energy wastage, and adjusts control strategies to make savings. An example of a company offering a BMS bureau service, amongst others, would be Matrix Sustainable Energy.

## Construction Managers

Used on large projects as independent managers to protect clients' interests.

## Contractors

Delivery of energy-saving technologies or projects, usually operating on normal contracting principles and models.

## Energy Consultants

Provide advice on energy-saving opportunities on a fee-for-service model. Typically they provide initial energy surveys and investment-grade audits, but some specialize in training and motivation schemes. They range in size from sole traders and small companies right up to major international engineering companies which offer energy consultancy amongst other services. Examples include EnergyExcel, NIFES and AECOM.

## Energy Procurement Advisers

Assist with procurement of energy through data collection and tendering of energy supplies in competitive markets such as the UK. Utilyx and Utiliwise are examples of energy procurement advisers.

## Energy Service Company (ESCO)

Integrated company that identifies and delivers energy efficiency improvements, usually with a guaranteed level of savings. They can range from small to large, although the larger companies are more appropriate for true Energy Performance Contracts in which the ESCO is providing a guarantee of performance. For the guarantee to be effective, the ESCO requires a large enough balance sheet. Examples include Ameresco (USA and Canada), MCW (Canada), Johnson Controls (international) and Cynergin (UK). The term ESCO is a source of confusion in the market and I would argue that it is time to ditch the term altogether. ESCOs are developers of projects and projects can also be developed by consultants, hosts, vendors and even communities.

## Energy Suppliers

Suppliers of electricity, gas and fuels. The energy supply market in most countries is dominated by gas and electricity suppliers, although in some markets, for example Denmark, there are also heat suppliers. The market structure of energy supply varies between monopoly, oligopoly and various forms of competition. Energy suppliers include EDF, RWE, Eon, Duke Energy, Pacific Gas and Electric.

## Equipment Vendors

Suppliers of energy efficiency equipment. Equipment vendors range from small early stage ventures through to global companies such as ABB, Siemens, GE and Philips. Technology developers are aiming to become equipment vendors or develop technologies that can be purchased by vendors.

## Facilities Management (FM) Companies

Providers of FM services; split into hard FM (the physical maintenance of buildings and equipment) and soft FM (services such as catering and cleaning). The activity of many FM companies overlap the energy management market in different ways, including provision of M&T and other services as well as capital project design and development. Many FM companies are moving into energy services and management. Traditional FM contracts do not incentivize FM companies to reduce energy usage, although there has been some contract innovation.

## Information Services

An emerging class of company offering transparency on energy use and projects for property owners. An example is Honest Buildings.

## Measurement and Verification (M&V) Service Providers

Specialized independent providers of M&V services can be used to provide M&V for investment programmes, particularly those involving third-party financing. This is a relatively new area, particularly in the UK, which could usefully be used in internally funded investment programmes to give greater certainty around reported savings. These companies usually implement M&V schemes using the International Performance, Measurement and Verification Protocol (IPMVP) as a guide. EEVS is an example of an independent M&V provider.

## Monitoring and Targeting (M&T) Bureaus

Providers of bureau services for M&T. These are used by companies which do not want to, or cannot justify, running their own internal M&T service.

M&T bureaus provide regular consumption data against targets and identify areas of energy wastage. They can also provide their own software. TEAM (see below) is also an M&T bureau.

## Monitoring and Targeting (M&T) Software Companies

Vendors of software packages to provide M&T, bill validation and assist with energy procurement. Typical companies include TEAM and Stark in the UK.

## Retro-Commissioning Companies

Apply a systematic process to bringing the building controls and operation back to a high standard of energy efficiency in line with the building owner's/ occupier's requirements. This can be achieved by conventional recommissioning or by the application of software overlays, sometimes sold as a software as a service (SAAS) package.

## Retrofit Developer

A developer of energy efficiency retrofit projects. Traditionally these have been end users themselves, energy consultants or ESCOs. With the advent of new opportunities, as well as new contract forms such as Managed Energy Service Agreements (MESAs), a new type of developer is emerging that can sometimes also bring third-party finance.

## Retrofit Fund

Specialist fund established to provide third-party finance to energy efficiency projects. To date there are very few, if any, specific retrofit funds, although we expect to see some formed in the next few years.

## Technology Developers

Developers of new energy efficiency products (and sometimes services). Companies are usually backed by the founders, high-net worth individuals, venture capital investors, and/or corporates. Examples include Soladigm, Energetix and Enlighted.

## Transaction Vehicle

A company established solely to facilitate investment in energy efficiency projects/retrofits. Transaction vehicles may use different contractual and business models.

# Appendix 2:
# Energy Conversion Table

Table A2.1    Energy conversion table

| Unit | Multiplied by | Conversion factor | = | Unit | Notes |
|---|---|---|---|---|---|
| kilowatt hours (kWh) | × | 3.6 | = | megajoules (MJ) | |
| kilowatt hours (kWh) | × | 3,412 | = | British thermal units (BTU) | |
| | | | | | |
| therms | × | 100,000 | = | British thermal units (BTU) | |
| therms | × | 29.31 | = | kilowatt hours (kWh) | |
| | | | | | |
| tonnes of oil equivalent (toe) | × | 396.83 | = | therms | |
| tonnes of oil equivalent (toe) | × | 41.868 | = | gigajoules (GJ) | |
| tonnes of oil equivalent (toe) | × | 11,630 | = | kilowatt hours (kWh) | |
| | | | | | |
| cubic feet of gas | × | 1,025 | = | British thermal units (BTU) | Depending on calorific value of gas |
| | | | | | |
| gigajoule (GJ) | × | 947,950 | = | BTU | |
| gigajoule (GJ) | × | 278 | = | kilowatt hours (kWh) | |
| Horsepower (hp) | × | 746 | = | watts (W) | |
| | | | | | |
| Quadrillion BTU (QBTU) | × | 293 | = | terawatt hours (TWh) | QBTU is also called a 'Quad' |
| Quadrillion BTU (QBTU) | × | 25.1996 | = | million tonnes oil equivalent (mtoe) | |

## Table A2.1    Energy conversion table *concluded*

| Unit | Multiplied by | Conversion factor | = | Unit | Notes |
|------|------|------|------|------|------|
| Quadrillion BTU (QBTU) | × | 1.055 | = | exajoule (EJ) | |
| | | | | | |
| terawatt hour (TWh) | × | 11.63 | = | million tons oil equivalent (mtoe) | |
| terawatt hour (TWh) | × | 277.78 | = | exajoule (EJ) | |

# Index

**Green Outcomes in the Real World**
**Global Forces, Local Circumstances,**
**and Sustainable Solutions**
Peter McManners
Hardback: 978-0-566-09179-7
e-book PDF: 978-0-566-09180-3
e-book ePUB: 978-1-4094-5966-8

**Outsourcing Energy Management**
**Saving Energy and Carbon through Partnering**
Steven Fawkes
Hardback: 978-0-566-08712-7

**Sustainable Growth in a Post-Scarcity World**
**Consumption, Demand, and the Poverty Penalty**
Philip Sadler
Hardback: 978-0-566-09158-2
e-book PDF: 978-0-566-09159-9
e-book ePUB: 978-1-4094-5961-3

**The Business Leader's Guide to the Low-carbon Economy**
Larry Reynolds
Hardback: 978-1-4094-2351-5
e-book PDF: 978-1-4094-2352-2
e-book ePUB: 978-1-4094-7127-1

Visit **www.gowerpublishing.com** and

- search the entire catalogue of Gower books in print
- order titles online at 10% discount
- take advantage of special offers
- sign up for our monthly e-mail update service
- download free sample chapters from all recent titles
- download or order our catalogue

For Product Safety Concerns and Information please contact our EU
representative GPSR@taylorandfrancis.com Taylor & Francis Verlag GmbH,
Kaufingerstraße 24, 80331 München, Germany


Printed and bound by CPI Group (UK) Ltd, Croydon, CR0 4YY
01/05/2025
01858426-0012